The SportingNews

P R E S E N T S

A Century of Greatness

YANKEES

Photo Credits

Front cover—main image: The Sporting News Archives; background image: The Sporting News Archives; left top to bottom: Robert Seale/The Sporting News; AP/Wide World Photos; The Sporting News Archives; The Sporting News Archives.

Back cover: Albert Dickson/The Sporting News.

The Sporting News Archives: 2-3, 14, 15TL, 20-21, 24-53, 54TR, 54B, 55B, 56-57, 58TL, 58C, 58BR, 59TL, 59C, 59B, 60TL, 60BL, 60C, 61-76, 77TR, 77B, 79TR, 80TR, 82TR, 82BR, 83BR, 84BL, 84BR, 89TL, 90TL, 90B, 91TL, 91CR, 92, 96CL, 100, 101T, 102, 103TL, 104-105, 106, 107TR, 109TR, 109BR, 110, 111-114, 115T, 116B, 117, 118R, 119-121, 124-126, 127TL, 127TC, 127C, 12-135, 138-139, 140-143, 151-154, 155T, 156-162, 164-168, 169L, 170-171, 172TC, 172TR, 172C, 173-179, 191-193, 196T, 197B, 200B, 201B, 202T, 210, 212-214, 215B, 216-217, 224, 227B, 230-253, 254T, 256.

Albert Dickson/The Sporting News: 12, 16, 95BR, 127TR, 137, 146T, 147T, 148, 150T, 184-185, 186T, 188, 189BR, 218BR, 219, 222, 223B, 254CL.

Bob Leverone/The Sporting News: 93TR, 95TL, 95BL, 186B, 187B, 189T.

Robert Seale/The Sporting News: 13, 147B, 150B, 187TL, 187TR, 189BL, 190, 218BL, 223T, 254BL.

Dilip Vishwanat/The Sporting News: 96TR, 97L, 101BR, 122, 255TL, 255BL.

John Dunn for The Sporting News: 90TR, 93TL, 94, 95TR, 96TL, 96BL, 97R, 103BL, 149, 228-229, 254TR, 255BR.

Bernie Nunez for The Sporting News: 97B, 108-109, 255CR, 255TR.

Major League Baseball Photos: 17, 55T, 78-79, 79TL, 79C, 80L, 80B, 81TR, 81L, 81B, 85TL, 86R, 115C, 208-209, 221.

NBLA/MLB Photos: 58TR, 59TR.

Rich Pilling/Major League Baseball Photos: 8-9, 81TL, 84TL, 84TR, 85C, 86BL, 87TL, 87TR, 88TL, 88TR, 88BL, 89BR, 91TR, 98-99, 103R, 118BL, 146B, 211, 220.

Paul Cunningham/Major League Baseball Photos: 6-7, 18-19.

Louis Requena/Major League Baseball Photos: 23, 77TL, 82TL, 82C, 82BL, 83TR, 83BL, 85BL, 86TL, 86BC, 87B, 89TC, 116TL, 123, 136, 218T, 227T.

AP/Wide World Photos: 10-11, 15TR, 54TL, 93L, 106-107, 109BL, 144–145, 163, 180–183, 194-195, 196B, 197T, 198B, 199, 200T, 201T, 201C, 203, 204B, 205-206, 207B, 215T, 225-226.

Bettmann/CORBIS: 169R, 172TL, 198T, 202B, 204T, 207T; Underwood & Underwood/CORBIS: 60TR.

Nancy Hogue: 88BR-89BL.

Jeff Carlick: 91BL.

Robert Thom/Photo Illustration: 155B.

Acknowledgements

They do not wear pinstripes or make their living staring down 96-mph fastballs, but *The Sporting News* team members who contributed to this volume are no less efficient than the New York Yankees—baseball's most successful and celebrated franchise.

To create and execute a book like *Yankees* requires a monumental commitment from editors, designers, proofreaders and photo enhancers, many of whom work quietly behind the scenes, often performing functions in addition to their weekly duties. Their efforts are appreciated.

A special thanks goes to editorial director Steve Meyerhoff, without whose vision and leadership this project might have died, and prepress director Bob Parajon, who keeps things on an even keel on the production side with his tireless work ethic. Yeoman effort also was provided by August Miller, who was responsible for gathering more than 500 photographs.

The personality of any book is in its design and credit for the Yankees' upscale look goes to art director Angie Pillman. The job of making the photographs look great was handled by David Brickey, with able assistance from fellow prepress specialists Steve Romer, Pamela Speh and Vern Kasal.

It's hard to understate the contribution of associate editor Dave Sloan, who added to his weekly responsibilities by providing valuable editing and proofreading help. And other special contributions were made by Mike Dubester, Peter A. Spina, Jason Kint, Adam London, Dave Weiner and Joe Hoppel.

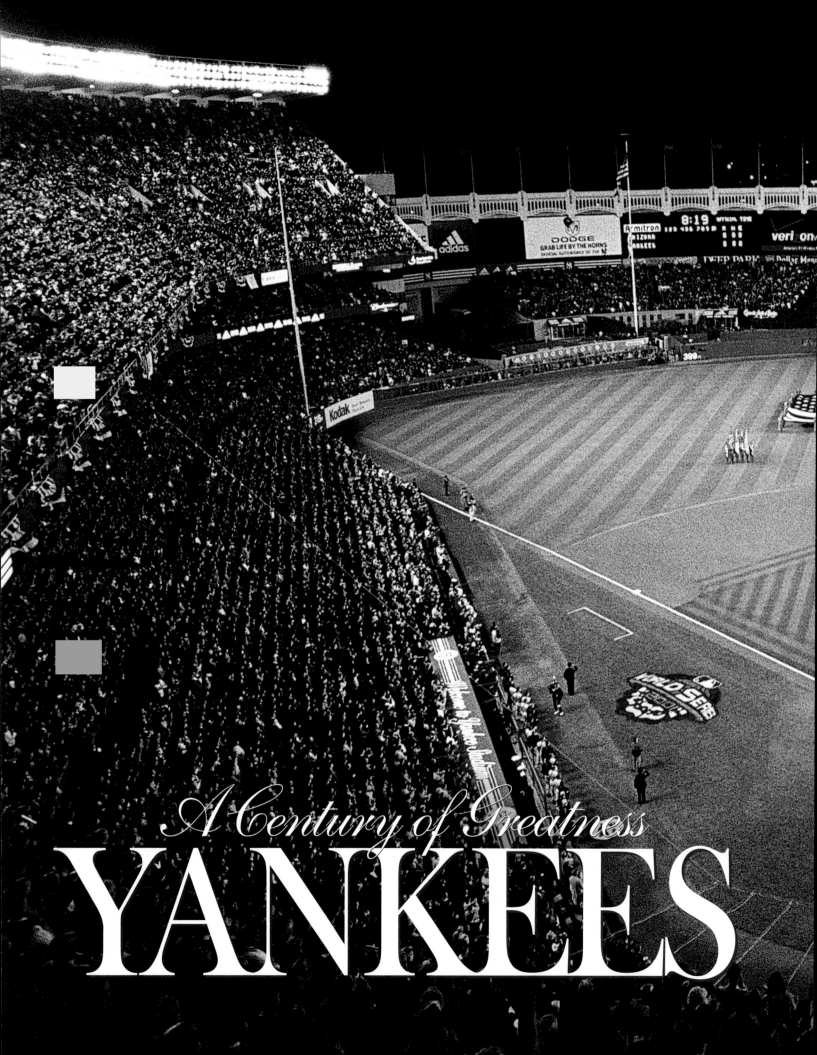

A Century of Greatness
YANKEES

Contents

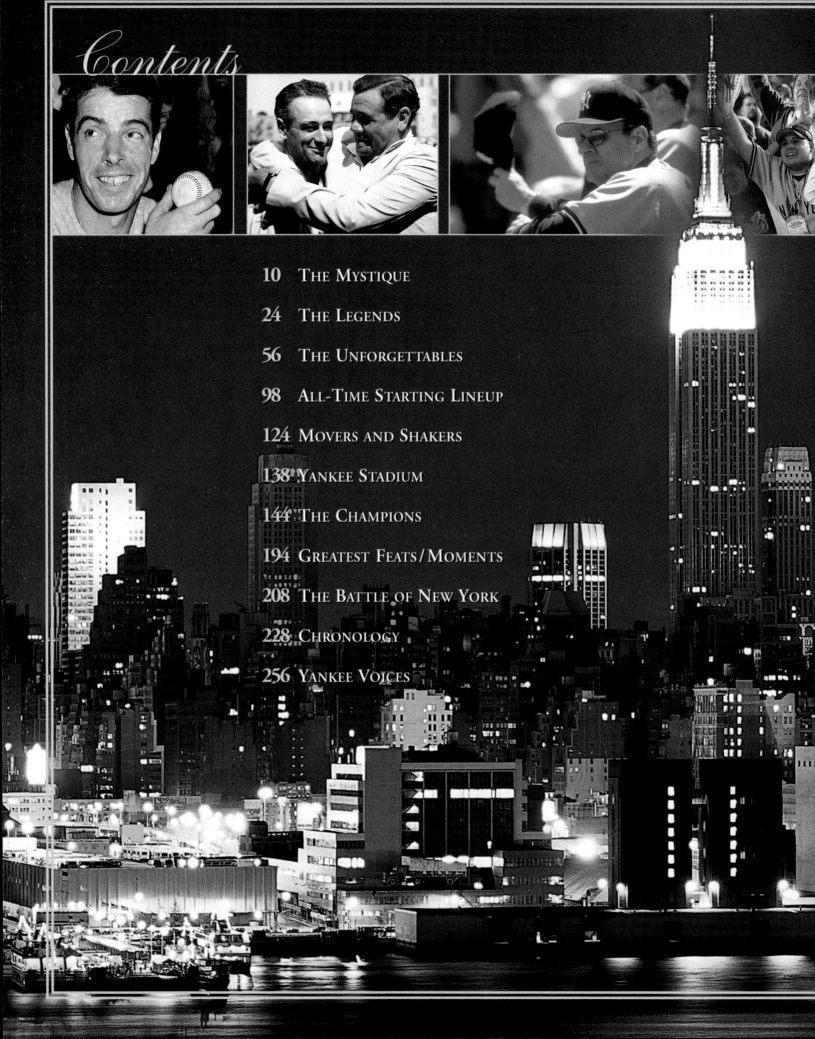

The MYSTIQUE FOUR

Iť's that uniform. Energy and confidence emanate from its distinctive blue pinstripes; the interlocking "N" and "Y", displayed proudly on the chest and dark blue cap, suggest power and success. Put it on—carefully, respectfully—and experience the instant transformation from ballplayer to "Yankee"—from Clark Kent to Derek Jeter.

It's also that stadium, with its awe-inspiring size, distinctive facade and proud history. And the monuments bearing names like Ruth, Gehrig, Huggins, DiMaggio and Mantle. And the championship aura. The city. The traditions. The memories.

To be or not to be a Yankee is not a choice, it's a calling that defines a career and gives it special meaning. And make no mistake, the Yankees uniform empowers. Those guys wearing pinstripes seem to play baseball more crisply, carry themselves with more dignity and win more dispassionately. Teamwork, fundamentals, work ethic, discipline—it's all part of the Yankee Mystique.

"You're in the batter's box one day and you say to yourself, 'Damn, I've got this number on my back that says 44, and my uniform says New York on the front of it.' And I have no idea how I'm going to get a hit, but I've got to act like it and understand the fundamentals and go forward and maybe something will happen. And it happens. Wearing a Yankees uniform helps you believe. Your footsteps are louder. You go somewhere and it's, 'The Yankees are here!' You're part of that. You're part of that makeup."

—*Reggie Jackson*

Nothing says 'Yankees' more than the pinstriped uniform, a team trademark since the early ownership years of Jacob Ruppert, and the interlocking 'NY' logo, no matter how it's displayed.

Yankee Mystique is all about perception—legendary players and feats, front-office vision, lavish spending, tightfisted management, a business-like, sometimes-insensitive approach to player dealings and, of course, that incredible winning legacy. The name "Yankees" is synonymous with "championships" and overmatched opponents have long compared the franchise's seemingly aloof and no-nonsense style to U.S. Steel and other faceless corporations.

To really understand the mystique, you first must appreciate the roots established by Col. Jacob Ruppert, who dedicated his life to providing a brand of baseball that would measure up to the grand New York stage upon which it was played. More than anything, the stylish, well-manicured, meticulously coifed New York beer baron was a man who coveted perfection in his business dealings and lifestyle—an obsession Yankee teams forever would reflect in their appearance, operation, play and success.

It was Ruppert who adopted pinstripes as the official look of the Yankees when he became part owner in 1915 and made numbers a permanent part of the team's uniform in 1929—each number corresponding to the player's slot in the batting order. Yankee Stadium, traditionally billed as The House That Ruth Built, actually was a Ruppert contribution in 1923—the biggest, grandest and most modern sports facility in America.

It was Ruppert who hired legendary manager Miller Huggins, "empire builder" Ed Barrow and George Weiss, longtime czar of the Yankees' vaunted

Ruppert (above right) demanded excellence, which he got from such players as second baseman Joe Gordon (left) and longtime cleanup hitter Lou Gehrig. The Iron Horse's locker (above, right photo) has been preserved as an emotional reminder of early Yankees success for fans touring baseball's Hall of Fame in Cooperstown, N.Y.

farm system. Ruppert purchased Babe Ruth in 1920 from cash-strapped Boston owner Harry Frazee for a cool $125,000 and he followed that theft by plundering Frazee's talent-rich Red Sox roster, setting the franchise on its championship course.

By the end of the 1920s, Ruppert's Yanks had won six pennants, three World Series and the contempt of fellow A.L. owners who could not match his deep pockets. Ruppert's free spending and obsession for winning became Yankee trademarks, a spirit captured by the directive he delivered to Joe McCarthy when he hired him as manager in 1930. "I will stand for you finishing second this year," he said, "but remember, McCarthy, I do not like to finish second."

Ruppert did like a 10-game lead by the All-Star break, a clinched pennant by Labor Day and champagne showers—the kind that typically follow World Series victories. Under McCarthy, the championship pace hit warp speed (consecutive World Series wins from 1936 through '39) and Yankee Mystique gained a new, deeply felt dimension.

"In more northerly sectors, such as Boston, Chicago, Detroit or Cleveland, 'Yankee' is a word that strikes upon the ear with a horrid sound. It means a ballplayer who sweeps down like a wolf on the fold, lays waste to the green meadows to the local playground, and swaggers off in a burst of mocking laughter. Compared to the sentiments inspired by Joe DiMaggio in Fenway Park, (William Tecumseh) Sherman is revered in Atlanta."
—*Red Smith, New York Herald Tribune, 1952*

McCarthyism, New York style, formed a perfect backdrop for the 1930s Yankees—and a blueprint for winning that still is followed today. Not only was Marse Joe a master baseball tactician and strategist, he was a Ruppert-like obsessive

Joe McCarthy (far left) set a high standard for Yankees success during his managerial tenure from 1931-46 and Joe DiMaggio (near left) exuded class and pride as the poster boy for the franchise's championship mystique.

who understood the trappings of success and the discipline it takes to sustain it.

McCarthy's first act as manager in 1931 was to chop up the clubhouse card table, explaining "I want the players in here to think of baseball and nothing else." He outlawed shaving in the clubhouse, saying players should arrive at the office ready to work, and he established a strictly enforced dress code that required jacket and tie for travel and all dining room appearances.

A McCarthy clubhouse was always professional and business-like, a sense of pride that extended to the field. He expected his players to act like gentlemen and he shot down clubhouse jokesters with the one-time admonition, "You're a Yankee, young man. Act like it." New York players not only had to be champions, they had to look and act like champions as well.

With Barrow and Weiss feeding him a steady stream of top-flight talent, McCarthy gave the term "champions" new meaning. A stickler for fundamentals and dismissive of anybody who couldn't grasp his all-for-one team concept, the former Chicago Cubs boss built his squads around quiet, conservative players like Lou Gehrig and Joe DiMaggio, who led the charge to eight pennants and seven championships in McCarthy's 16 seasons.

Always the psychologist, McCarthy played mind games with both his team and opponents. He had Barrow give his players uniforms a half-size larger than necessary and squared-off caps—all the better to look menacing. Every player, supplied with three sets of uniforms, was expected to show up clean and groomed for a game—menacing AND dignified.

It was under McCarthy that the franchise developed its swagger and relentless consistency, inspiring cries of "break up the Yankees." Not surprisingly, the Yankees became universally hated for their success and resented for their classy approach

The green facade of yesteryear has been replaced by a sparkling white concrete facsimile that stretches across center field, connecting the left field and right field grandstands. The facade remains a deeply rooted Yankee tradition.

and lack of emotion, which outsiders perceived as smug arrogance. By the time McCarthy departed during the 1946 season, the franchise was operating on a different baseball plane than its competitors.

"It's great to be a Yankee. Once you don a Yankee uniform, you never become careless on the playing field. If you do, there will be 15 Yankees privately telling you that's not the Yankee way. Loafing is taboo. Yankees are always proud of each other. Never in my three years of association with the Yankees have I ever seen or heard an argument between the players. Yankees expect competition and thrive on proving they're better. They never sleep on the bench. They figure plays in advance—become offensive players from the start. ... Once you've won your spurs with the Yankees, you'll never have trouble getting a big-league job whenever some other player crowds you off the Yankee roster." —Casey Stengel, 1952

During an amazing 12-year span from 1949-60, Stengel got a close-up and personal view of Yankees Mystique. While guiding the Bronx Bombers through an incredible run of 10 pennants and seven World Series wins, he noted the power of the pinstripes—stars who shined brighter, position players with more focus, more dedicated reserves and rejuvenated veterans. It was, indeed, great to be a Yankee in 1952—and apparently still is.

"To play for the Yankees, you just feel like you're carrying on a tradition," said righthander David Cone, a key pitcher for teams that won four championships in a five-year span from 1996-2000. "You know that there's no way to compare to Babe Ruth or Lou Gehrig. You know there's nothing you can do that will match their accomplishments. Yet, at the same time, you sort of carry the torch. I think we all feel that. We're lucky to be here. We're lucky to play for the Yankees. And we want to do something to continue that legacy, no matter what it is."

From Waite Hoyt to Cone, from Ruth to Paul O'Neill and Bernie Williams, there has been a special bond between the player and his Yankees uniform. That uniform is handed out with lofty expectations. A true Yankee is workmanlike and dedicated; proud and focused; willing to sacrifice individual honors for team goals. Flamboyant players like Ruth, Lefty Gomez and Jackson have thrived in pinstripes, but the franchise is better defined by the quiet, more elegant leadership of Gehrig, DiMaggio, Mickey Mantle, Don Mattingly and Jeter.

For every Bill Dickey, Yogi Berra, Red Ruffing, Whitey Ford and Thurman Munson there have been 50 Mark Koenigs, Monte Pearsons, Nick Ettens, Gene Woodlings, Bucky Dents and Joe Girardis—players who have performed admirably for four or five years and collected a few World Series checks before giving way to a new wave of Yankee-ready talent. While other teams have struggled to put nine quality starters on the field, the Yankees typically have had reserves as good as their starters.

Many were the product of baseball's best farm system during the Yankees' golden years. But when roster holes needed to be plugged, the team found other sources. In the 1920s, Barrow simply raided the Red Sox roster; in the 1950s and early '60s, the Yankees used the struggling Kansas City Athletics as a "big-league" farm team. George Steinbrenner does it today with his checkbook, shamelessly outbidding all competitors for free-agent talent.

And when a promising youngster like Roger Maris arrives via trade, or veterans like Johnny Mize and Enos Slaughter are acquired to help during a stretch run, something just seems to click. Potential becomes reality and sagging fortunes magically reverse.

The Yankees uniform empowers the players who wear it, a statement supported by the incredible championship tradition that has given the team status as baseball's premier franchise.

"I show up every day and do the same things I did when I had a Braves' uniform on and the same things I did when I had a Cleveland uniform on," said outfielder David Justice, who hit 20 home runs for the 2000 Yankees after being acquired at midseason from the Indians. "Now, the difference is that you just think about the history of the organization and you realize a whole lot of bad boys wore this uniform. I think there is a mystique, but it's because of the tradition."

A winning tradition that's hard to ignore—six pennants in the 1920s, five in the '30s, five in the '40s, eight in the '50s, five in the '60s, three in the '70s, one in the '80s and five since 1996. From 1936-43, the Yankees played in seven of eight World Series, winning six; from 1949-64, they appeared in 14 of 16 fall classics, winning nine. From 1921-64, the team never went more than three years without winning a championship. They have appeared in 38 of the 98 World Series played and won 26—even though they didn't claim their first pennant until 1921.

"We Yankees aren't built from a special mold. But we're conscious of the Yankees tradition and know that we must live up to it. Every Yankee feels that way the moment he steps through the clubhouse door on Ruppert Place. The stands are somehow bigger and more awesome. The beautifully tended diamond looks like no other diamond in the world. That dugout ... the game's greatest stars have sat there and then gone forth to conquer the baseball world.

"Remember that Silver Anniversary game a year ago, the Babe lugging his bat up the

Yankee Stadium, fondly remembered as The House That Ruth Built, still intimidates first-time visitors and Yankee opponents, starting with the 'Championships' banner that stretches across the outside facade and lists the team's World Series winners.

steps for the last time with the ghost of Gehrig at his side? And among the gray-haired men of middle age who awkwardly took their places on the diamond were baby-faced Waite Hoyt and towering Wally Pipp and durable Everett Scott. And Bob Meusel of the mighty arm and Jumping Joe Dugan and fellows who had played with me 10 years before—Ruffing and Lefty Gomez, Bill Dickey and Ruby Red Rolfe ... and the younger fellows, Keller and Henrich and Gordon.

"Seeing them all together put me in my place. Tears came into my eyes, tears of gratefulness that I was and still am a Yankee."

—*Joe DiMaggio, writing for Baseball Digest in 1949*

First-time visitors are gripped, shaken and overwhelmed by the mystique of Yankee Stadium. It is equal parts expansive, elegant, intimidating and inspirational—reeking of success and affected by the inordinate amount of drama that has unfolded there. This is a house of heroes: The Babe and Murderer's Row, the Iron Horse and Yankee Clipper, Lefty, Red and Whitey, Yogi and the Scooter, the Old Professor, the M&M Boys, Mr. October and Donnie Baseball.

For years, the Yankees paid homage to former greats Babe Ruth, Lou Gehrig and Miller Huggins with monuments that provided obstacles for center fielders in front of the fence. The monuments were moved to a newly created Monument Park beyond the left-center field fence when the ballpark was renovated in 1974-75.

If you don't believe how overpowering this baseball cathedral can be, just go there and see for yourself. And be prepared. If the facade, monuments and championship banners don't get you, the soothing, dignified voice of longtime Stadium announcer Bob Sheppard probably will.

"All you have to do is walk out in front of Yankee Stadium and look at those pennants on the wall," said Chili Davis, an outfielder/designated hitter for the 1998 and '99 World Series champs. "I don't think you see one of them that says, 'Division Champions' or 'American League Champions.' Twenty-four (26 now) world championships. That's a pretty big difference right there.

"I've gone to other baseball stadiums and they've got banners hanging around— you know, 'Wild-Card Champions' and 'Division Champions' and whatever. But they don't even hang those banners here. I think they're in the batting cage or somewhere."

Yankee Stadium is a tale of two eras. The first (1923-73) speaks to the dignified elegance of Ruppert, Barrow, Weiss, Huggins and McCarthy. The second (1976-present) is more reflective of the Bronx Zoo-like atmosphere inspired by Steinbrenner, Billy Martin, Sparky Lyle, Jackson, Munson and Dave Winfield.

From the beginning, The House That Ruth Built was defined by its winning legacy. Massive beyond imagination, it reflected the corporate-minded city that surrounded it and the ego-inflated teams that played there. The pale green facade and lush green grass gave it a regal air; the short right field porch and "death valley" left-center field gave it a special personality. For years, on-field monuments honoring Huggins, Gehrig and Ruth provided obstacles for fielders who tried to play balls hit to the distant center field fence.

This was a more dignified Yankee Stadium, unlike the rollicking, zany atmosphere of Brooklyn's Ebbets Field. Fans at the Stadium, more refined and less vocal, reflected the "We're better than you" arrogance of a team that always seemed to win with business-like efficiency. Everything at Yankee Stadium was grand and elegant, from its World Series tradition to the special moments, player tributes and Old Timers Days—an annual event unmatched emotionally by any other stadium or organization.

Today's Yankee Stadium is younger and rowdier, filled with fans who demand excellence and express their dissatisfaction with zeal and impatience. The monuments, which now include DiMaggio and Mantle, have been moved to a Monument Park area beyond the left-center field fence, where they are joined by 17 plaques honoring Ruppert, Barrow, McCarthy, Stengel and other team officials and players.

Everything at renovated Yankee Stadium is cleaner, brighter and more efficient. Modern technology and convenience have replaced some Stadium nuances, but that has not affected the aura—or the fans' passion for winning.

This, still, is the house of champions.

"There's a lot of pride. It's a great honor to associate at all with excellence. I'll never forget the time ... they offered me the job as general manager three years ago. And I was thinking real quick in my head, 'My God, the most storied franchise in sports. What an honor this is to have the opportunity presented to me, just to be associated with the Joe Torres, the Jeters, the Bernies, the O'Neills, even if it's only in a very small way.' And

The 1958 championship pennant was the last in a banner decade that produced eight American League pennants and six World Series winners.

being a non-player, it probably means even more to me. These guys are true champions and I know it means a lot to them, too. The history and tradition are extremely special. It's a unique experience. It's one in a million. It really is." —G.M. Brian Cashman

So what, exactly, is a Yankee? What separates him from the typical player and allows him to compete in that intense New York spotlight?

"I would say it's the championships," said former Yankees first baseman Tino Martinez, a key figure for five pennant-winners and four World Series champs from 1996-2001. "You try to win championships and that's the bottom line about being a Yankee. It doesn't matter how great your individual seasons have been, or how great your career has been. It's all about winning championships. That's all about being a Yankee."

For all his gaudy numbers and spectacular achievements, Ruth's most lasting legacy is that championship aura he helped bring to the Yankees. The Babe played for four Yankee World Series winners. Gehrig played for six, Gomez for five, Red Ruffing for six, Bill Dickey for seven, Berra for 10, Mantle for seven, Ford for six. Yankee Hall of Famers are defined by their championship rings, but no more so than the hundreds of complementary players who have contributed so much to Yankee success.

For the select few, wearing pinstripes can mean fame, fortune and postseason paychecks. But it also comes with intense pressure to succeed and minimal job security. The Yankees can be dispassionate. This is the organization that let a frustrated Ruth play his final season (1935) in Boston rather than give him the managerial job he desperately wanted. It's the organization that released Hall of Fame shortstop Phil Rizzuto, a 13-year Yankee, on Old Timers' Day in 1956. Managers Stengel and Berra were fired after leading the Yankees to pennants—but losing in the World Series.

"On the Yankees, you've got to produce," pitcher-turned-Yankees coach Jim Turner told *The Sporting News* in 1952. "That is vital. Because if you don't produce, there's someone else ready to step in and take your place. There's no loafing on Yankee teams—even the men on the bench. They've got to holler. That's part of their job and if they don't holler and pull for the guys who are playing, they don't hang around long. ... There is no such thing as going through the motions."

What amazes Yankee haters is that the pinstripe mystique and team-first dedication has endured for more than eight decades—evolving, sustaining, surviving and rejuvenating through changes in management, winning droughts (1965-75, 1982-95) and well-publicized controversy. And when the Yankees of the '90s reclaimed the championship spotlight, they mirrored the World Series winners of yesteryear with their all-business, no-nonsense, everybody-contributes approach. It's the Yankee way.

"There's a quiet confidence that this team has, and I think there is some kind of magic working here. I think we all knew that when it was time to turn it up again, we knew how to do it because we'd been there before. Everybody steps it up. And it hasn't been one hero. It's been a lot of different heroes." —Jim Leyritz, 1999

One of the special days of every season is Old Timers' Day at Yankee Stadium, when former greats get to relive a little of that old magic for appreciative New York fans. More than a few tears were shed (opposite page) in 1972 when DiMaggio (5) and Mickey Mantle (7) made a memorable joint appearance.

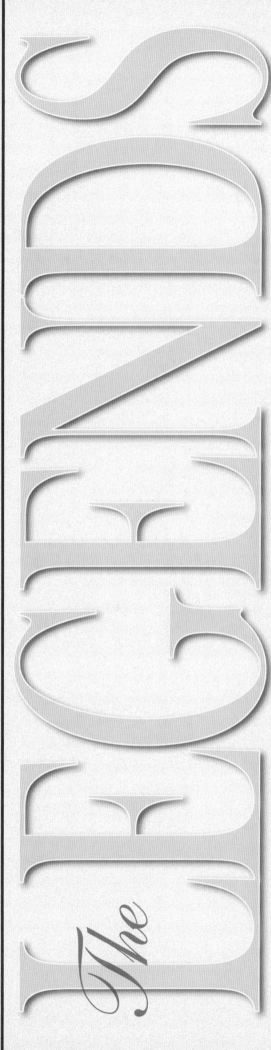

The LEGENDS

Babe Ruth

B abe Ruth. The name still sends emotional shivers through the baseball world, more than a half century after his death. It also retains a relentless hold on New York, a hard-edged metropolis that sets high standards for heroes who come with battle scars and an unexplainable mystical flair.

But what's not to like about the man who saved our National Pastime. ... who ignited the championship fires of the game's greatest franchise. ... who introduced us to the sporting concept of power over finesse? In retrospect, the great Ruth was equal parts ambassador, showman, lovable buffoon, man of the people and baseball artist—the greatest offensive batsman of the game's first full century.

He also was the Bambino, the Sultan of Swat, the Big Bam, the Babe and, to his teammates, "Gigge." By any name, he rewrote the baseball record books and supplied the offensive standards by which future generations would be judged. A long home run or great accomplishment became "Ruthian" feats, and the infectious smile and indomitable spirit became Yankee cornerstones.

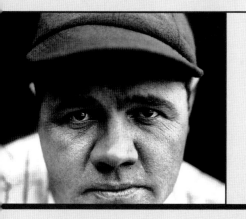

"To play on the same club with Ruth was not only a pleasure—it was a privilege, an experience which comes once in a lifetime. Babe was no ordinary man. He was not alone the idol of the fans, he was superman to the ball players. He was their man, their guy. ...

"Ruth possessed a magnetism that was positively infectious. When he entered a clubhouse—or a room—when he appeared on the field, it was as if he was a whole parade. There seemed to be flags waving, bands playing constantly. If atomic formulas could be applied to personality, Ruth's measurements were definitely atomic."

—*Former Yankee teammate Waite Hoyt*

The Ruth legend began inauspiciously in Baltimore when a 6-year-old youngster, unable to get the home care he needed from working parents, was sent to St. Mary's Industrial School, a Catholic facility that specialized in the rearing of orphans and other needy children. From local sandlots and school leagues, George Herman Ruth rose to baseball prominence through a powerful left arm and pitching poise that attracted the attention of Baltimore's International League team and eventually the Red Sox of the American League.

The career offensive numbers—714 home runs, 2,213 RBIs, 2,174 runs scored, a .342 average, a .690 slugging percentage—define Ruth as a baseball legend. But his ability to throw pitches past overmatched hitters is what defined his early career. Ruth made his major league debut in 1914 and twice scaled the 20-win plateau for the Red Sox while helping them win three World Series.

As the talented lefty piled up victories, he also provided glimpses of the future. In a dead-ball era of small, fast players who could slap, poke and line hits to all fields, the burly 6-foot-2 Ruth displayed an uncanny ability to hit the ball hard and far. By 1919, the Red Sox were using him as a part-time pitcher/outfielder and he responded by hitting a single-season-record 29 home runs.

"There was an explosion and I, playing deep off second, looked up and saw a white dot streaking through the sky above me. The ball continued to soar and finally dropped out of sight in the upper seats of the far-distant bleachers. We players as well as the spectators gasped. It was by far the longest home run anyone present had ever seen.

"And it was (one of) Babe Ruth's first magnificent four-ply wallop(s). Though we did not know it (in 1915), a great career had begun."

—*Former Indians second baseman Bill Wambsganss, writing for the Central Press Association in 1936*

Whether crossing the plate after another home run (above center) or mixing into the more mundane social world of Yankees owner Jacob Ruppert (above right), Babe Ruth's distinctive face was part of the New York sports scene for many years.

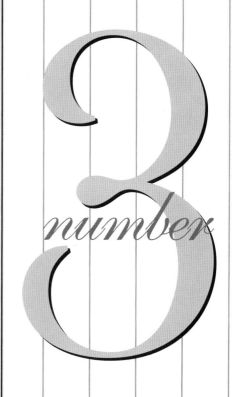

3
number

Ed Barrow (seated left), an important figure in Yankees history, was Red Sox manager in 1918 when Harry Frazee (seated right) signed Ruth and Stuffy McInnis.

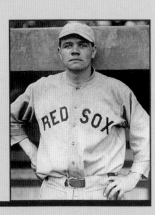

Ruth helped Boston win three World Series as a power pitcher before taking his talents to a higher level with the Yankees.

Yankees fans might disagree with that sentiment. For New Yorkers and the majority of baseball fans, Ruth's career really began on January 5, 1920, when the Yankees purchased his contract from cash-strapped Boston owner Harry Frazee for $125,000. Yankees co-owner Jacob Ruppert, intrigued by Ruth's batting prowess, looked past his 89-46 pitching record and announced that his 25-year-old prodigy would become a full-time right fielder.

"His left arm, geared for pitching, had to be adjusted to throws from the out-field," *New York Sun* columnist Frank Graham reported in 1935. "When this adjustment had been made, there wasn't a more powerful or more accurate thrower in either league. Bob Meusel won acclaim for the rifle-shot pegs he made from the outfield, but he never was a match for the Babe in accuracy. It took enemy players a little time to learn this, but when they learned it they never forgot it."

Neither would they forget the balls that began sailing at record pace out of New York's Polo Grounds (the park the Yankees shared with the New York Giants) and other ballparks throughout the American League. Fans, players and baseball officials watched with open mouths as Ruth hit 54 home runs in 1920 and followed with 59 a year later. He also batted .378 and drove in a whopping 171 runs in his shocking 1921 season.

Because of Ruth, the New York Yankees were suddenly on the baseball map. And the game itself, still reeling from the aftershocks of the Black Sox World Series scandal, was suddenly sharing Ruth's enormous spotlight. As fans flocked to the Polo Grounds and other major league parks to get a look at the longball-hitting phenom they had been reading about, owners began scurrying to find big, strong hitters who, like Ruth, could decide a game with a single swing of the bat.

"... The lanky kid had a pitching arm of rawhide, in his thin-waisted, long-legged, 6-foot-2 inch frame and 200 pounds was limitless stamina. In his mind, schooled to industrial trades, was baseball genius.

"But from the very start his clouting ability vied with his lefthanded pitching prowess until finally the first overshadowed the second and sent him to the outfield to become the greatest slugger and home run hitter of all time."

—*Associated Press writer Edward J. Neil*

Gift wrapped within the aura of Ruth's 1921 explosion was the Yankees' first-ever A.L. pennant after two decades of futility. They were easy World Series marks for the battle-tested Giants in a struggle for New York bragging rights, but the championship die had been cast. So had Ruth's growing reputation as a fun-loving, hard-living night owl who was driven to physical excesses.

The Bambino traveled the streets of New York as comfortably and enthusiastically as he attacked a pitched ball. Big, friendly and jovial, Ruth was easy to spot with his moon face, round nose, barrel chest and spindly legs. He interacted easily with the people, quick to smile or sign an autograph, and he was generous to a fault. Children loved him, an affection he returned with plenty of interest, and the gregarious personality combined with a showman flair that captivated his legions of fans.

Ruth and catcher Al DeVormer cut dashing figures in the early 1920s, when the excitement-craving Bambino became a familiar face in the New York social scene.

"... That Billiken face, topped by an inevitable fawn-colored cap, makes him easily recognizable. Children love him. He obliges all who ask for an autograph.

"Babe calls everyone, even some close friends, 'Kid' because it is easier than trying to remember names. He is full of kiddish pranks himself. Two years ago in St. Louis, he threw cakes of soap from a hotel window into a fountain to splash passers-by.

"He is superstitious. He never wears underwear, summer or winter. In his locker are horseshoes. He believes he cannot hit unless he uses an eye lotion before every game. He always touches second base between innings on his jog from right field to the dugout."

—*Newsweek magazine*

Make no mistake: Ruth was no saint. He baited umpires and opponents with off-colored remarks, engaged in power struggles against manager Miller Huggins, threw temper tantrums and even challenged the authority of baseball's hierarchy. But his susceptibility to indiscretion also was one of his greatest charms. He was just like everyone else, a true man of the people.

"Babe was just a big kid," former teammate Meusel recalled. "Babe was on the go all the while. He craved excitement. He couldn't sit still. He had tremendous nervous tension. When you went anyplace with him, you were on the move constantly. Ruth never worried much about anything."

If he had a major fault, it was his unquenchable appetite for more. More fun, more drink, more home runs—and more food. His eating habits, particularly his affection for the hot dog, were legendary.

"Ruth eats today (in 1930) as he did in the old days, with utter disregard for his digestion. An ordinary dinner for Ruth consists of a whole capon, potatoes, spinach, corn, peas, beans, bread, butter, three to six cups of coffee, pie and ice cream. He has been known to eat 18 eggs and three portions of ham with a dozen slices of buttered toast for breakfast."

—Harry T. Brundidge for
The Sporting News

It was Ruth's constant struggles with self-discipline that added color and personality to a Yankees team that grew stronger with every season. But it created consternation among the Yankees hierarchy and headaches for Huggins, who had trouble keeping his superstar in rein.

During the 1921 offseason, Ruth and teammates Meusel and Bill Piercy defied commissioner Kenesaw Mountain Landis' ban on barnstorming—a decision that cost them the first six weeks of the 1922 season. Then, playing under a stunning $52,000, three-year contract, Ruth had his tonsils removed at midseason and was suspended for throwing dirt in an umpire's face and chasing an

Ruth and Bob Meusel (right) were suspended by baseball commissioner Landis (center) after the 1921 season, but they all found reason to smile in a later meeting.

abusive fan through the stands. He capped his forgettable 110-game, 35-homer season by hitting .118 in the World Series—another loss to the Giants.

If the 1922 season did not bring Ruth to his knees, it at least gave him pause. He bounced back in 1923 to bat a career-high .393 with 41 homers, 131 RBIs and 151 runs scored and he even hit a home run in the grand opening of Yankee Stadium (The House That Ruth Built), emphasizing his flair for the dramatic. With the Bambino pulling the offensive trigger, the Yankees roared to their third straight pennant and first World Series championship, courtesy of a sweet six-game victory over the Giants.

It was more of the same in 1924 (.378, 46 homers, 121 RBIs) as the Yankees finished second to the Washington Senators, but the 1925 season would present the biggest obstacle of his career. Again haunted by an inability to control his personal excesses, Ruth collapsed on a spring exhibition tour and was rushed to the hospital with a serious intestinal disorder that required surgery. Dick Williams, writing for The Ring, offered this account:

Ruth's classic home run swing transformed baseball from a finesse to power game.

"On an early April day of 1925, in a railroad station in Asheville, high up in the serene Carolina hills, there occurred the first ominous rumblings of the most celebrated digestive disorder of our time.

"It took place in the capacious middle of a great man, George Herman Ruth, and when he opened his mouth and gave vent to the first startled gasp of agony, men and women and little children all over our nation heard it and gave anxious and attentive ear. He was seen to pale beneath his tan. His eyes dilated and his nostrils distended. Slowly one knee began to buckle. Slowly he sought his middle with two hamlike hands and bent forward, and then, as the second knee gave way, he crashed to the station platform.

"The great man was leveled. Babe Ruth had collapsed. One little hot dog, piled upon many, many thousands of hot dogs, had done this hideous thing.

"The stomach ache of all stomach aches had arrived. Babe Ruth had it.

"Two hours after its arrival, the Western Union and Postal Telegraph services were inundated with inquiries from all parts of the country. Newspapers demanded thousands and thousands of words. Private citizens anxiously inquired to the seriousness of the seizure. There was hell to pay.

"The great figure was lifted tenderly and hustled away to a hospital. Learned men of science trundled out their X-rays and other gear and peered into the cavernous body. Then they wrapped the sufferer carefully, placed him aboard a special car and sent him to New York, the while he continued his mighty lamentations and the world waited.

"For days there was unprecedented anxiety. Eventually the object of it opened his eyes and, mistaking the attending physician in his white attire for one of Mr. Harry Stevens' catering agents of Yankee Stadium, asked if he might have a hot dog.

" 'No,' said the doctor. 'Not now or ever again.' The great man looked upon the anxious faces about him and sighed. 'OK, doc,' he said weakly. 'I'm off 'em for life if you say so.'

"This news was flashed to the waiting world outside. Babe Ruth had eschewed the hot dog! A new era was born!"

Ruth's undisciplined lifestyle sometimes made life difficult for Miller Huggins (left), who managed to keep his powerful Yankees on course for three World Series championships.

Ruth's new era would get off to a shaky start. The stomach problem limited him to 98 games and 25 homers in 1925, but the best was yet to come. With first baseman Lou Gehrig joining a lineup that included Tony Lazzeri, Meusel

Ruth and Lou Gehrig (left), maybe the best 1-2 punch in baseball history and perfect complements in the Yankee lineup, seldom crossed paths in off-field social circles.

and Earle Combs, the Bronx Bombers returned to pennant-winning form in 1926 and then laid claim to lasting status as "the greatest team in baseball history" a year later.

The 1927 Yankees bashed their way to 110 wins and then swept away the Pittsburgh Pirates in a quick-and-easy World Series. The highlight of the regular season came on September 30 when Ruth, a .356 hitter, broke his own single-season record with his 60th home run—a standard that would hold up for the next 34 years.

"When the Babe stepped to the plate in that momentous eighth inning, the score was deadlocked. Koenig was on third base, the result of a triple, one man was out and all was tense. ...

"The first Zachary offering was a fast one, which sailed over for a called strike. The next was high. The Babe took a vicious swing at the third pitched ball and the bat connected with a crash that was audible in all parts of the stand. It was not necessary to

follow the course of the ball. The boys in the bleachers indicated the route of the record homer. It dropped about halfway to the top. No. 60 was some homer, a fitting wallop to top the Babe's record of 59 in 1921.

"While the crowd cheered and the Yankee players roared their greetings, the Babe made his triumphant, almost regal tour of the paths. He jogged around slowly, touched each bag firmly and carefully and when he imbedded his spikes in the rubber disk to record officially homer 60, hats were tossed into the air, papers were torn up and tossed liberally and the spirit of celebration permeated the place."

—*The New York Times, October 1, 1927*

Ruth hit 54 homers as the powerful Yankees returned to the championship circle in 1928 and swept the St. Louis Cardinals. He capped another big season by batting .625 in the World Series and hitting three home runs in Game 4—matching his three-homer Series feat against the same Cardinals two years earlier.

Ruth, carrying more weight and aging quickly, would never again reach the 50 plateau, but he continued to set a fast home run pace. He hit 182 over the next four seasons, a total overshadowed by his previous accomplishments and the rise of the Philadelphia Athletics to championship form. But glory would come again. The Bambino, playing against the Chicago Cubs in Game 3 of the 1932 World Series at Wrigley Field, brushed his career with one mystical stroke that would be discussed in baseball circles for decades to come.

"That autumn afternoon in 1932, the Chicago Cubs were on Babe Ruth. They ribbed him and rode him and made him fume. And that was a bad mistake. The Babe good-natured was dangerous enough, but with his dander up he was a holy terror. So this aging immortal, this huge, potato-nosed man with the powerful shoulders, expansive chest and chorus-girl legs, barked to the windy Windy Cityites in the dugout that he was going to belt the next pitch clear out of the park for a home run. With heroic confidence, he motioned menacingly with his bat toward Wrigley Field's center field bleachers, letting the spectator in on his plan, too.

"Then, to paraphrase the poet, the Chicago pitcher held the ball, and then he let it go, and then the pill was plastered by the force of Babe Ruth's blow. He had kept his threat. The oval sailed high and far, and finally landed in the area he had indicated, for what was probably the most dramatic home run in World Series annals."

—*Baseball magazine writer Harold Winerip*

The Yankees swept the Cubs and Ruth's career began its inevitable decline. He slipped to 34 home runs in 1933 and 22 in 1934, his final season with the Yankees. He did have his moments—a two-run homer that helped the

Ruth, instant excitement whenever he stepped to the plate, was the greatest gate attraction in New York history.

Ruth mixed well with the New York public, especially with the kids who lined up for his autographs. The affection was always mutual.

American League win the inaugural All-Star Game in 1933, career homer No. 700 in a 1934 game against Detroit—but the years of hard living had taken their toll and he was forced to pass the leadership baton to Gehrig, the man with whom he would be linked in Yankees posterity.

Ruth's career came to a strange conclusion in 1935 when, at the age of 40, he returned to Boston to play 28 games for the lowly National League Braves. Struggling to remain respectable, the Bambino would enjoy one more moment in the spotlight—a May 25 game against the Pirates at Pittsburgh.

"I have never seen three home runs hit harder than the Babe hit them that day," recalled former Pirates star Arky Vaughan. "Especially the last one. That one was powered over the right field grandstand at Forbes Field. They say it bounded into the street and rolled over to Schenley Park, and I'm here to tell you it was the longest hit ever made in Pittsburgh. Babe hit three homers in succession and tagged a single on his fourth trip. Then he left the game. That's a day I'll never forget."

Eight days after hitting homers 712, 713 and 714, the great one retired. Ruth, holder of virtually every slugging record, hoped to manage in the major leagues, but the opportunity never came. He died of throat cancer in 1948, a year after baseball set aside a "Babe Ruth Day" that included emotional ceremonies at Yankee Stadium.

The legend lives on.

In pre-integration America, Ruth's incredible appeal crossed color lines and gave him status as a true man of the people.

"One other thing he had—and retained through all his playing days. That was a terrific enthusiasm for baseball. He lasted so long as a big leaguer and made so many home runs because, apart from the skill he possessed, he got so much fun out of it all. He liked to hit home runs in championship games and in World Series—but he liked to hit them just as well in exhibition games. Through Florida and on the way north in the spring ... in towns like Indianapolis and Louisville and St. Paul on off days during the season ... I've seen him get just as big a jolt out of belting the ball out of sight as he did when there was a pennant or a pot of World Series gold at stake."

—*New York Sun columnist Frank Graham*

Lou Gehrig

His slashing lefthanded swing terrorized major league pitchers, a bolt of lightning that followed Babe Ruth's thunder. Lou Gehrig was the silent-but-deadly enforcer for a championship machine that ran roughshod over baseball from 1926 through 1938. Big, strong, powerful and indestructible, Gehrig was the slow, plodding Iron Horse that blossomed into a Yankee thoroughbred.

Baseball fans remember Gehrig as the man who played 2,130 consecutive games, a durability standard that stood for more than half a century. But that was only part of his legacy. Gehrig also was a relentless run producer who batted .340 over 15 full seasons and collected 1,995 RBIs, topping the 100 plateau for 13 straight years and the 150 barrier seven times. His 493 home runs, 1,888 runs scored and mild-mannered professionalism often were lost in the glare of Ruth's showmanship.

From 1925, Gehrig's first full season with the Yankees, through 1934, Ruth's last, they formed the best 1-2 offensive punch the game has ever known. Teams couldn't pitch around No. 3 hitter Ruth because of No. 4 Gehrig; the Babe's incredible on-base percentage fed Gehrig's mind-boggling RBI totals. Gehrig, the quiet, no-nonsense, methodical homebody, will forever be linked with Ruth, the gregarious, fun-loving, spotlight-hogging Sultan of Swat.

"I'm not a headline guy," Gehrig once said. "I know that as long as I was following Ruth to the plate, I could have gone up there and stood on my head and nobody would have noticed the difference. When the Babe was through at the dish, whether he hit one or fanned, nobody paid any attention to the next hitter. They were all talking about what Babe had done."

"The tragedy of Gehrig's tremendous records and stunning career was not only that he lacked the flashy showiness so popular during the era in which he played, but that he always seemed to rise to his greatest heights at the precise time when it would be least noticed. And no matter what he did, that wonderful, flamboyant, cussed but naturally beloved Babe Ruth seemed to have been born to outshine him and dim the glory that should have been Gehrig's."

—*Jack Sher writing for Sport magazine in 1948*

Gehrig, the son of German immigrants who found their way to New York City in 1900, was not destined for baseball greatness. His dream took hard work and perseverance. The 220 pounds of muscle he packed into a 6-foot-1, broad-shouldered, wrestler-like frame camouflaged a wealth of athleticism and the shy, colorless, gentle personality he brought to the locker room belied the competitive spirit he delivered on the field.

The giveaway on Gehrig was the way he swung the bat: From a motionless stance, tree-trunk legs planted firmly and wide shoulders hunched slightly forward, he would uncoil suddenly at the ball, driving it with amazing force to all parts of the ballpark. If Ruth was king of the towering, majestic home run, then Gehrig was master of the vicious, fence-busting line drive. It was that powerful bat-meeting-ball force that caught the eye of Yankees superscout Paul Krichell when he watched Gehrig play a 1922 game for Columbia University.

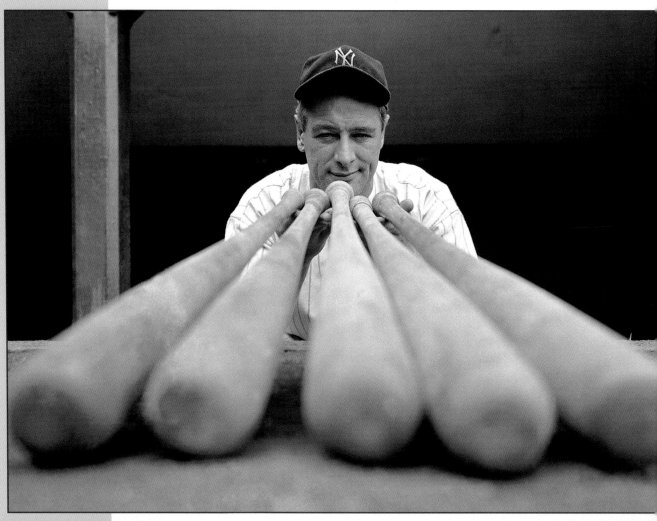

There was nothing flashy or flamboyant about the no-nonsense Lou Gehrig, who let his bats do the talking.

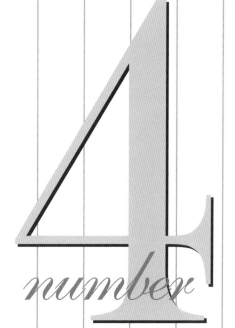

Gehrig's powerful swing intimidated Yankee opponents and his dimpled smile and friendly manner endeared him to once-skeptical fans.

" 'I saw another Ruth today,' the awed Krichell told (Yankees boss) Ed Barrow that night. Barrow laughed. The Yankees also laughed when Krich brought his prize discovery to the Stadium, a shy, overgrown kid with the shoulders and build of a wrestler.

"But no one laughed when they saw him hit a ball. Oddly enough, he hit it with a bat he borrowed from Babe Ruth. There might have been something symbolic about that unconscious act."

—*New York Times columnist Arthur Daley*

The Yankees signed Gehrig for $1,500 and the youngster spent the 1923 and '24 seasons splitting time between New York and Hartford of the Eastern League. Gehrig, who had pitched at Columbia, worked hard in his 193 games at Hartford to turn himself into a competent first baseman and batted .369 for the Senators in 1924. When the Yankees opened the 1925 season with Gehrig on their roster, he was ready for the big test.

But it wouldn't be that easy. Wally Pipp had been entrenched as Yankee first baseman since 1915 and he opened the season in that role. Pipp remained in the lineup until June 2, when a twist of fate gave Gehrig his first opportunity.

"Whatever the reason for Pipp's headache, manager Miller Huggins sympathetically advised Wally to take the day off and let the kid from Columbia take over. In later years, Pipp was to make quite a joke of the headache. 'Some day off,' Wally chuckled. 'I never got back to first base for another season and then in another league—with Cincinnati in the National.'

"This was the start of the legend of indestructible Lou, a record taken so matter of factly by teammates and the public that the very nonchalance with which it was accepted was in itself a tribute to Gehrig. It was taken for granted mainly because Lou took it for granted."

—*Sport magazine writer Tom Meany*

At first, the aggressive, fast-moving, always-intense New York fans didn't know what to make of their new first baseman. He was slow, plain, plodding and far removed from the color and excitement that always seemed to swirl around Ruth. He was dubbed "Old Biscuit Pants" and "Piano Legs" by early critics, but he eventually won them over with his never-yielding class, that shy, dimpled smile and the work ethic that would come to define his Hall of Fame career.

And, of course, those line drives that he dropped all over Yankee Stadium and other major league parks. Quietly, Gehrig became Ruth's protection in a

Gehrig was devoted to the important women in his life—an overprotective mother and wife Eleanor (above), with whom he shared the last six years of his life.

Gehrig (left) regarded Babe Ruth with a sense of awe and often credited him as a baseball mentor and inspiration.

"Murderer's Row" lineup that included Tony Lazzeri and Bob Meusel and he became the model of durability, out there every day playing a solid first base and driving in important runs.

What Ruth was to the home run Gehrig was to the RBI. He was an outstanding clutch hitter who drove in 112 runs for the pennant-winning 1926 Yankees and then put together a magnificent 1927 season—.373 with 47 home runs and 175 RBIs for what many regard the greatest team ever assembled. But in what would become a career pattern for Gehrig, his contributions were lost in the glare of the team's 110 wins, Ruth's record 60 home runs and a World Series sweep of the Pittsburgh Pirates. As always, he chose to downplay his seeming subservience to Ruth.

"How did I learn to hit a long ball? ... Whatever I know about it I owe to Babe Ruth. He has been an untiring instructor and has spent hours of his time showing me how to swing. I really didn't know much about Ruth until 1927, when we began rooming together on the road, but I'll tell you now that there is no man in the world with a bigger heart than Babe. He has the constitution of 10 lions. ... The saddest day of my life will be when the Babe swings the last time. I can tell you, too, that the biggest kick I have gotten out of baseball was in the last few days of the 1927 season when the Babe hit his 60th home run for a new record."

—Harry T. Brundidge for The Sporting News

In retrospect, the Ruth-Gehrig match must have been choreographed by the baseball gods. Ruth craved the spotlight, and Gehrig was only too happy to let him have it. Gehrig wanted to stay in the background, and the Babe provided a perfect foil. While never close off the field, the duo became inexorably linked in Yankees legend. Gehrig happily allowed Ruth to grab the headlines and never strayed from his simple convictions—devotion to his mother and his Yankee teammates, who reveled in his quiet dignity.

By 1928, the New York fans also were reveling in the workmanlike contributions of their big first baseman. Gehrig batted .374 with 27 homers and 142 RBIs in a pennant-winning 1928 season, then followed with a .545 average and four homers in a World Series sweep of the St. Louis Cardinals. In 1930 and '31, non-pennant-winning seasons for the Yankees, Gehrig piled up shocking RBI totals of 174 and 184—a still-standing American League record.

The 1932 season provided a perfect example of the Gehrig curse—spectacular achievements, bad timing. On June 3 against Philadelphia, he became the first player in the 20th century—the third all-time—to hit four home runs in a major league game. But top-of-the-page headlines the next day trumpeted the unexpected retirement of longtime New York Giants manager John McGraw. When Gehrig capped his season with another spectacular World Series performance against the Chicago Cubs—.529, three homers, eight RBIs—he was upstaged by Ruth's called-shot home run.

"I didn't think I would ever see a ballplayer that good," said impressed Cubs manager Charlie Grimm after the fall classic. Grimm was discussing the unsung Gehrig, not Ruth.

It wasn't until Ruth left the Yankees after the 1934 season that Gehrig had the spotlight all to himself—and that would last only until the 1936 arrival of another rising Yankee star—Joe DiMaggio.

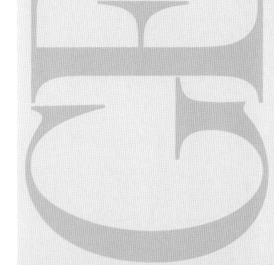

One of the memorable moments of Gehrig's farewell party at Yankee Stadium was the warm embrace delivered by an emotional Ruth.

"In 1935, Lou Gehrig was out from beneath the shadow of Babe Ruth. The Babe was no longer with the Yankee team. Wear and tear and time had tapped Ruth. But actually, Gehrig had begun to emerge even before Ruth's retirement. For toward the end, as the figures indicate, not even the Babe could cast a shadow large enough to blanket the Iron Horse.

"Gehrig's modesty and self-depreciation continued to keep him in the background, but his deeds, his amazing vitality, durability and quality of play refused to be submerged any longer."

—*Paul Gallico for Cosmopolitan magazine*

Indeed, the 1934 season, Ruth's last with the Yankees, was a Gehrig showcase. He won an A.L. Triple Crown—.363, 49 homers, 165 RBIs—and hit four of his major league-record 23 grand slams. Having already passed former Yankee Everett Scott's iron-man record of 1,307 straight games in 1933, he continued his relentless march toward baseball immortality.

With DiMaggio on board in 1936, Gehrig led the A.L. with 49 homers, drove in 152 runs and claimed the A.L. Most Valuable Player award. He stood as the unquestioned leader of a Yankee team that would win the first of four consecutive World Series. A 37-homer, 159-RBI performance in 1937 was typical Gehrig, but a 1938 dropoff to .295 and 114 RBIs sounded an ominous note.

When he reported to 1939 spring training, it became obvious that something was wrong. "That was my first year on the club," recalled former Yankee outfielder Charlie Keller. "I had heard so much about him. He worked so hard in spring training. Lou was having trouble already at that time. But it just seemed to get worse after that."

Gehrig opened the season at first base and continued giving his best effort—with diminishing returns. Finally, without warning, Gehrig accepted his fate and removed himself from the Yankees lineup for the first time in 14 years. On May 2, 1939, news spread throughout the baseball world that the Iron Horse was human.

"I decided last Sunday night (April 30) on this move. I haven't been a bit of good to the team since the season started. It would not be fair to the boys, to Joe (manager Joe McCarthy) or to the baseball public for me to try going on. In fact, it would not be fair to myself, and I'm the last consideration.

Nobody appreciated baseball's Iron Horse more than Joe McCarthy (left), who formed a personal relationship with his big first baseman and stood by his side through the difficult final days of his career.

"... McCarthy has been swell about it all the time. He'd let me go until the cows came home, he is that considerate of my feelings, but I knew in Sunday's game that I should get out of there. ... Maybe a rest will do me some good. Maybe it won't. Who knows? Who can tell? I'm just hoping."
—*Lou Gehrig to New York Times reporter James P. Dawson*

Gehrig would not play another game. Less than a month after ending his streak, Gehrig traveled to the Mayo Clinic in Rochester, Minn., where he was diagnosed with amyotrophic lateral sclerosis, a neurological disorder with no known treatment. It would be fatal.

Gehrig remained with the team, unable to play, through the 1939 season. The highlight of what would be another Yankee championship campaign came early on July 4, when Lou Gehrig Appreciation Day was staged at Yankee Stadium between games of a double-header against Washington. With former and current teammates joining more than 62,000 fans to pay tribute, Gehrig capped an emotional afternoon with a heart-wrenching speech during which he proclaimed himself "the luckiest man on the face of the earth."

A little less than two years later, on June 2, 1941, Gehrig, who had remained upbeat and cheerful to the end, died. "Lou set the greatest example of courage I've ever seen," Keller said. That sentiment was shared by everyone.

"He was described as a plain, humdrum fellow without much color. He never considered himself either unusual or outstanding. It was the American public with its close to infallible common sense that made Lou Gehrig a national hero.

"Because what happened to Lou Gehrig, his life, his struggles, his one love and his ending, far transcends that evanescent, glittery, surface stuff called color. It outweighs sport and the figures of sport. Gehrig entered the hearts of the American people because he was to the end a great and splendid human being."
—*Paul Gallico for Cosmopolitan magazine*

A somber Gehrig, flanked by members of both the Yankees and Washington Senators and cheered on by more than 62,000 fans at Yankee Stadium, fights back his emotions during 'Lou Gehrig Appreciation Day' ceremonies on July 4, 1939—one of the most poignant player tributes ever staged.

Joe DiMaggio

He was the reluctant superstar—aloof, mysterious and unprepared for the demands that face a genuine American icon. Try as he might, Joe DiMaggio could neither escape nor enjoy the fruits of his greatness. From the anonymous sandlots of San Francisco to the thunderous applause of Yankee Stadium, he rose to a hero status he never wanted and adulation he could never understand.

The moment DiMaggio set foot in New York, he was handed the baton of Yankee greatness once carried by Babe Ruth and Lou Gehrig. By the time he left 16 years later, he had carved out a Hall of Fame career, led the Yankees to 10 American League pennants and nine World Series championships, won three Most Valuable Player awards and captured the heart of a nation mesmerized with his graceful style and quiet dignity.

This was the Yankee Clipper, Joltin' Joe and Giuseppe, immortalized in song, married to movie idol Marilyn Monroe and portrayed by a doting media as the most multi-talented star in the game. Indeed, DiMaggio covered Yankee Stadium's vast center field with an effortless, gazelle-like grace, hit for high average and power and played with a mistake-free instinct that amazed teammates and opponents.

"It's funny to think about it," former teammate Bill Dickey once said, "but I think DiMaggio was underestimated as a player. He did things so easily, people didn't realize how good he was."

DiMaggio's only flaw was his susceptibility to illness and injury, a problem that cost him many games and frustrated managers, teammates and fans. But when he was healthy, no player provided a more consistent impact on a franchise's success.

"The Yankee Clipper was the heart of the Yankees just as Babe Ruth had been before him. Each was the leader, the man who extricated them from difficulties. Their personalities were as far apart as the poles, but in action they were blood brothers.

"... It was amazing the way DiMag could respond to pressure, a money player with few equals. Rarely did he falter when the chips were down. He was eternally making the big play and it didn't matter what it had to be—the big hit, the big catch or the big throw. He could make them all in flashing style."

—New York Times columnist Arthur Daley

The DiMaggio legend took root a continent away from the bright spotlight he would command one day in New York. At first, baseball fans dismissed 1933 rumors about a San Francisco Seals phenom as typical Pacific Coast League hype. But soon they were hearing daily reports about 18-year-old Joe DiMaggio's amazing hitting streak, which would balloon to 61 games en route to a .340 average and 169 RBIs. The second of three outfielder brothers who would reach the major leagues (Vince played for 10 seasons with five National League teams, Dom for 11 with the Boston Red Sox), he was described as a 6-2, 193-pound baseball prodigy, a dark-haired, good-looking Italian kid who could chase down fly balls like a young Tris Speaker.

The irony of 1934 will never be lost on Yankee fans. As the great Ruth was playing his final season in pinstripes, the promising DiMaggio was battling a career-threatening knee problem—a fortuitous injury for New Yorkers. One by one, interested major league teams backed off, leaving Yankees scout Bill Essick as the only player in the DiMaggio sweepstakes.

For the bargain price of $25,000 and five journeyman players, DiMaggio became a Yankee. With the knee repaired by minor surgery, the youngster batted .398 and drove in 154 runs for the 1935 Seals. The hype was pouring all over New York City sports pages in 1936 when DiMaggio reported to St. Petersburg, Fla., for spring training with the Yankees.

"It couldn't have been too easy for him in the beginning, for everyone expected so much of him. Remember, every club in both leagues had wanted him until a knee injury had caused all but the Yankees to lose interest in him. ... He reached St. Petersburg with a relined reputation as the best ballplayer to come out of the Coast League since ... well, Lazzeri? The Waner brothers? O'Doul? They weren't quite sure.

number
5

Lou Gehrig passed his leadership baton to DiMaggio in a late 1930s changing of the Yankee guard. The veteran Gehrig (left) works with the young DiMaggio during a 1936 spring training drill.

"When they saw him at St. Petersburg, they knew he couldn't miss. They had seen a lot of guys with big minor league reputations curl up when the pitchers started to throw curves at the training camp. Not this one, though. He was up to stay."

—New York Sun columnist
Frank Graham

DiMaggio's timing was perfect. With Ruth retired and Gehrig entering the twilight of his career, New York needed a new engineer for its Yankees championship express. Young, good looking, mysterious and blessed with classic baseball skills, DiMaggio was the perfect candidate. Glowing spring training reports only heightened the fervor.

Hungry Yankee fans couldn't wait to get their first look—which is exactly what they had to do. After bruising his foot in a spring game, DiMaggio suffered severe burns when he was left unattended with his foot in a diathermy machine. He missed opening day and the Yankees' first 17 games before making his long-awaited debut. Nobody was disappointed.

The Yankees routed the St. Louis Browns, 14-5, before 25,530 fans in a May 3 contest at Yankee Stadium and DiMaggio signaled his arrival with a triple, two singles, one RBI and three runs scored. It was love at first sight.

DiMaggio did nothing to discourage this early infatuation, batting .323 with 29 home runs and 125 RBIs in his rookie season. He also teamed with Gehrig to lead the Yankees to a pennant and World Series championship—the first of four straight the team would win with DiMaggio in the lineup. The New York fans watched with reverence as their rookie prize glided around the outfield and established himself as one of the most feared hitters in the game.

DiMaggio followed his big first season with a .346, 46-homer, 167-RBI 1937 effort and a .324, 32, 140 outburst in '38. His first of three MVPs and two A.L. batting titles (.381) came in 1939, the year Gehrig's iron man streak came to a stunning end, and signaled his ascendance to the throne as Yankee leader.

"As long as I can remember, when the Yankees took the field, they all waited for Joe to make the first break. Nothing was said about this ritual, but everybody held back and waited for Joe to lead us out."

—Former DiMaggio teammate Joe Page in The Sporting News, 1951

DiMaggio might have been the engineer, but he wasn't happy about the perks that came with the job. Fame was instant, privacy was no longer possible. He didn't understand his sudden celebrity and never learned how to make it work for him.

Ruth had enchanted New York with his colorful antics and magnetic personality. Gehrig had won over fans with his boyish charm and quiet charisma. DiMaggio was shy, aloof and withdrawn off the field, powerful, showy and dominating on it. His athletic flair and dramatic accomplishments brought back memories of the Bambino—and the adulation he had commanded.

It was the idolatry that DiMaggio detested. He disdained public appearances, did his best to avoid aggressive fans and deflected credit whenever possible to his teammates. Always gracious to fans and writers, the classy Clipper lived in fear of his powerful aura. Few people, not even the teammates who admired and looked up to him, were allowed to penetrate his inner shell.

DiMaggio often would remain secluded in the Yankees clubhouse until the wee hours of the morning, hoping to avoid the masses. But inevitably they would be waiting outside and, forced into a corner, he would sign autographs and shake hands as long as it took to break free.

"Fame irritated DiMaggio. He is one of the loneliest men I've ever met and usually he moved (as fast as possible) through crowds. The flattery most men enjoy embarrasses him. I've spent most of my adult life in the newspaper business. Joe DiMaggio is the shyest public man I've met. ... He is more a spectator than a participant in any group. He is concealed and withdrawn."

—New York Post columnist Jimmy Cannon

The classic swing was a big part of DiMaggio's aura—a mystique that still hangs over the tradition-rich Yankees franchise.

A classic DiMaggio moment came in Game 4 of the 1939 World Series when he slid home (left) as Reds catcher Ernie Lombardi 'snoozed.' DiMaggio circled the bases on a 10th-inning single, thanks to an error and a home-plate collision that stunned Lombardi.

There was nothing shy about DiMaggio when he stepped to the plate. He was relaxed and patient, a pull hitter who could uncoil into the pitch with power from his wide, motionless stance. He seldom struck out, putting the ball into play with a Ted Williams-like consistency.

Over a relatively short 13-year big-league career that was interrupted in its prime by three years of military duty in World War II, DiMaggio batted .325 and topped the 100-RBI plateau nine times—a testament to his ability in the clutch. He always seemed to be in the middle of World Series action, pounding out eight home runs and 30 RBIs in 10 fall classics. Amazingly, only three of his major league seasons (1940, '46 and '48) were not followed by World Series and only four did not yield championships.

DiMaggio had plenty of help in a powerful Yankees lineup that also included outfielder Charlie Keller (left).

If there was one single season that cemented DiMaggio's name in Yankees lore, it was 1941—the Year of the Streak. For two glorious months, from May 15 to July 17, he put together the longest, most exhilarating stretch of hitting excellence ever witnessed. Over an incredible 56-game span, he collected 91 hits, drove in 55 runs, batted .408 and led the Yankees to a 41-13 record with two ties.

First he passed former Browns first baseman George Sisler's modern major league record of 41 straight games (1922), then former Baltimore outfielder Willie Keeler's all-time record of 44 (1897). The streak finally ended at Cleveland Stadium on July 17, as reported in the next morning's *New York Times* by John Drebinger:

"In a brilliant setting of lights and before 67,468 fans, the largest crowd ever to see a game of night baseball in the major leagues, the Yankees tonight vanquished the Indians, 4-3, but the famous hitting streak of Joe DiMaggio finally came to an end.

"Officially it will go into the records as 56 consecutive games, the total he reached yesterday. Tonight in Cleveland's Municipal Stadium the great DiMag was held hitless for the first time in more than two months.

"Al Smith, veteran Cleveland lefthander and a Giant castoff, and Jim Bagby, a young righthander, collaborated in bringing the DiMaggio string to a close. Joltin' Joe faced Smith three times. Twice he smashed the ball down the third base line, but each time Ken Keltner, Tribe third sacker, collared the ball and hurled it across the diamond for a putout at first. In between these two tries, DiMaggio drew a pass from Smith.

"*Then, in the eighth amid a deafening uproar, the streak dramatically ended. ... With the bases full and only one out, Bagby faced DiMaggio and, with the count at one ball and one strike, induced the renowned slugger to crash into a double play. ... the crowd knew the streak was over.*"

That streak, and another 16-game run that immediately followed, helped DiMaggio post a final .357 average. Another 1941 headline-maker was Boston left fielder Williams, who posted the first .400 average (.406) since 1930—and the last of the 20th century. DiMaggio outpolled his career rival in 1941 MVP voting and came back six years later to edge him again, this time by a single vote.

By the late 1940s, the minor injuries that had cost DiMaggio playing time in virtually every major league season began taking a more serious toll. A left heel problem required surgery and sent him to the sideline; then his right heel required surgery and cost him half of the 1949 campaign. After missing the first 65 games of that season, DiMaggio returned to action in a crucial July series against the Red Sox and hit four home runs in three games—a Yankee sweep.

That regular season ended on an emotional note when 69,551 fans paid tribute to

Everything about DiMaggio was classy, from his quiet, no-nonsense demeanor to his gliding artistry in center field and his powerful, run-producing swing.

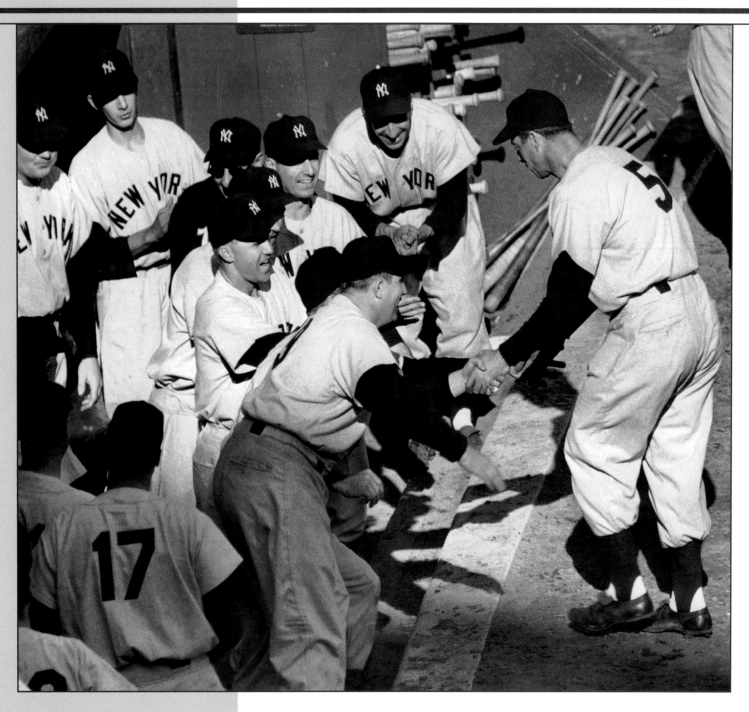

DiMaggio gets a warm welcome after hitting his final career home run—a Game 4 blow against the Giants in the 1951 World Series.

their Yankee Clipper during Joe DiMaggio Day ceremonies at Yankee Stadium. "I'd like to thank the Good Lord for making me a Yankee," he told the cheering throng.

Two years later, at age 36 after an injury-plagued 116-game 1951 season, a subdued DiMaggio announced his retirement. Fittingly, his final hit, a double, came in Game 6 of the Yankees' World Series win over the New York Giants.

"If he wasn't the greatest player we've ever seen in 20 years of watching the American League, he'll do until his counterpart comes along. He could run and field and hit. ... He could clear the fences and he had the speed for extra bases inside the park.

"DiMaggio was at his best against good pitching and in the clutch. He was a born big leaguer who picked up the polish and style of a champion with effortless ease. There never was any question but what he'd make the grade."

—Chicago Daily News columnist John P. Carmichael

Mickey Mantle

Greatness makes for strange bedfellows, which explains why it did not seem so preposterous back in 1951 that a naive boy from tiny Commerce, Okla., could one day share a New York sports pedestal with the likes of Babe Ruth, Lou Gehrig and Joe DiMaggio. It was never a matter of talent for Mickey Mantle, who arrived at his first Yankees training camp wearing a cheap straw hat and lugging a four-dollar cardboard suitcase. It was a matter of survival and perseverance.

As baseball genius goes, Mantle's required patience, understanding and lots of bandages, the kind he wrapped around his aching knees for 18 major league seasons. Touted as the offensive reincarnation of Ruth and the center field heir to the great DiMaggio, Mantle stumbled early before carving out his own record of excellence that carried him to Hall of Fame glory and the Yankees to new championship heights.

That the Mick was able to overcome unrealistic expectations and knee problems that dogged him virtually every day of his career is a tribute to the almost perfect blend of physical skills in his muscular 5-foot-11, 195-pound body. He was worth the price of admission, a switch-hitter with unheard of power from both sides of the plate and a swing tailored to fit his thick 17½-inch neck, powerful shoulders, strong back and bulging forearms and biceps.

Young sluggers Mickey Mantle (left) and Eddie Mathews were well on their way to 500-homer renown when they posed together in 1955.

"Once inside the batter's box, he digs his spikes hard in the dirt, planting his rear foot as firmly as a stake. He sets his front foot down more lightly, bends slightly at the waist and swishes his bat back and forth. As the pitcher winds up, Mantle abruptly cocks his bat. For an instant, he is a motionless, outrageously muscular figure that might have been hewn from solid oak. Then he swings and there is the sound of distant thunder."
—Roger Kahn for Newsweek magazine in 1956

The Mantle aura was all about thunder—loud, gargantuan tape-measure home runs that exploded beyond the boundaries of everyone's imagination. He didn't just hit the ball out of the park; he pounded it into oblivion. Mantle hit the ball with Gehrig-like force and Ruthian distance, a combination nobody had ever guessed possible.

"I thought when I was playing with Ruth and Gehrig I was seeing all I was ever gonna see," said former Yankees catcher Bill Dickey, a coach with the team in 1956. "But this kid ... Ruth and Gehrig had power, but I've seen Mickey hit seven balls, seven, so far ... well, I've never seen nothing like it."

From the right side in 1953, he hit a drive off Washington lefthander Chuck Stobbs that sailed over the 50-foot outer wall at Griffith Stadium and came to rest in the back yard of a house 565 feet from home plate. Batting lefthanded in 1956, he hit a skyscraper shot off Washington's Pedro Ramos that bounced off the

The name of Mantle's game was power, which generated from the picture-perfect swing he unleashed from either side of the plate.

facade above Yankee Stadium's third deck—370 feet from the plate, 117 feet high and 18 incredible inches away from leaving the stadium.

Soon, every Mantle arrival in another American League city was being preceded by newspaper accounts of titanic blasts—at Chicago's Comiskey Park, Kansas City's Municipal Stadium, Detroit's Briggs Stadium ... or wherever he happened to play last. But fans, enticed by the quality of his home runs, got much more than they bargained for. They often left the park marveling at the blazing speed (3.1 seconds from home to first), the great instincts and the powerful arm that made Mantle one of the most complete players in baseball history.

"(Yankees manager Casey) Stengel will describe by the hour Mantle's natural power at the plate ('He hit one into those upper right field stands in Detroit. Seats were flyin' round for five minutes.'). And, for another hour, Mickey's speed on the basepaths and in the outfield ('The boy can fly.'). Then, if you're still with him, Casey will go into Mantle's overall quickness and coordination."

—Tom Meany for Collier's magazine

There was never any doubt Mantle would be a major league player. The swing, the instincts and the intensity were instilled early and groomed by his father, Elven "Mutt" Mantle, a frustrated sandlot star who supported his family as an Oklahoma miner. The elder Mantle worked out his son relentlessly and insisted that he learn to switch hit, a tool that would serve him well.

Yankees scout Tom Greenwade liked what he saw in 1949 and signed the blond, grey-eyed kid, then a shortstop, for $1,000. By the time young Mick got a call to join the Yankees for 1951 spring training, reports already had circulated through New York that Stengel was grooming a phenom—he "could hit the ball farther than Ruth, run like the wind"—to replace the aging and injury-prone DiMaggio as a center fielder and to carry the Yankees' torch of greatness.

It wouldn't be that simple. Playing in DiMaggio's vast shadow was bad enough. But Mantle had never played above the Class C level and was totally unprepared for the transition from rural America to the bright lights of New York. As words like "yonder", "that there" and "shucks" captivated the New York media, his shy, withdrawn personality wilted in the city's intense spotlight. He was as far away from DiMaggio's poise and Ruth's articulate color as he was from Commerce, Okla.

By midseason of his rookie year, it had become apparent that Mantle, starting in

A young Mantle takes his turn in the spring training sliding pit. Before suffering knee injuries that would plague him throughout his career, Mantle was one of the fastest players in the game.

right field, was overwhelmed. He was shipped to Kansas City of the American Association, a failure in his own mind and a disappointment for New York fans who had expected instant success. Mantle regained his confidence and was recalled late in the 1951 season; it took Yankee fans the better part of a decade to embrace him with star-quality affection.

"What is a superstar? It is a great player who has a strange, mysterious rapport with the fans. The player must have exceptional talents, but it is the magnetic spark from the fans that give him the glamor, the ability to thrill, the ability to draw fans through the turnstiles.

"Mantle came to New York as a shy, retiring teenager and gradually became a living legend as he hit homers lefthanded and righthanded for tremendous distance. ... He was always an exciting crowd-pleaser, but in his earlier days received his share of boos, even in New York. It was as if the fans, some of them, resented the young giant's prowess."

—Jim Ogle for The Sporting News in 1968

A career pattern was set in the 1951 World Series when Mantle, chasing a Game 2 fly ball, stepped on a Yankee Stadium drain and tore tendons in his already delicate knee. Seldom would he run again without pain and never would he get through a whole season without missing playing time. Months after his World Series mishap, young Mick was stunned when his 40-year-old father died of cancer.

Mantle celebrates his Game 5 home run in the 1953 World Series—a grand slam that lifted the Yankees to an 11-7 win over Brooklyn.

Everybody knew about Mantle's physical problems, but opponents never really understood the extent of his pain until they saw him dressing over the years at All-Star Games.

"I always knew he was bandaged," former shortstop Dick Howser once said. "I thought he just wrapped the usual Ace bandage around his leg. Then I saw him wrap all that wide, foam rubber bandage around his legs and couldn't believe it. I wondered how he not only could play bandaged like that, but run as he did."

As Mantle became acclimated to New York and more comfortable with media demands, fans began seeing the flashes of greatness. The home runs became longer and more spectacular, he used his blazing speed more often on the basepaths and his center field defense improved. Few runners dared challenge his rifle arm.

His breakout season came in 1956 when, now the driving force of the Yankees offense, he won an American League Triple Crown, batting .353 with 52 home runs and 130 RBIs. His first of consecutive MVPs established him among the game's elite players and gave him renewed status as a New York icon. But Mantle never felt the full adulation of fans until 1961, the season he played second fiddle to teammate Roger Maris in the great home run chase.

EXIT

Mantle suffered his first serious knee injury when he tripped on a Yankee Stadium drain and tore his tendons in Game 2 of the 1951 World Series. Center fielder Joe DiMaggio catches a fly ball (left) as right fielder Mantle sprawls in pain.

As both players mounted a serious rush on Ruth's single-season home run record of 60, New York fans suddenly embraced Mantle, the "true Yankee," and openly rooted for him to top Maris, who was in his second year with the team. As the tension mounted for Maris, Mantle could do no wrong and was afforded the love he always had been denied. That Mantle, injured down the stretch, would fall short with 54 homers while Maris would break the record with 61 did nothing to tarnish the birth of a hero.

Mantle, the rookie, posed with center field predecessor DiMaggio (left photo) in 1951. Mantle, the veteran, posed a decade later with home run partner Roger Maris (right photo).

"Suddenly, as he became the underdog to the interloper, Mickey became a favorite to the crowd. ... the pendulum swung so abruptly to the well-scrubbed, dimple-cheeked slugger who became his last several seasons a folk hero. Pestered everywhere for his time and autograph ... he became bigger than life, a legend in his time."

—Bob Broeg for The Sporting News

The Mantle aura became almost mystical as he limped his way through the rest of his career. Once lost in the city's bright glare, he now mixed comfortably in its nightlife, often acccompanied by teammate buddies Billy Martin and Whitey Ford. Once intimidated by the fans and the media, he learned how to work them to his advantage.

Mantle was still 'a kid' in 1952 when he celebrated a World Series victory over the Dodgers with Yankees shortstop Phil Rizzuto.

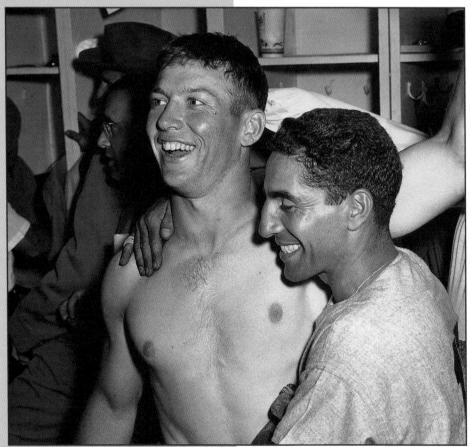

Stories still circulate about the moody Mantle, prone to glare away unwanted questions from the press and brush aside autograph-seeking kids. He could be surly and brusque, but he also could be open and disarming. Many a New Yorker was charmed by the shy smile and innocence that still emanated from his round face years after his career had ended in 1968.

And it's hard not to be charmed by his career accomplishments, which include a .298 average, 536 home runs and 1,509 RBIs—most of them compiled in unyielding pain. And like the Ruth-Gehrig-DiMaggio Yankee superstar line he completed, Mantle claimed an amazing World Series legacy. In 12 of his first 14 major league seasons, the Yankees won A.L. pennants and seven championships. He still owns World Series records for runs (42), homers (18), RBIs (40), total bases (123) and walks (43). Nobody was more prolific in Series play.

"I can remember what a scared, tongue-tied kid Mantle was when he first broke into the big leagues in 1951. And I can still remember the awed look on his face the first time he ever met DiMaggio.

" 'Wanna know something?' said the Mick, 'I'm still awed by him. And I'm still awed by (Ted) Williams, too. When I look back on how I was a kid, I marvel at the kids who come up today. No one awes them. And they all are so articulate. I was five years in the big leagues before I got up enough nerve to talk to any of the stars.' "

—*New York Times columnist Arthur Daley in 1968*

Mantle's Hall of Fame plaque tells the story of a success-filled career.

There are two schools of thought. One says Mantle could have been better, maybe the greatest player ever, if he had worked a little harder than he played. Another says his numbers are remarkable considering he played most of his career on one leg. Perhaps his legacy lies somewhere between the extremes.

Hard living certainly took a toll on his body, which already was being stretched to the limit. "If I knew I was going to live this long, I would've taken better care of myself," he said in 1995, shortly before his death at age 63 of liver cancer. Mantle was only half joking. He had lived in morbid fear since 1952 that, like his father and two uncles, he would die young.

But it's hard to imagine that he could have endured the knee pain any more than he did or perform more admirably in the clutch, the quality that best defined his outstanding career. It's no coincidence that the Yankees, as Mantle edged into the twilight of his career after 1964, stopped dominating baseball.

There were, simply, no more legends on the horizon to carry on the championship tradition of Ruth, Gehrig, DiMaggio ... and Mantle.

Mickey Mantle Day, staged at Yankee Stadium in 1965, was filled with tears, cheers and an emotional speech from one of the great sluggers in baseball history.

"It was always hard for me to understand how a man, who knew he was dying, could stand here and say he was the luckiest man in the world. Now I know how Lou Gehrig felt. Now I understand.

"I feel about the same as I did the first day I walked into Yankee Stadium. I had no words to describe that feeling. I have none to describe my feelings now. Playing 18 years in Yankee Stadium for you folks has to be the best thing that ever happened to a ballplayer."

—*Mantle, speaking to 60,096 fans at Yankee Stadium, during ceremonies to retire his No. 7 in June 1969.*

THE UNFORGETTABLES

JACK CHESBRO

The Yankees' first Hall of Fame pitcher compiled a 129-92 record over six-plus New York seasons (1903-09), highlighted by an extraordinary 41-win 1904 effort that still ranks as the century's highest win total. The sturdy spitballer completed 48 of 51 starts and worked 454⅔ innings in his prolific season, but he is best remembered for throwing a final-day wild pitch that allowed Boston to clinch the A.L. pennant.

WILLIE KEELER

He was on the downside of his Hall of Fame career and nowhere near his 1890s form, but "Wee Willie" still ranks as the Yankees' first legitimate superstar. He played right field instead of center from 1903-09 and batted .294, far below his .341 career average. The speedy "hit it where they ain't" lefthander batted .343 in 1904, when the Highlanders lost the pennant on the season's final day.

KID ELBERFELD

Colorful, intense and always ready for a good fight, Elberfeld was the first regular shortstop and second manager in the Yankees' "New York" history. The .271 career righthanded hitter anchored the team's infield through 1907 and became manager midway through the 1908 season when he replaced Clark Griffith. Elberfeld returned as a player only in 1909, his final New York campaign.

CLARK GRIFFITH

The "Old Fox," nearing the end of his Hall of Fame pitching career, was the first manager hired and fired after the franchise's move to New York. He posted a 419-370 managerial record from 1903-08 and a 32-24 mark on the mound. Griffith, who compiled a 237-146 record over 20 major league seasons, gained later fame as manager and longtime owner of the Washington Senators.

AL ORTH

The hard-throwing righthander formed a solid 1-2 pitching punch with Jack Chesbro during a career-ending 1904-09 stint with the Highlanders. Orth was ill during much of Chesbro's 41-win 1904 campaign, but he was 18-16 in '05 and 27-17 in '06, when he led the A.L. in innings (338⅔) and complete games (36). The 204-game winner posted only 16 victories over his final three seasons.

RUSS FORD

The most prolific rookie in Yankees history posted a 26-6 record with 209 strikeouts in 1910. The righthanded spitballer followed with win totals of 22, 13 and 12, bringing his career record to 73-56. Then, without warning, it was over. Ford jumped to the outlaw Federal League in 1914, pitched two seasons and abruptly retired. He still ranks first all time in career ERA (2.54) among Yankee pitchers with 1,000 or more innings.

HAL CHASE

One of the more controversial and free-spirited Highlanders, "Prince Hal" was a popular star and regular first baseman from 1905-13—a defensive wizard and .291 career hitter who mesmerized fans with outstanding talent and angered them with indifferent play. Chase also was a known gambler who played most of his 14 big-league seasons under the scrutiny of managers who suspected him of throwing games.

JACK QUINN

The center of a bitter contract dispute between the White Sox and Yankees after playing five years in the Federal League and Pacific Coast League, the righthander was forced to return to New York in 1919 and posted 15-14 and 18-10 records before going 8-7 as a starter and reliever for the franchise's first pennant-winner. Quinn, a 247-game big-league winner, was 40-34 in his first Yankees stint from 1909-12.

WALLY PIPP

Best remembered for a headache that allowed Lou Gehrig to begin his ironman streak in 1925, Pipp actually was a 10-year starter at first base (1915-24) and a member of the Yankees' first championship team. A .281 career lefthanded hitter with power, he typically batted fourth or fifth and posted five New York seasons of 90 or more RBIs. In 1916 and '17, Pipp led the A.L. with homer totals of 12 and 9.

FRANK "HOME RUN" BAKER

Although he never matched the heights of his seven seasons with the Athletics, the future Hall of Famer gave the Yankees four solid seasons as a regular third baseman (1916-19) and ended his one-year retirement to supply part-time help for the franchise's first two pennant-winners in 1921 and '22. Baker's best New York season was 1919, when he batted .293 with 10 homers and 83 RBIs.

BOB SHAWKEY

The four-time 20-game winner anchored Yankee staffs from 1916-24 and won 54 games over the 1921-23 run that produced three pennants and the franchise's first championship. The former Athletics righthander, who was 1-2 in seven World Series contests, won 168 games over 13 Yankee seasons before retiring in 1927 to become a coach. Shawkey took the managerial reins in 1930, after Miller Huggins' 1929 death, but lasted only one season.

ROGER PECKINPAUGH

The starting shortstop in all nine of his New York seasons (1913-21), Peckinpaugh helped mold the Yankees into a contender. A pesky righthanded hitter with good defensive range, he anchored the franchise's first pennant-winning team in 1921 before finishing his 17-year career at Washington and Chicago. At age 23, Peckinpaugh served as Yankees manager for the last 20 games of 1914.

EVERETT SCOTT

He was the outstanding defensive shortstop for the Yankees' first championship team in 1923. But "Deacon" is better remembered as the man who held baseball's ironman record (1,307 straight games) before Lou Gehrig. The 5-8 Scott, a Yankees starter from 1922-24 after eight years with the Red Sox, saw his streak end May 6, 1925, when manager Miller Huggins benched him in favor of Pee Wee Wanninger.

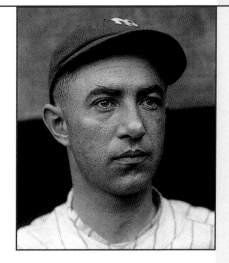

WAITE HOYT

Best remembered for the 45-14 record he compiled as ace for the 1927 and '28 Yankees, Hoyt actually was the team's most consistent starter throughout the 1920s. From 1921-29, the Hall of Fame righthander compiled a 155-96 mark for teams that captured the franchise's first six pennants and three World Series titles. The sophisticated and articulate former Red Sox hurler was 6-3 for the Yankees in fall classic play.

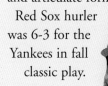

CARL MAYS

The submarining righthander was the winning pitcher in the Yankees' first World Series game and the man who threw the 1920 pitch that struck and killed Cleveland shortstop Ray Chapman. Mays also was part of a Boston pipeline that built the Yanks into championship contenders. Acquired from the Red Sox in 1919, he was 26-11 in 1920 and 27-9 in 1921—the season the Yankees won their first pennant.

JOE DUGAN

"Jumping Joe" was the starting third baseman on five pennant-winners and all three Yankee championship teams in the 1920s. Acquired in 1922, he filled a defensive void and provided a solid righthanded bat for the team's "Murderer's Row" lineup until 1928. Dugan, a close friend and drinking companion of Babe Ruth, holds distinction as the first Yankee to hit a World Series homer at Yankee Stadium.

SAM JONES

"Sad Sam," part of the early Red Sox pipeline to New York, posted a 21-8 record in 1923 to fuel the Yankees' first championship. Jones, a 229-game winner in a career that stretched to 1935, also contributed to pennant-winning teams in 1922 and '26 over five Yankee seasons. The righthander, who was traded to the Browns before the 1927 campaign, was 0-1 in five Yankee World Series appearances.

JOE BUSH

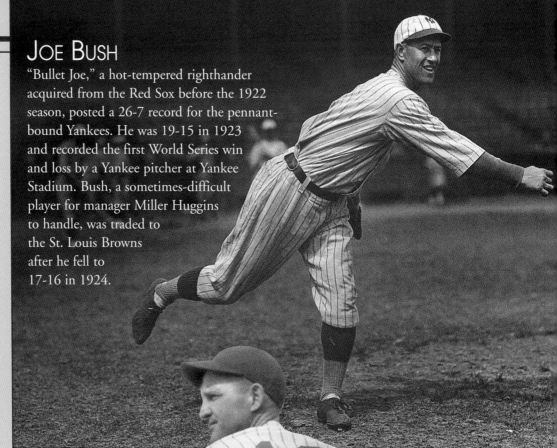

"Bullet Joe," a hot-tempered righthander acquired from the Red Sox before the 1922 season, posted a 26-7 record for the pennant-bound Yankees. He was 19-15 in 1923 and recorded the first World Series win and loss by a Yankee pitcher at Yankee Stadium. Bush, a sometimes-difficult player for manager Miller Huggins to handle, was traded to the St. Louis Browns after he fell to 17-16 in 1924.

GEORGE PIPGRAS

The hard-throwing righthander won 10 games for the 1927 Yankees in his first full season and 80 more over the next five years, during which he served as staff ace for two more title teams. He was 24-13 in 1928 with an A.L.-high 300⅔ innings and 16-9 for the 1932-champion Yankees. Pipgras started one game in each of his three World Series and won them all.

HERB PENNOCK

Acquired from the Red Sox in 1923 at age 29, the clever lefthander began an 11-year Yankees association that would yield a 162-90 record and four championships. A control artist who changed speeds and kept hitters off balance, the slender Hall of Famer was 19-6 for the 1923 champs, 21-9 in 1924 and 23-11 in 1926, a pennant-winning season. He was 36-14 overall for the 1927 and '28 Yankees and 5-0 in World Series play.

MARK KOENIG

He outhit Babe Ruth and Lou Gehrig in the 1927 World Series, but Koenig was best known as an outstanding defensive shortstop for what many consider the greatest team in history. He also was a good contact switch-hitter who batted second between Earle Combs and Ruth. Koenig was a starter for pennant winners from 1926-28 before taking on a utility role in '29. He was traded in 1930 to Detroit.

PEE WEE WANNINGER

Wanninger spent only one season in New York, but his name is prominent in Yankees lore. He was the light-hitting shortstop who replaced Everett Scott in the lineup on May 6, 1925, ending Scott's ironman streak at 1,307 games. And he was the scheduled hitter who gave way to pinch-hitter Lou Gehrig on June 1, thereby beginning the Iron Horse's consecutive-games streak of 2,130.

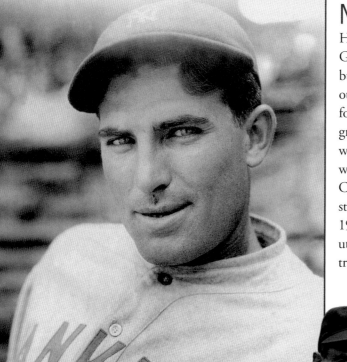

EARLE COMBS

The speedy center fielder and leadoff man for the "Murderer's Row" Yankees batted .325 and scored 1,186 runs in a Hall of Fame career that stretched from 1924-35. Combs, who ranks second on the team's all-time triples list with 154, also was a .350 hitter in four World Series, three of which produced championships. He batted .356 with a league-leading 231 hits and 23 triples in 1927.

URBAN SHOCKER

Having traded Shocker in 1918 to the St. Louis Browns, for whom he became a four-time 20-game winner, the Yankees reacquired him in December 1924. Over the next three seasons, the righthanded spitballer became an important figure for one of the great teams in history. Shocker was 19-11 for the 1926 pennant-winners and 18-6 for the powerful 1927 Yankees, a season complicated by heart problems. He appeared in one 1928 game and died later that season at age 35.

JOE SEWELL

Baseball's ultimate contact hitter was near the end of his Hall of Fame career when he took over third base for the 1931 Yankees. He held the job for three years, including a memorable 1932 campaign that produced the franchise's fourth World Series title. Sewell, a .282 hitter with the Yankees, averaged 94.7 runs scored in his New York stay while batting No. 2 ahead of Babe Ruth and Lou Gehrig.

BILL DICKEY

The Hall of Famer backstopped eight Yankee pennant-winners and seven World Series champions over a brilliant 17-year career (1928-43, 1946). He was a masterful catcher as well as a .313 career lefthanded hitter and four-time 100-RBI man. A team leader and post-career tutor of Yogi Berra, Dickey couldn't avoid the spotlight. He played in eight All-Star Games and posted World Series totals of 37 hits, five homers and 24 RBIs.

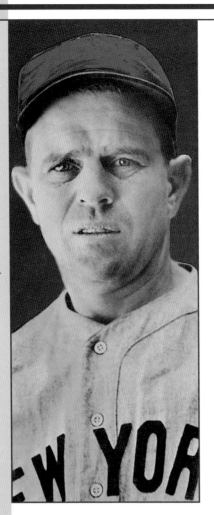

MILLER HUGGINS

The first in a line of great Yankee managers, Huggins (right) was the strategic mastermind of the franchise's first six pennants and three World Series titles. The 5-6, 140-pound "Hug" fought obstinate players, ill health and an antagonistic owner to carve out a 12-year New York record of 1,067-719 (.597). The manager of the powerful 1927 Yankees died unexpectedly in September 1929, news that rocked the Yankees organization.

WILCY MOORE

As a 30-year-old rookie for the 1927 Yankees, the sidearming righthander posted a 19-7 record and 13 saves while staking claim as the team's first great reliever. Plagued by arm problems, Moore still was reliable in 1928 and '29—as well as '32 and '33, when he closed out his career with the Yankees after a short stay in Boston. He was 2-0 with a 0.56 ERA in World Series play.

BEN CHAPMAN

Fiery and intense, the speedy outfielder could win games with his bat, glove, arm or legs. A .305 hitter over six-plus Yankee seasons (1930-36), Chapman was a three-time stolen base champ and two-time 100-RBI man who could adapt his hitting style to any situation. He batted .299 and drove in 107 runs as a left fielder in 1932, capping the season with six RBIs in a World Series sweep of the Cubs.

RED ROLFE

Rolfe provided a steady glove and disciplined bat for teams that won five World Series and six pennants from 1936-42. Always reliable defensively after becoming the regular third baseman in 1935, the contact-hitting lefthander topped .300 four times and scored 100 or more runs in seven of his 10 New York seasons—including an A.L.-best 139 in 1939. Rolfe was a .284 hitter in six World Series.

FRANK CROSETTI

He was the regular shortstop on five World Series champions and a backup on three others. Crosetti's playing career spanned 17 seasons (1932-48) and his 20-year coaching career gave him 37 straight seasons in a Yankees uniform. Never flashy, the .245 career hitter did little things to help his team win. He stole bases, drew walks, made all the routine plays and led quietly, by example.

MONTE PEARSON

Overshadowed by fellow starters Lefty Gomez and Red Ruffing, Pearson still was an important cog in the Yankees machine that won four straight World Series from 1936-39. In five New York seasons, he posted records of 19-7, 9-3, 16-7, 12-5 and 7-5. The 6-foot righthander started one game in each of his four World Series, winning all of them while carving out a 1.01 postseason ERA.

JOHNNY MURPHY

One of the game's most proficient early firemen, Murphy helped bring respectability to the art of relief pitching. The righthanded curveballer won 93 games and saved 104 in a 12-season Yankees career that stretched from 1932-46 and presaged the closer role as we know it today. "Fordham Johnny," who produced win totals of 14-10, 13-4, 12-4 and 10-5, won or saved games in each of the six World Series he helped the Yankees win.

ATLEY DONALD

As a 28-year-old rookie in 1939, Donald won his first 12 games (an A.L. rookie record) and finished 13-3. The fire-balling righthander spent the rest of his eight-year career complementing such Yankee starters as Lefty Gomez, Red Ruffing, Spud Chandler, Tiny Bonham and Marius Russo. A 65-33 career pitcher and member of three championship teams, Donald later became a successful Yankees scout.

BUMP HADLEY

Ten-year veteran Hadley joined the Yankees in 1936 and helped pitch them to four straight World Series titles. The stocky righthander compiled consecutive records of 14-4, 11-8, 9-8 and 12-6 before accepting a relief role in 1940, his final Yankee season. Hadley, a 161-game big-league winner, is remembered for throwing the 1937 beanball that prematurely ended Hall of Famer Mickey Cochrane's career.

LEFTY GOMEZ

The fast-quipping, hard-throwing Hall of Famer combined with righthander Red Ruffing to dominate the A.L. during the 1930s. A four-time 20-game winner, Gomez was a big-game pitcher—6-0 in five World Series and 3-1 in All-Star Game competition. The colorful, always-witty Lefty, who carved out a 26-5 record in 1934 and a 24-7 mark in 1932, ranks third all-time in Yankee victories with 189.

BABE DAHLGREN

The Yankees' other "Babe" holds distinction as the first baseman who replaced Lou Gehrig when the Iron Horse ended his consecutive-games streak at 2,130 on May 2, 1939. Dahlgren hit a homer and double that day, driving in three runs, and went on to record 15 homers and 89 RBIs during the season. Dahlgren, who also homered in the '39 World Series, drove in 73 runs in 1940, his final New York campaign.

GEORGE SELKIRK

Faced with the overwhelming burden of replacing Babe Ruth in right field, Selkirk responded well and contributed to five World Series titles from 1936-41. The man dubbed "Twinkletoes" replaced Ruth in 1935 and drove in 94 runs. Five times he batted .300 and twice he topped 100 RBIs over a nine-year career that ended in 1942. Selkirk batted .265 in six fall classics with 10 RBIs.

TOMMY HENRICH

"Old Reliable" was exactly that—a clutch, fundamentally perfect player who contributed to seven World Series championships. The .282 career-hitting right fielder and first baseman could beat you with his glove, dangerous left-handed bat or leadership, all of which he displayed from 1937-50. Typical Henrich was the ninth-inning home run he hit to beat the Dodgers and Don Newcombe, 1-0, in Game 1 of the 1949 World Series.

CHARLIE KELLER

"King Kong" Keller was a muscular lefthanded home run threat and part of an outstanding outfield that included Joe DiMaggio and Tommy Henrich. The bushy-browed left fielder, one of the game's most feared sluggers until back problems diminished his effectiveness, recorded three 30-homer and 100-RBI seasons from 1939-46, a period in which the Yanks captured four pennants and three World Series titles.

HANK BOROWY

Borowy was front and center from 1942-45, when the Yankees won two war-time pennants and a World Series. The 26-year-old rookie righthander was 15-4 for the 1942 A.L. champs and 14-9 in 1943, when they won a championship. After a 17-12 effort in 1944, Borowy was 10-5 in '45 when the Yankees shockingly sold his contract to Chicago. He won 11 of 13 decisions for the Cubs and finished the season 21-7.

TINY BONHAM

The 6-2, 215-pound "Tiny" jumped into the Yankees' pennant parade from 1940-46. The righthander was 9-3 as a late-season callup in 1940 and 21-5 and 15-8 in pennant-winning 1942 and '43 campaigns. His 2.73 career ERA ranks fourth all time among Yankee pitchers with 1,000 or more innings. Bonham, after pitching his third season for Pittsburgh in 1949, died of complications following abdominal surgery at age 36.

JOE GORDON

As the replacement for second baseman Tony Lazzeri in 1938, Gordon hit 25 homers and won over skeptical fans. He went on to top 100 RBIs three times—including his MVP-winning 1942 effort—over a seven-season Yankee career interrupted by two years of military service. "Flash" was a six-time All-Star Game selection and key member of four World Series champions before he was traded to Cleveland in 1946.

PHIL RIZZUTO

"Scooter" was the sparkplug shortstop who anchored 10 pennant-winners and eight World Series champions during the 1940s and '50s. The 5-6, 160-pound Brooklyn-born Hall of Famer was the glue that held together the Yankees' dynasty from 1941-56, both physically and emotionally. Rizzuto's greatest contribution was the energy he always brought to the game, for 13 years as a player and another four decades as a popular Yankees broadcaster.

SPUD CHANDLER

The .717 winning percentage (109-43) over 11 seasons defines Chandler, who didn't make his first big-league appearance until age 29. The 6-foot righthander was 20-4 with a 1.64 ERA in 1943, earning the A.L. MVP award. He also posted seasons of 20-8, 16-5, 14-5 and 10-4 while contributing to teams that won seven pennants and six championships from 1937-47. Chandler was 2-2 in World Series play.

SNUFFY STIRNWEISS

A free-spirited second baseman who could beat you with his bat, glove or legs, Stirnweiss was a popular Yankee from 1943-50 and a contributor to three championship teams. His signature season was 1945 when he led A.L. hitters in average (.309), runs (107), hits (195), triples (22) and stolen bases (33). Stirnweiss, who also played third, batted .319 with A.L.-best totals of 205 hits, 125 runs and 55 steals in 1944.

NICK ETTEN

Etten, a solid first baseman and run producer during the war years of 1943-46, enjoyed a short-but-sweet Yankees career. He hit 14 homers and drove in 107 runs for the 1943 team that defeated the Cardinals in the World Series and he posted A.L.-leading totals of 22 homers in 1944 and 111 RBIs in '45 before being dispatched to Philadelphia after the 1946 campaign.

JOHNNY LINDELL

A converted pitcher, Lindell was Joe DiMaggio's center field replacement during the 1943-44 war years and the starting left fielder from 1946-47. The rest of his nine-plus New York seasons (1941-50) were spent as a valuable reserve. Lindell (right photo with DiMaggio), a member of three championship teams, hit a pennant-saving home run against Boston on the next-to-last day of the 1949 season, enabling the Yankees to tie for first place.

BILL BEVENS

A sore shoulder ended Bevens' career after only four major league seasons, but his name lives in Yankees lore. Bevens, a big righthander, came within one out of pitching baseball's first postseason no-hitter in Game 4 of the 1947 World Series, only to lose the no-hitter and the game when Dodgers pinch-hitter Cookie Lavagetto hit a two-run double. Bevens did post 13-9 and 16-13 records in 1945 and '46.

JOE PAGE

Desperately looking for a relief ace to replace Johnny Murphy, the Yankees turned to Page in 1947. Unspectacular as a spot starter/reliever over his first three years, the fireballing lefthander reeled off win-save totals of 14-17, 7-16, 13-27 and 3-13 while helping the Yanks claim three championships. Page, a workhorse in the 1947 and '49 World Series, hurt his arm in spring 1951 and was released.

BUCKY HARRIS

In his first New York season, Washington's former "Boy Wonder" manager guided the Yankees to a 1947 pennant and victory in one of the most exciting World Series ever played. When the Yankees finished third in 1948, new general manager George Weiss, looking for an excuse to hire Casey Stengel, fired Harris and set the stage for one of the most glamorous periods in the team's history.

BOBBY BROWN

A part-time third baseman from 1946-54, Brown made his biggest impact as a .439 World Series hitter. He collected 18 hits in 41 at-bats over four fall classics, playing key roles in a 1949 win over Brooklyn and a 1950 sweep of Philadelphia. Brown, who attended medical school during his years with the Yankees, went on to become a Texas cardiologist and served 11 years as A.L. president.

VIC RASCHI

His 120-50 record from 1946-53 was a key factor in six championships and nobody symbolized the Yankee work ethic of that period more than Raschi. The big righthander posted three straight 21-win seasons (1949-51) and beat Boston in the final game of 1949 to clinch a pennant. A 5-3 pitcher in World Series play, Raschi once fired a 15-0 shutout at Detroit and drove in seven runs himself.

ALLIE REYNOLDS

"The Chief" was equally adept as a starter or reliever—a clutch righthander in any role and a key figure for six Yankee World Series champions. He never won fewer than 13 games over eight Yankee seasons (1947-54) that yielded a 131-60 record and 41 saves. Reynolds, a 7-2 performer in World Series play, is best remembered for his two 1951 no-hitters, the second of which clinched a tie for the pennant.

ED LOPAT

Smart, clever and always one step ahead of the hitter, Lopat displayed his mound magic for the Yankees for seven-plus seasons and played a big role in their five-straight championship run from 1949-53. The 5-10 lefty averaged more than 14 wins while compiling such records as 21-9 (1951), 18-8 (1950) and 16-4 (1953). His 4-1 World Series mark included two 1951 wins against the Giants.

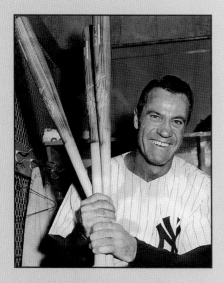

HANK BAUER

The hard-nosed former Marine spent most of his 12 Yankee seasons (1948-59) as a platoon outfielder who pushed and prodded teammates to championship heights. Bauer, a .277 career hitter, helped the Yanks win nine pennants and seven World Series, several with memorable performances. His bases-loaded triple and spectacular ninth-inning catch saved Game 6 of the 1951 classic and his four home runs sparked a 1958 Series win over Milwaukee.

JOE COLLINS

A 10-year Yankee, Collins retired in 1958 when the team sold his contract to Philadelphia. He was the regular first baseman from 1952-54 and a platoon player in other seasons—a quiet leader for seven pennant-winning teams and five World Series champions. Collins was a lefthanded hitter who could pull the ball into Yankee Stadium's short right field porch, a feat he performed four times in World Series play.

GENE WOODLING

It's no coincidence the Yankees posted five straight World Series wins from 1949-53—the first five of six seasons Woodling spent in New York. He was the primary left fielder during those years and a dangerous lefthanded hitter who twice topped .300. Woodling, a longtime Yankees scout after ending his 17-year career, was a .318 World Series hitter who, unfortunately, is remembered for a fly ball he lost in the sun in the finale of the 1950 classic.

JERRY COLEMAN

Coleman was a slick-fielding second baseman who started for three World Series champions (1949-51) and performed backup duty for another (1956). Fans remember the articulate righthander as the smooth double-play partner of Phil Rizzuto and a clutch hitter who batted .364 in the 1957 Series and supplied two game-winning hits in the 1950 fall classic. He later became a familiar voice in the Yankees broadcast booth.

JOHNNY SAIN

A four-time 20-game winner for the Braves, the 6-2 righthander spelled relief for Yankee teams that won three straight World Series. Sain, known for his guile and wide assortment of curveballs, was a spot starter and reliever who posted a 33-20 record from 1951-55 and an A.L.-high 22 saves in '54. Working in relief, the future Yankee pitching coach (1961-63) won the opener of the '53 Series.

ANDY CAREY

Carey took over at third base in 1954 and held the job until 1959, when back problems and illness limited him to 41 games. He batted .302 in '54 and tied for the A.L. lead with 11 triples a year later. A solid defender who played on four championship teams before leaving in May 1960, Carey is best remembered for his Game 1-winning single in the 1957 World Series off Warren Spahn.

JOHNNY MIZE

A Hall of Fame performer during his early career with the Cardinals and Giants, Mize provided valuable bench help in a career-ending stint with the Yankees (1949-53). The "Big Cat" played for five straight World Series champions, primarily as a pinch-hitter and backup first baseman. He played often enough to hit 25 homers in 1950 and his three-homer, six-RBI effort in the 1952 Series helped the Yanks win a seven-game classic against Brooklyn.

BILL SKOWRON

"Moose" was a key figure for seven pennant-winners and four World Series champions from 1954-62. The strong, righthanded-hitting first baseman was a four-time .300 hitter and 20-homer man in regular-season action, but he ranks among all-time World Series leaders with 39 hits, 29 RBIs and eight home runs, including a grand slam in Game 7 of the Yanks' 1956 win over Brooklyn.

BILLY MARTIN

A fiery, battling second baseman for Yankee teams that won six pennants and five World Series, "Billy the Kid" went on to later fame as the manager who was hired and fired five times by owner George Steinbrenner. Martin the player is best remembered for his World Series-saving catch of a popup in Game 7 of the 1952 classic and his World Series-ending single in 1953. Martin the manager is remembered for his celebrated off-field fights, tirades against Reggie Jackson and Steinbrenner and the two pennants (1976, '77) and one World Series winner (1977) he delivered.

ENOS SLAUGHTER

After building a Hall of Fame resume with the Cardinals, "Country" made two New York stopovers as veteran insurance for pennant-bound teams. The always hustling right fielder made his biggest contribution in the 1956 World Series when he batted .350 and hit a decisive Game 3 homer against Brooklyn. He also provided bench help for pennant-winners in 1957 and '58 before ending his 19-year career in 1959 at age 43.

GIL MCDOUGALD

The versatile infielder, the only Yankee to start regularly at second, third and shortstop, was a valuable member of eight pennant winners and five World Series champions from 1951-60. McDougald, the man who felled Indians pitcher Herb Score with a line drive to the face in 1957, was 1951 A.L. Rookie of the Year and a two-time .300 hitter. He still ranks among the leaders in numerous World Series offensive categories.

Don Larsen

He was a journeyman righthander who won 45 games over five New York seasons (1955-59), but few players hold a more exalted place in Yankees lore. On October 8, 1956, the 6-4, 225-pounder with the new no-windup delivery pitched the only perfect game—the only no-hitter—in World Series history. His 97-pitch masterpiece was one of three wins Larsen recorded in four New York World Series.

Ralph Terry

Terry's first signature moment came in 1960 when he served up a World Series-ending home run to Pittsburgh's Bill Mazeroski. His second came in 1962, when he finished off a World Series-deciding shutout of the Giants by retiring Willie McCovey on a dramatic Game 7-ending line drive. The 6-3 righthander was at his Yankee best from 1960-63 when he posted win totals of 10, 16, 23 and 17 for pennant-winning teams.

Ryne Duren

Fans cheered wildly when the squinting righthander with the thick glasses entered from the bullpen and fired his first 95-mph warmup off the screen. Duren was colorful and unpredictable in three full New York seasons (1958-60) and hitters lived in fear. Duren played on that fear to record an A.L.-high 20 saves in 1958 and he posted a 1.93 ERA with a win and save in that season's World Series win over Milwaukee.

Bob Grim

Grim, the last A.L. rookie to win 20 games, was 20-6 during a 1954 Rookie of the Year season in which he started 20 times and won eight games in relief. Arm problems forced the hard-throwing righthander to the bullpen in 1956 and he won 12 games and recorded a league-leading 19 saves for the 1957 A.L. champs. Grim was traded to Kansas City in 1958.

ELSTON HOWARD

He was the first black player in Yankees history (1955) and the American League's first black MVP (1963). "Ellie" was steady, whether playing outfield in his early years or behind the plate in the 1960s as the successor to Yogi Berra. In a New York career that lasted 12-plus seasons, Howard played for nine pennant winners and four World Series champions and appeared in six All-Star Games.

CASEY STENGEL

Clown, sage, buffoon, genius, master motivator—the "Old Professor" was all of the above during an amazing 12-year managerial run (1949-60) that brought the Yankees 10 pennants and seven World Series titles. Unsuccessful during two previous managerial stops, the former outfielder used his platoon system and superior Yankee talent to carve out a 1,149-696 record and all-time best 37 fall classic games won. A New York fan favorite, the 70-year-old Stengel was forced to retire in 1960 but he resurfaced two years later as manager of the expansion Mets.

BOB TURLEY

"Bullet Bob," one of the hardest-throwers in Yankees history, reached baseball heaven in 1958 when he finished 21-7, earned World Series MVP honors with two key wins in New York's seven-game come-back win over Milwaukee and captured Cy Young honors. His next-best seasons were 17-13 and 13-6 in a Yankees career that stretched from 1955-62, and he posted a 4-3 record in five fall classics.

CLETE BOYER

An outstanding third baseman, Boyer played for five World Series teams and two champions in a Yankees career that stretched from 1959-66. A career .242 righthanded hitter with occasional power, Boyer is best remembered for a glove that was overshadowed by the defensive work of Baltimore contemporary Brooks Robinson. Boyer, one of seven baseball-playing brothers, collected 20 hits and 11 RBIs in World Series play.

TONY KUBEK

Kubek spent nine seasons (1957-65) as a steady shortstop and occasional outfielder for Yankee teams that won seven pennants and three World Series. A .266 hitter over a career that ended prematurely because of back and neck problems, Kubek is remembered as the victim of a bad-hop grounder. He was rushed to the hospital after being struck in the throat in Game 7 of the 1960 World Series against Pittsburgh.

BOBBY RICHARDSON

This little second baseman played for the Yankees from 1955-66, anchoring teams that won seven pennants and three championships. The always-reliable Richardson was an offensive catalyst from his leadoff or No. 2 batting slot and a five-time Gold Glove winner. Richardson became the first World Series MVP to play for the losing team when he totaled a record 12 RBIs in a 1960 binge against Pittsburgh.

JOE PEPITONE

The Brooklyn-born "Pepi" was a flaky, fun-loving first baseman with a lefthanded swing tailored for Yankee Stadium. Although he never lived up to his vast potential, he topped 25 home runs four times from 1962-69 and played for three pennant-winning teams. The long-haired Pepitone, a fan favorite who won three Gold Gloves, hit a memorable grand slam in Game 6 of the 1964 World Series against St. Louis.

LEFT TO RIGHT: BOYER, KUBEK, RICHARDSON AND PEPITONE.

LUIS ARROYO

The cigar-smoking little lefthander with the nasty screwball was a bullpen force during the Yankees' memorable 109-win 1961 season. Arroyo posted A.L. highs in games (65), relief wins (15, 12 in a row) and saves (29) while recording a victory in Game 3 of the World Series. A 1962 arm injury kept Arroyo from becoming a long-term force and his four-year New York stay ended in 1963.

HECTOR LOPEZ

From 1959-66, Lopez was one of the game's most versatile and reliable role players. He could play second base, third and the outfield while handling life as a regular, platoon player or pinch-hitter. Lopez, a slashing righthanded batter, was dangerous in the clutch and a contributor to five straight pennant-winners from 1960-64. He drove in seven runs in nine at-bats in the 1961 World Series against Cincinnati.

ROGER MARIS

Everybody remembers Maris' record-setting 61-homer onslaught in 1961, but he also won an A.L. MVP award in 1960 (39 homers, 112 RBIs) and drove in 100 runs for the 1962 Yankees. The talented right fielder was a key figure on five pennant-winners and two World Series champions after being acquired from Kansas City. Never popular or comfortable in the New York spotlight, Maris was traded to St. Louis after the 1966 season and helped the Cardinals win two N.L. pennants.

RALPH HOUK

A former Yankee backup catcher, the "Major" replaced Casey Stengel as manager in 1961 and led the team to three straight pennants and two World Series titles before becoming general manager in 1964. Houk returned to the dugout in 1966, replacing Johnny Keane, and was prominent in the franchise's rebuilding years from 1966-73. He resigned after the 1973 season and later managed at Detroit and Boston.

JIM BOUTON

Best remembered as the author of *Ball Four*, a post-New York baseball book that invaded the previously sacrosanct locker room, Bouton actually was a talented righthander who posted 21-7 and 18-13 records in 1963 and '64, both pennant-winning seasons. Bouton, known for his cap-shedding delivery, injured his arm and never won more than four games again before being sold to Seattle in October 1968.

TOM TRESH

The son of former big-league catcher Mike Tresh was a hard-hitting switch-hitter who started and ended his career at shortstop but spent the majority of his Yankee years (1961-69) in left field. The 1962 Rookie of the Year was a four-time 20-homer man and member of four pennant-winning teams. His three-run, eighth-inning homer beat the Giants in Game 5 of the 1962 World Series.

BOBBY MURCER

"The next Mickey Mantle" fell short of those expectations, but he was a solid run-producing Yankees outfielder from 1969-74 before making a memorable return from 1979-83. The .277 career hitter left New York in a shocking 1974 trade and returned in '79, just in time to become chief spokesman and eulogist after close friend Thurman Munson died in a plane crash. The popular Murcer has been broadcasting Yankee games since his retirement in 1983.

AL DOWNING

The hard-throwing left-hander made his first Yankee appearance in 1961 and his first impact two years later when he posted a 13-5 record while starting 22 games. Downing was 13-8 in 1964, the Yankees' final pennant year of the decade, and went on to record win totals of 12, 10 and 14 before suffering an arm injury in 1968. He left New York in 1969 with a 72-57 record.

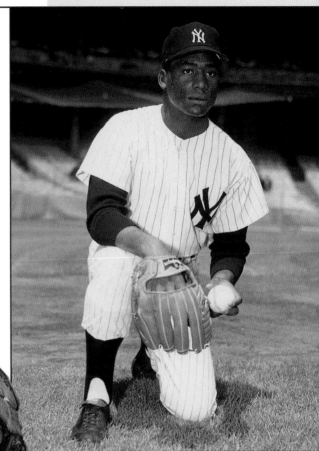

JOHN BLANCHARD

He was a valuable role player for Yankee teams that won five consecutive pennants and two World Series from 1960-64, an outfielder-catch-er-first baseman who supplied power off the bench. The lefthanded-swinging Blanchard was a dangerous clutch hitter, whether spot starting or pinch-hitting with the game on the line. He batted .455 in the 1960 World Series and homered twice in the 1961 fall classic.

MEL STOTTLEMYRE

A three-time 20-game winner, he was a bright spot for Yankee teams that suffered through a humbling pennant drought from 1965-75. The righthanded sinkerballer posted a 9-3 rookie record and one World Series win in 1964 and proceeded to win 164 games before a shoulder injury ended his career in 1974. Stottlemyre, who has served as Yankees pitching coach under manager Joe Torre since 1996, pitched in four All-Star Games.

Doc Medich

The big righthander posted win totals of 14, 19 and 16 for 1973-75 Yankees teams—seasons that set the stage for a return to World Series glory. Medich, an offseason medical student who eventually became a doctor, was the ace of '74 and '75 teams that contended for East Division titles. He was sent to Pittsburgh in a 1975 trade that brought Willie Randolph to New York.

Stan Bahnsen

The 6-2 righthander won A.L. Rookie of the Year honors in 1968 when he compiled a 17-12 record and sparkling 2.05 ERA for the Yankees. He continued as a rotation workhorse through 1971, never making fewer than 33 starts or pitching fewer than 220 innings while compiling a 55-52 record. Bahnsen, traded to Chicago after the 1971 season, posted a 21-16 mark in 1972 for the White Sox.

Thurman Munson

His tragic death in a 1979 plane crash rocked the Yankees and millions of fans, who had watched the hard-nosed catcher rise from 1970 Rookie of the Year to 1976 MVP and fearless captain of two World Series champions. Munson, a five-time .300 hitter and three-time 100-RBI man, was one of the most feared clutch hitters in the game and winner of three Gold Gloves. He was a .357 hitter in postseason play—.373 in 67 World Series at-bats.

Ron Blomberg

He never reached potential because of injuries, but the lefthanded-hitting first baseman does hold one baseball distinction. He became the game's first DH on April 6, 1973, when he batted against Boston's Luis Tiant and drew a bases-loaded walk. Hailed as a future star when he was drafted in 1967, Blomberg batted .302 and hit 47 homers in 400 games over seven New York seasons.

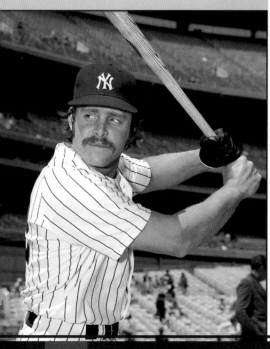

Roy White

The popular left fielder, a steady hand for teams that failed to win a pennant from 1965-75, provided a veteran influence from 1976-78, when the Yankees won three pennants and two World Series. A dangerous switch-hitter, White compiled a .271 career average, drove in runs, stole bases and contributed in many other ways. He still ranks high in many of the Yanks' all-time offensive categories.

SPARKY LYLE

The colorful lefthander with the long sideburns, handlebar mustache and nasty slider appeared in 420 games and recorded 141 saves from 1972-78—the Yankees' "Bronx Zoo" era. His showcase season was 1977, when he finished 13-5 with 26 saves, led the Yankees to a championship and became the first A.L. reliever to win a Cy Young. Lyle lost his closer job to Goose Gossage in 1978 and was traded after the season to Texas.

FRITZ PETERSON/ MIKE KEKICH

These Yankee lefthanders gained lasting infamy when they swapped wives, families, homes and even pets in a bizarre revelation before the 1973 season. Peterson (far left) was a talented starting pitcher who won 20 games in 1970 and 109 over a Yankees career that stretched from 1966-74. Kekich (left) won only 31 games from 1969 to '73, when he was traded to Cleveland.

RON DAVIS

The big righthanded sidearmer was primarily a setup man for closer Goose Gossage over four New York seasons (1978-81). Davis, who once struck out eight straight batters, was 14-2 with nine saves in 1979 and 9-3 with seven saves a year later. He appeared in four World Series games in 1981 before being traded to Minnesota, where he piled up season saves totals of 22, 30, 29 and 25.

WILLIE RANDOLPH

He was the Yankees' quiet man for 13 seasons, the slick-fielding second baseman who could spark an offense with his patience and ability to get on base. Randolph, a .276 career hitter, was a rock for the "Bronx Zoo" Yankees and key contributor to five pennant- and division-winning teams from 1976-81. The four-time All-Star, who left as a free agent in 1988, has served as a Yankees coach since 1994.

MICKEY RIVERS

"Mick the Quick" was the go-get-'em center fielder and leadoff man for three pennant-winners and two World Series champions from 1976-78, his only three full New York seasons. The slouching little lefthander stole bases (43 in 1976), hit for average (.326 in '77) and used his blazing speed to spark the team's powerful offense. As a Yankee, Rivers averaged .299 and swiped 93 bases.

RON GUIDRY

Remembered historically for his 25-3, 1.74-ERA, Cy Young-winning 1978 season, "Louisiana Lightning" was a New York favorite for 14 seasons, three of which produced 20-win records and two of which ended with World Series titles. The 160-pound lefty overpowered hitters with a 95-mph fastball and nasty slider, strikeout pitches that inspired a rhythmic clap from Yankee fans when he reached two strikes on the hitter. Guidry posted a 170-91 record and five postseason wins over a career that ended in 1988.

CATFISH HUNTER

After reaching championship heights with the Athletics, Hunter signed a free-agent contract and helped the Yankees win three straight pennants and two World Series from 1976-78. The clever righthander was 23-14 in 1975 and 17-15 in '76, but tailed off to 9-9 and 12-6 before ending his Hall of Fame career in 1979. Hunter was the starter and winner in Game 6 of the 1978 Series—the victory that completed the Yankees' miracle season.

CHRIS CHAMBLISS

The big first baseman with the classic swing ended an 11-year World Series drought for Yankee fans when he hit his dramatic ALCS-winning home run against the Royals in 1976, a shot that touched off a near riot at Yankee Stadium. Chambliss was a lineup fixture and run producer from 1974-79, a steadying influence for teams that won three pennants and two World Series.

LOU PINIELLA

The fiery, emotional Piniella, one of baseball's most feared clutch hitters, was an 11-year fan favorite on Yankee teams that won four pennants from 1976-81. Adequate in the outfield, "Sweet Lou" was a .291 career hitter who always seemed to be center stage with the game on the line. After retiring in 1984, the former Royals Rookie of the Year coached under Billy Martin and managed the Yankees for two-plus seasons.

BOB LEMON

The former Cleveland pitching great holds a special place in the hearts of Yankee fans, even though he never managed a full season in New York. It was Lemon who guided the Yanks through the dramatic 1978 pennant race after replacing Billy Martin in July with the team trailing the Red Sox by 10 games. Under Lemon, the Yankees posted a 48-20 record, won a division-deciding playoff game at Fenway Park and defeated the Royals and Dodgers in the ALCS and World Series. The laid-back Lemon also managed parts of the 1979, '81 and '82 seasons.

GOOSE GOSSAGE

Free-agent signee Gossage, a big, intimidating righthander, took over the closer role from Sparky Lyle and posted 150 saves for teams that won two pennants and a World Series. Goose pitched for the Yankees from 1978-83 and was involved in many spotlight moments. New Yorkers will never forget 1978, when Goose dramatically retired Boston's Carl Yastrzemski on a popup to end the one-game East Division playoff and then recorded final outs in both the ALCS and World Series.

BUCKY DENT

He was a light-hitting shortstop for Yankee teams that won four pennants and two World Series from 1977-81, but everybody remembers Dent for the dramatic three-run homer he hit in a one-game playoff at Boston to secure the 1978 East Division title. That blast gave Dent, who hit only 40 career homers, lasting hero status if not job security. He was gone by 1982, although he did return to manage the Yankees for parts of the 1989 and '90 seasons.

ED FIGUEROA

He was the Yankees' biggest winner from 1976-78, a stretch in which they won three straight pennants and two World Series. The 6-1 righthander won 55 games over that span, which included a 20-9 mark that helped fuel the incredible pennant run of 1978. After an elbow injury shortened Figueroa's 1979 season, he was sold to Texas in 1980. He left New York with 0-2 records in both the ALCS and World Series.

REGGIE JACKSON

Brash, proud, articulate and controversial, the power-hitting right fielder was "the straw that stirred the drink" from 1977-81—a five-season span in which the Yankees won four division titles and two World Series. The Hall of Fame-bound lefthanded hitter with the big, corkscrew swing was not too shabby during the regular season (41 homers, 111 RBIs in 1980; 32-110 in '77), but he always excelled in the postseason spotlight. "Mr. October" is best remembered for his dramatic three-home run explosion against the Dodgers in Game 6 of the 1977 World Series.

TOMMY JOHN

From 1979-82, John won 62 games for Yankee teams that captured two division titles and a pennant. From 1986-89, the 6-3 lefty won 29 more in a New York return that served as the finale to his incredible 26-year career. A sinkerballer who became the poster boy for recovery from serious arm surgery, John was 21-9 in 1979 and 22-9 a year later. He was 1-0 in both the 1981 ALCS and World Series.

BRIAN DOYLE

The backup infielder played 93 games over three New York seasons, batting .170. But Doyle found himself dead center in the spotlight when he replaced injured second baseman Willie Randolph in the 1978 postseason. In the World Series, he batted .438 (7-for-16), scored four runs and helped the Yanks win their second straight championship. He finished his four-year career in 1981 at Oakland.

OSCAR GAMBLE

The free-spirited Gamble contributed 17 homers and much-needed locker room chemistry to the Yankees' 1976 pennant run. After two-plus years with other teams, he returned in 1979 for six more seasons as a part-time outfielder and DH, helping the Yanks win two more division titles and another pennant. Gamble, a lefthanded pull hitter, belted two homers and drove in six runs in the 1981 postseason.

KEN GRIFFEY SR.

His 1982 arrival signaled the departure of Reggie Jackson, who didn't want to become a full-time DH. Griffey, the former Big Red Machine star in Cincinnati, was shuffled among four positions—all three outfield spots and first base—and never really adjusted to the Yankee spotlight. He did bat .306 in 1983 and he was hitting .303 in June 1986 when he was traded to Atlanta.

DAVE RIGHETTI

Righetti, the A.L.'s 1981 Rookie of the Year, was one of the more popular Yankees of the 1980s. The hard-throwing lefty spent three seasons as a starter, a period highlighted by his memorable July 4, 1983, no-hitter against Boston at Yankee Stadium. In 1984, "Rags" replaced Goose Gossage as closer and went on to pile up 224 saves. He recorded a then-record 46 in 1986 and never dropped below 25 from 1984-90.

BOB WATSON

A burly first baseman and outstanding hitter over 14 seasons in Houston, Watson batted .307 for the division-champion 1980 Yankees and hit .318 with two homers and seven RBIs in the 1981 World Series. Watson later returned to the Yankees as general manager, a job he held in 1996 and '97 after two years in the same post with the Astros. He was responsible for hiring Joe Torre as manager.

DAVE WINFIELD

His 205 homers, 818 RBIs and five Gold Gloves helped Winfield pad his Hall of Fame credentials over eight-plus Yankee seasons (1981-90), but he never attained hero status in New York. One reason was his constant feuding with owner George Steinbrenner over contract and personal issues. Another was his timing—the 6-6 left fielder, lured to New York by an incredible 10-year contract, played for only one World Series team—and batted a dismal .045 in the 1981 fall classic.

RUDY MAY

The tall lefthander with the sweeping curveball made two visits to New York—from 1974-76, when he compiled a 26-19 record, and from 1980-83, when he was 28-27. May, a part-time starter and reliever, was 14-12 with a 3.06 ERA for the 1975 Yankees, but his best season was 1980, when he finished 15-5 with a 2.46 ERA for the A.L. East Division champions.

DON BAYLOR

The former Angels MVP brought intensity and toughness to a Yankees team that was short of both. From 1983-85, the muscular righthanded hitter handled DH duties and showed his young teammates how to hustle, battle, break up double plays and play without fear—a quality illustrated by the 60 pitches that hit him over that span. Baylor also averaged 24 homers and 88 RBIs for the Yankees.

JIM ABBOTT

A popular if not overly successful member of the Yankees' pitching staff in 1993 and '94, the inspirational lefthander compiled a 20-22 record. Abbott, who overcame the handicap of being born without a right hand, enjoyed his signature New York moment on September 4, 1993, when he pitched a 4-0 no-hitter against Cleveland— the first Yankee no-hitter since Dave Righetti's 10 years earlier.

DON MATTINGLY

"Donnie Baseball" was one of the most popular players in Yankees history, even though he never played in a World Series. Mattingly batted .307 from 1982-95, but his six-year stretch from 1984-89 was phenomenal. He topped 100 RBIs in five of those seasons, won a batting title (1984), captured an MVP (1985) and tied a big-league record by homering in eight straight games. Fans loved his first base artistry (nine Gold Gloves), tireless work ethic and enthusiasm, even though he didn't play in a postseason game until 1995—his final campaign.

JIM LEYRITZ

His three-run, Game 4 homer off Atlanta reliever Mark Wohlers revived the gasping Yankees in the 1996 World Series and set the stage for four championships in five years. The backup catcher, a Yankee since 1990, was traded after that dramatic season, but he returned to New York in 1999 to provide late-season help for another pennant-winner. Leyritz hit eight postseason homers—four for the Yankees, four for the Padres.

WADE BOGGS

What irony! Boggs, former Red Sox star third baseman, dressed in pinstripes and sitting atop a policeman's horse with fist raised in celebration of the Yankees' 1996 World Series win over Atlanta. Boggs, picked up as a free agent in 1993, batted .313 over five Yankee seasons (.311 for the 1996 champs) before ending his Hall of Fame career at Tampa Bay in 1998 and '99.

RICKEY HENDERSON

From 1985-89, Henderson performed his leadoff magic for New York fans. His four-plus seasons were filled with stolen bases (seasons of 80, 87 and 93, all Yankee records), impressive power numbers (nine leadoff homers in 1986, seasons of 24 and 28), high runs totals (146, 130) and high on-base percentages (.423, .422). He also filled a center field void before moving to his natural left field spot. Mired in a contract dispute, Henderson was traded to Oakland in June 1989.

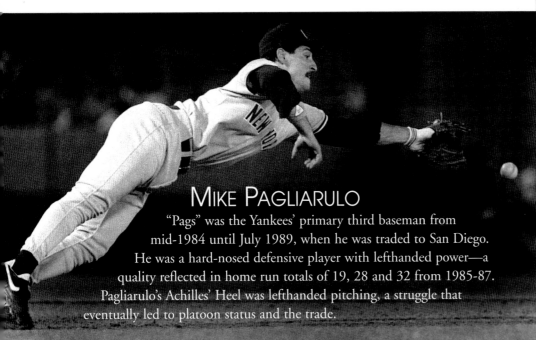

MIKE PAGLIARULO

"Pags" was the Yankees' primary third baseman from mid-1984 until July 1989, when he was traded to San Diego. He was a hard-nosed defensive player with lefthanded power—a quality reflected in home run totals of 19, 28 and 32 from 1985-87. Pagliarulo's Achilles' Heel was lefthanded pitching, a struggle that eventually led to platoon status and the trade.

DANNY TARTABULL

He signed a big five-year, free-agent contract in 1992 and spent much of his three-plus Yankee seasons battling lofty expectations. The muscular right fielder/DH did post homer-RBI seasons of 25-85 and 31-102 in 1992 and '93, but he struggled in 1994 and was traded to Oakland midway through the '95 campaign.

DARRYL STRAWBERRY

The former Mets slugger contributed 11 homers as a part-time outfielder/DH in the 1996 Yankees championship season. He was better in 1998, hitting 24 homers before being diagnosed with colon cancer—a revelation that inspired the team in its run to another World Series win. Strawberry, plagued by early career drug abuse problems, has fought a tragic battle against drugs and other personal problems since appearing in 24 games in 1999.

SCOTT BROSIUS

The former Oakland third baseman was an anchor for four Yankee pennant-winners and three World Series champions from 1998 until his retirement in November 2001. A .257 career regular-season hitter, he batted .314 in four World Series with four homers. His 1998 postseason was special. He batted .383 overall with four homers, two of which came in Game 3 of the fall classic. He claimed Series MVP honors with a .471 average.

PAUL O'NEILL

From 1993 until his retirement in 2001, the intense and popular former Cincinnati right fielder quietly led the new-era Yankees to four World Series titles. The slashing lefthanded hitter, a consistent 100-RBI threat, was a constant in the Yankees' return to power from 1996-2000, a .303 hitter over nine New York seasons. O'Neill hit 10 homers and drove in 34 runs in postseason play for the Yankees.

DAVID CONE

The former Mets 20-game winner matched that win total in 1998 for a Yankees team that won 114 games and the second of four championships in a five-year span. The veteran righthander was 64-40 from his mid-1995 arrival to his free-agent departure after the 2000 season—6-1 in postseason play. Cone's signature New York moment came July 18, 1999, when he fired a perfect game against Montreal at Yankee Stadium.

JOE GIRARDI

Girardi was the cerebral, defensive catcher who backstopped the 1996 Yankee championship team and the backup for young Jorge Posada for World Series winners in 1998 and '99. A .272 career hitter over his four Yankee seasons, Girardi signed a free-agent contract with the Cubs after the 1999 campaign, returning to the city where he had started his career 10 years earlier.

JOHN WETTELAND

He wasn't a Yankee for long, but the big righthanded reliever parlayed his New York time into a championship ring. Acquired from the Expos in a 1995 trade to anchor the bullpen, Wetteland recorded 74 saves in two seasons, leading the A.L. with 43 in 1996. He posted four more in the '96 World Series, notching the final out of the Yankees' first championship since 1978.

CHUCK KNOBLAUCH

He was the second baseman for three Yankees World Series champions, the left fielder for another pennant-winner. Fans recall the strange throwing problem that threatened Knoblauch's career and forced a move to the outfield, but it's hard to ignore his contributions as a reliable leadoff hitter and double-play partner of shortstop Derek Jeter after his 1998 acquisition from Minnesota. Knoblauch was a .272 hitter over four Yankee seasons, a .242 batter in World Series play.

ROGER CLEMENS

Since the second half of the 2000 season, the former Red Sox and Blue Jays star has been the Yankees' top righthanded starter. Clemens compiled a sparkling 20-3 record and won his record sixth Cy Young Award in 2001 and he lifted his career victory total to 293 with a 13-6 mark in 2002. The big Texan, who was acquired by the Yankees before the 1999 season, posted a 3-0 record and 0.93 ERA in three straight World Series from 1999-2001.

TINO MARTINEZ

From 1996-2001, the popular Tino reached 25 homers and 100 RBIs five times while facing the enormous task of replacing Don Mattingly at first base. Quietly, efficiently, he succeeded while contributing to five pennant-winners and four World Series champions. Martinez, known for his clutch hitting, is best remembered for the shocking two-run, ninth-inning homer he hit off Arizona reliever Byung-Hyun Kim to tie Game 4 of the 2001 fall classic.

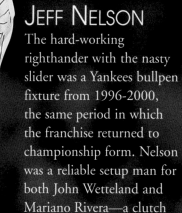

JEFF NELSON

The hard-working righthander with the nasty slider was a Yankees bullpen fixture from 1996-2000, the same period in which the franchise returned to championship form. Nelson was a reliable setup man for both John Wetteland and Mariano Rivera—a clutch performer who didn't allow an earned run over 10 World Series appearances in 1996, '98 and '99.

ANDY PETTITTE

The lefthanded anchor of Yankee staffs since his big-league arrival in 1995, Pettitte has consistently ranked among league leaders in victories while enhancing his reputation as a big-game pitcher. The 6-foot-5 bulldog became the first Yankee since Ron Guidry to reach 100 career wins in 2000 and he has been a rock in postseason play, compiling an 8-2 record for four championship teams—a 5-1 mark and 3.75 ERA in five ALCS.

ORLANDO HERNANDEZ

The former Cuban defector was called up from the minors in 1998 to replace injured David Cone and went on to compile a 12-4 record. His career-best 17-9 mark in 1999 was topped only by an amazing four-year run in which El Duque compiled a 9-2 postseason record (2-1 in World Series play) with a 2.48 ERA. Although injuries plagued the big righthander in 2001 and 2002, he remains a key figure for one of the A.L.'s most talented pitching staffs.

DAVID JUSTICE

The former Atlanta and Cleveland outfielder was acquired midway through the 2000 season and hit .305 with 20 homers for the pennant-bound Yankees. The hard-hitting left fielder/DH struggled through the postseason, although his dramatic three-run homer beat Seattle in Game 6 of the ALCS. Justice also struggled through an injury-plagued 2001 regular season and postseason before being traded to the Mets for Robin Ventura.

JORGE POSADA

The switch-hitting Posada, a part-time performer for the 1998 and '99 Yankee World Series champions, became the everyday catcher in 2000 and an integral part of a third straight title run. Posada has power (28 homers in 2000), run-producing skills (95 RBIs in 2001, 99 in 2002) and the ability to hit for average (.287 in 2000). He also handles one of baseball's most proficient pitching staffs and discourages basestealers with his strong arm.

BERNIE WILLIAMS

Continuing a long line of Yankee superstar center fielders, the switch-hitting Williams provides a classic blend of speed, power and defense. The 1998 A.L. batting champion (.339) has posted five seasons of 100-plus RBIs since becoming a full-time player in 1993 while anchoring four World Series champions and six division winners. One of the game's premier clutch hitters, Williams holds the career record for RBIs in Division Series play (26), ranks second in postseason RBIs (56) and is tied for second in postseason homers (17).

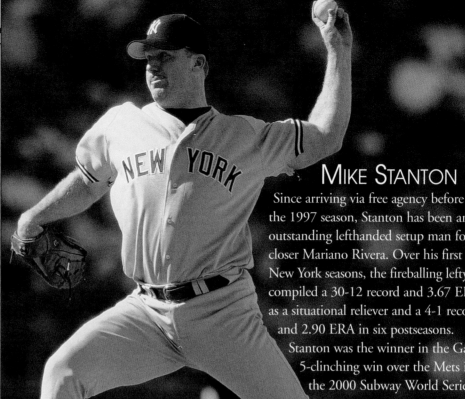

MIKE STANTON

Since arriving via free agency before the 1997 season, Stanton has been an outstanding lefthanded setup man for closer Mariano Rivera. Over his first six New York seasons, the fireballing lefty compiled a 30-12 record and 3.67 ERA as a situational reliever and a 4-1 record and 2.90 ERA in six postseasons. Stanton was the winner in the Game 5-clinching win over the Mets in the 2000 Subway World Series.

RAMIRO MENDOZA

Since 1996, the 6-2 righthander has filled a valuable role as long reliever and spot starter for the Yankees. Durable and consistent through 1999, Mendoza suffered arm problems in 2000 before rebounding strong in 2001. Over five Division Series and three ALCS, he has allowed four earned runs in 21⅓ innings. He is 1-0 as a three-time World Series performer and member of two championship teams.

JOE TORRE

Since taking the Yankees helm in 1996, Torre has carved out a 685-445 record while leading his teams to six East Division titles, five pennants and four championships—numbers that give him status among legendary Yankee managers Joe McCarthy, Casey Stengel and Miller Huggins. Torre's up-front, treat-everybody-the-same approach has provided stability, both in the locker room and front office. His managerial masterpiece was 1998, when the Yankees won a then-A.L. record 114 games, posted an 11-2 playoff mark and captured the first of four straight pennants and three straight World Series titles.

ALFONSO SORIANO

After showing flashes of his potential in 2001, the 6-1 second baseman emerged in 2002 as one of the game's premier offensive players. Soriano, handling leadoff duties, drove in 102 runs and scored 128 while batting .302. He barely missed distinction as baseball's third 40-40 man with spectacular totals of 39 homers and 41 stolen bases. In the 2001 World Series, the speedy Dominican delivered a Game 5-winning hit against Arizona and belted a Game 7 homer in a losing cause.

JASON GIAMBI

Giambi signed a free-agent contract with the Yankees before the 2002 season and contributed 40 home runs, 120 RBIs and a .312 average as a first base replacement for Tino Martinez. The stocky lefthanded slugger, who spent his first seven seasons with the Oakland A's, provided a much-needed power and run-production source for a lineup minus departed stars Martinez and Paul O'Neill. Giambi earned A.L. MVP honors for the A's in 2000 and finished as runnerup in 2001.

DAVID WELLS

In two stints with the Yankees, the unpredictable Wells has been durable and steady. He was 16-10 in 1997 and 18-4 in a spectacular 1998 championship season that featured his perfect game against Minnesota at Yankee Stadium and a 4-0 postseason record. Dealt to Toronto as part of a trade for Roger Clemens before the 1999 season, the 6-4, 240-pound lefty was resigned as a free agent in 2002 and led the East Division champs with a 19-7 record and 3.75 ERA.

STARTING
STAR

All-Time
Lineup
L.

MANAGER

1 Joe McCarthy
"Marse Joe"

2 **Casey Stengel**

*M*arse Joe was the man who put the word "dynasty" into New York's vocabulary. He also was the manager who introduced the concept of "Yankee Pride" and set the standards for excellence by which Yankee teams would forever be judged. McCarthy took the managerial reins in 1931, after the team had won six pennants and three World Series in the 1920s under Miller Huggins, and lifted the franchise to an even higher level. A stickler for teamwork, discipline and classy behavior, both on the field and off, McCarthy led the Yankees to a championship in 1932 and an unprecedented four straight World Series wins from 1936-39. By the time he left the Yankees in 1946, his teams had posted a 1,460-867 record, winning eight pennants and seven championships. The square-jawed, no-nonsense Hall of Famer also was an outstanding handler of pitchers and strategist who took full advantage of the superior player talent he was given.

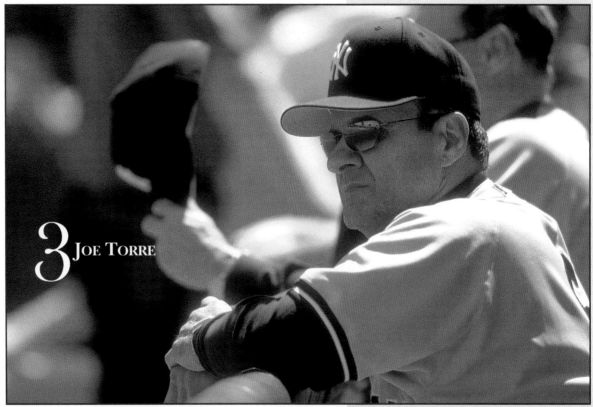

3 **Joe Torre**

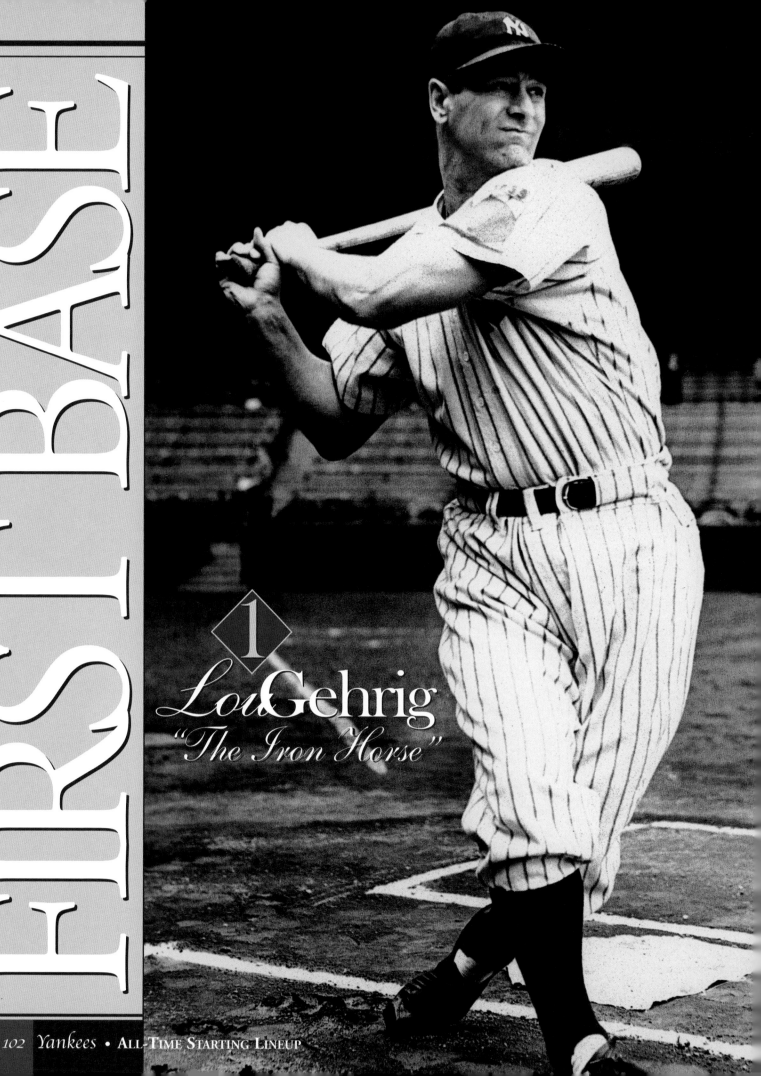

FIRST BASE

1

Lou Gehrig
"The Iron Horse"

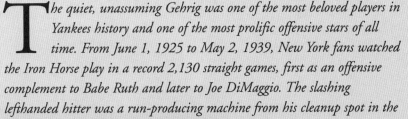

The quiet, unassuming Gehrig was one of the most beloved players in Yankees history and one of the most prolific offensive stars of all time. From June 1, 1925 to May 2, 1939, New York fans watched the Iron Horse play in a record 2,130 straight games, first as an offensive complement to Babe Ruth and later to Joe DiMaggio. The slashing lefthanded hitter was a run-producing machine from his cleanup spot in the

"Murderer's Row" lineup— a five-time RBI champion who topped the 100 plateau 13 straight seasons and posted a still-standing American League mark of 184 in 1931. From 1926-38, he averaged 147 RBIs and topped 150 seven times en route to a career total of 1,995. His career marks of .340 and 493 home runs also rank among all-time leaders. His other feats include a major league-record 23 grand slams, a four-homer game (1932), a Triple Crown season (1934) and a .361 World Series average with 10 homers and 34 RBIs. Gehrig, who played on six championship teams, could have reached greater heights if not for the fatal disease—amyotrophic lateral sclerosis—that ended his Hall of Fame career in 1939 and took his life two years later.

2
DON MATTINGLY

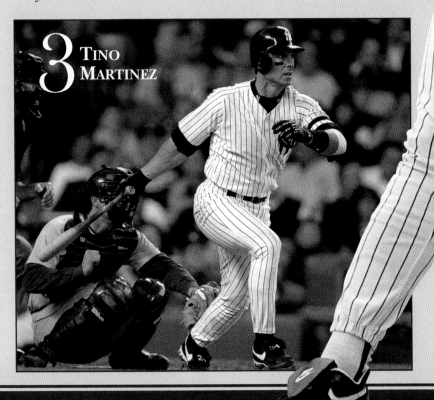

3 TINO MARTINEZ

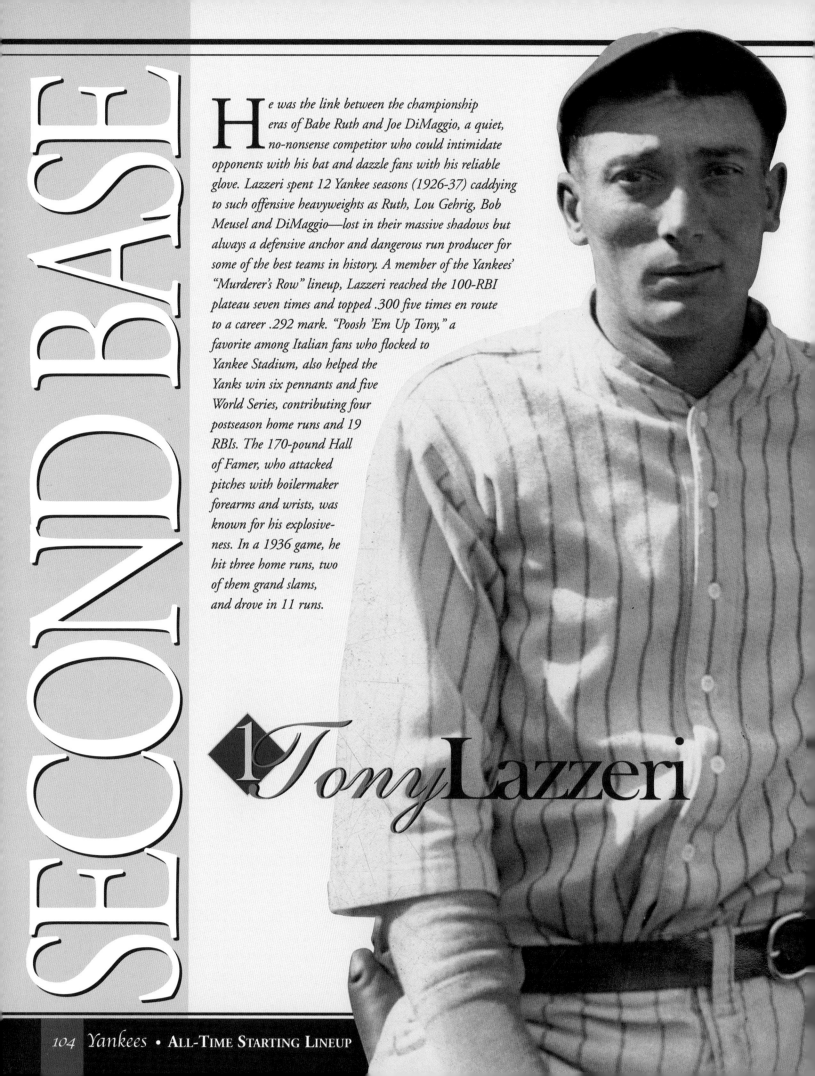

SECOND BASE

He was the link between the championship eras of Babe Ruth and Joe DiMaggio, a quiet, no-nonsense competitor who could intimidate opponents with his bat and dazzle fans with his reliable glove. Lazzeri spent 12 Yankee seasons (1926-37) caddying to such offensive heavyweights as Ruth, Lou Gehrig, Bob Meusel and DiMaggio—lost in their massive shadows but always a defensive anchor and dangerous run producer for some of the best teams in history. A member of the Yankees' "Murderer's Row" lineup, Lazzeri reached the 100-RBI plateau seven times and topped .300 five times en route to a career .292 mark. "Poosh 'Em Up Tony," a favorite among Italian fans who flocked to Yankee Stadium, also helped the Yanks win six pennants and five World Series, contributing four postseason home runs and 19 RBIs. The 170-pound Hall of Famer, who attacked pitches with boilermaker forearms and wrists, was known for his explosiveness. In a 1936 game, he hit three home runs, two of them grand slams, and drove in 11 runs.

Tony Lazzeri

3
BOBBY
RICHARDSON

2 JOE
GORDON

THIRD BASE

He broke the hearts of Dodgers fans with a Brooks Robinson-like fielding display in the 1978 World Series and pounded out 250 home runs in 11 New York seasons (1973-83), two of which produced championships. The sharp-tongued, no-nonsense lefthanded hitter, who won two Gold Gloves and represented the Yankees in five All-Star Games, showcased the best combination of power, defense and competitive fire of any third baseman in franchise history. Nettles, who was obtained in a 1972 trade from Cleveland, was at his best when going to his right

2 RED
ROLFE

to cut off ground balls headed for the left field corner. But he also was a dangerous run producer who led the American League with 32 homers in 1976 and jumped to 37 a year later, when he drove in a career-best 107 runs. A student of the game who contributed in subtle ways to four Yankee pennants, Nettles was stuck for most of his 22-year career between a rock and a hard place—the more flashy Robinson and George Brett, who dominated the A.L.'s third base spotlight.

3 CLETE BOYER

1 *Graig*Nettles

Derek ◇1 Jeter

No shortstop in Yankees history—not even Hall of Famer Phil Rizzuto—can match Jeter's combination of poise, confidence, speed, power, hitting and defense. He is the prototypical new-age shortstop who complements defensive wizardry with a big bat. It took him only five full seasons to reach the 1,000-hit plateau and his .317 career average ranks among the all-time Yankee greats. He is only the third Yankee to string together three straight 200-hit seasons and the only player in the last half century to score 100-plus runs in each of his first seven full seasons. But what really jumps out is his quiet poise and baseball savvy. New Yorkers still marvel at the heady play Jeter made in Game 3 of the 2001 Division Series against Oakland when he hustled to the first base side of the field to grab an errant cutoff throw and gun down the potential tying run at the plate, saving a 1-0 victory. It's no coincidence that Jeter anchored four championship teams in his first five seasons and collected a postseason-record 101 hits in 82 games covering seven playoffs.

3 FRANK CROSETTI

2 PHIL RIZZUTO

LEFT FIELD

◆1◆ Bob Meusel

The 6-foot-3, 190-pound Meusel was a fixture in the Yankees' "Murderer's Row" lineup during the 1920s, a .309 career righthanded hitter who was overshadowed by teammate and close friend Babe Ruth. Meusel, an integral part of teams that won the franchise's first six American League pennants and three World Series, led the A.L. with 33 homers and 138 RBIs in 1925, one of five seasons he topped the 100-RBI plateau. Fans remember his contributions to two of the most powerful teams in franchise history—.337 with 103 RBIs as the fifth-place hitter behind Ruth and Lou Gehrig for the 1927 Yankees; .297 with 113 RBIs in '28. But opponents marveled most at the cannon-like arm Meusel used to cut down careless baserunners over 10 New York seasons. Meusel, who played against older brother and Giants star Irish Meusel in the Yankees' first three World Series (1921-23), was fast enough to steal 142 career bases, including a season-high 26 in 1924.

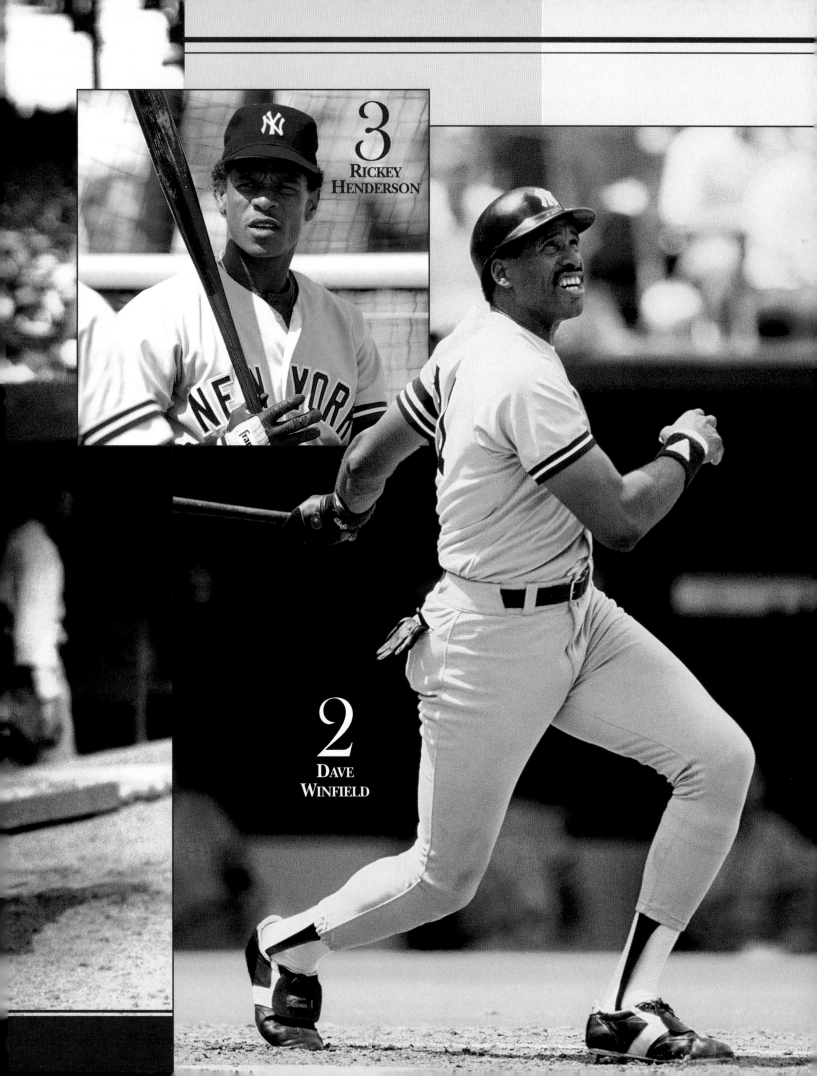

3
RICKEY
HENDERSON

2
DAVE
WINFIELD

CENTER FIELD

◆1 Joe DiMaggio
"The Yankee Clipper"

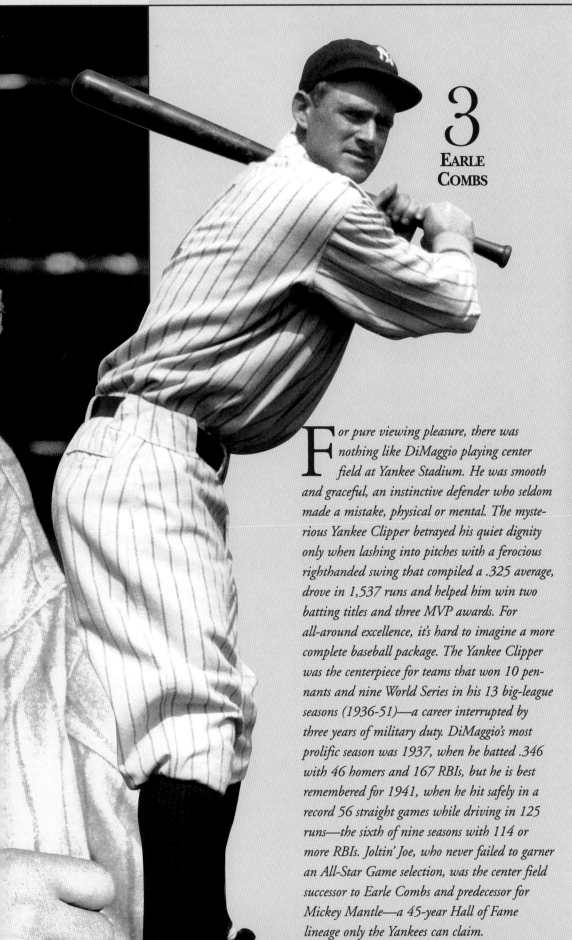

3
EARLE COMBS

F or pure viewing pleasure, there was nothing like DiMaggio playing center field at Yankee Stadium. He was smooth and graceful, an instinctive defender who seldom made a mistake, physical or mental. The mysterious Yankee Clipper betrayed his quiet dignity only when lashing into pitches with a ferocious righthanded swing that compiled a .325 average, drove in 1,537 runs and helped him win two batting titles and three MVP awards. For all-around excellence, it's hard to imagine a more complete baseball package. The Yankee Clipper was the centerpiece for teams that won 10 pennants and nine World Series in his 13 big-league seasons (1936-51)—a career interrupted by three years of military duty. DiMaggio's most prolific season was 1937, when he batted .346 with 46 homers and 167 RBIs, but he is best remembered for 1941, when he hit safely in a record 56 straight games while driving in 125 runs—the sixth of nine seasons with 114 or more RBIs. Joltin' Joe, who never failed to garner an All-Star Game selection, was the center field successor to Earle Combs and predecessor for Mickey Mantle—a 45-year Hall of Fame lineage only the Yankees can claim.

2
MICKEY MANTLE

RIGHT FIELD

◆1 *Babe* Ruth
"Sultan of Swat"

Nobody had more impact on baseball than the Bambino, a former outstanding Red Sox pitcher who changed the way the game was played with his prolific bat. Ruth is hailed as the game's savior, the man who ushered in the longball era and revitalized baseball when it was mired in the muck of the 1919 Black Sox scandal. His career numbers are overpowering and legendary—714 home runs, 60 in 1927; 12 American League homer titles and four seasons with 50 or more; six RBI crowns and five seasons with 150-plus; an .847 slugging percentage and 177 runs scored in a season; a .474 career on-base percentage ... the list goes on. And his colorful personality generated enough electricity to light up New York from 1920-34, a period that coincides with the Yankees' rise to glory. Ruth, a solid defensive right fielder, played in seven World Series with the Yankees, including the franchise's first four winners, and hit 15 postseason home runs, a record that stood until Mickey Mantle surpassed it in 1964. A charter member of baseball's Hall of Fame in 1936, Ruth is generally regarded as the greatest player of all time.

3 ROGER MARIS

2 REGGIE JACKSON

CATCHER

Not only was the oddly shaped (5-8, 195) and never-likeable Yogi the greatest Yankees catcher of all time, he was one of the best in baseball history. A three-time American League MVP who played in 15 All-Star Games and hit 358 home runs, Berra is most revered for his World Series legacy. He played in 14 classics, won 10 championships and compiled Series records for games (75), at-bats (259), hits (71) and doubles (10). Only Mickey Mantle and Babe Ruth hit more Series homers than Berra's 12 and only Mantle had more RBIs (40-39). Berra, a Hall of Famer whose Yankee playing career stretched from 1946-63, was a workhorse catcher who was tutored by former great Bill Dickey. He also was a dangerous bad-ball hitter, one of the most feared Yankees with a game on the line. Berra, who was versatile and fast enough to play in the outfield, holds numerous Yankee defensive records and still ranks high on most of the team's all-time offensive lists.

3 THURMAN MUNSON

2 BILL DICKEY

1 Yogi Berra

LEFTHANDED PITCHER

Ford was the winningest pitcher in Yankees history and one of the most efficient hurlers all time. His .690 winning percentage (236-106) is the best of the 20th century among pitchers with 200 or more wins and he holds team records for innings (3,170⅓), strikeouts (1,956) and shutouts (45). Ford was the ace of Yankee teams that won 11 American League pennants and six championships in the 1950s and '60s, a craftsman who carved up hitters with his brains as well as his accurate left arm. The colorful and quick-quipping Whitey, a master of location and changing speeds, posted such records as 18-6, 16-8, 18-7 and 19-6 under manager Casey Stengel, who often held him back to face the opposing team's best pitcher. But he was a phenomenal 25-4 in 1961 under Ralph Houk, winning Cy Young honors, and he was 24-7 in 1963. Stengel called Ford the best money pitcher in baseball and his World Series numbers support that praise—22 games, 146 innings, 10 wins and 94 strikeouts, all fall classic records. The Hall of Fame lefty, who pitched in six All-Star Games, also set a Series record for consecutive scoreless innings with 33.

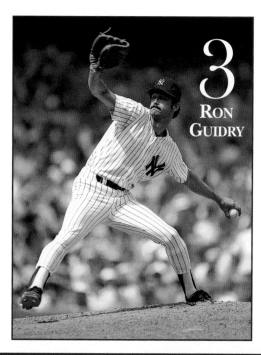

3 RON GUIDRY

2 LEFTY GOMEZ

Whitey $\Diamond$1 Ford

PITCHER

He was part of baseball's best lefty-righty pitching combination in the 1930s and a workhorse for 13 of his 15 New York seasons. Ruffing also was the best righthander in team history by virtue of his 231-124 record and the anchor he provided for six World Series champions. After a woeful 39-96 beginning to a career that started in Boston, the 6-2, 205-pound hard thrower was traded to the Yankees in 1930 and transformed immediately into Lefty Gomez's righthanded complement. Suddenly adept at changing speeds and mixing curves with his intimidating fastball, Ruffing finished 18-7 for the 1932-champion Yankees and posted consecutive seasons of 20, 20, 21 and 21 wins for teams that won four straight championships from 1936-39. He mirrored his regular-season success with a 7-2 World Series record, despite missing two years to military service in World War II. The Hall of Fame-bound redhead, who worked at least 220 innings every season from 1928-40 while completing 264 starts, posted 273 wins over 22 years, his final in 1947 with the Chicago White Sox.

2
ALLIE
REYNOLDS

1 *Red*
Ruffing

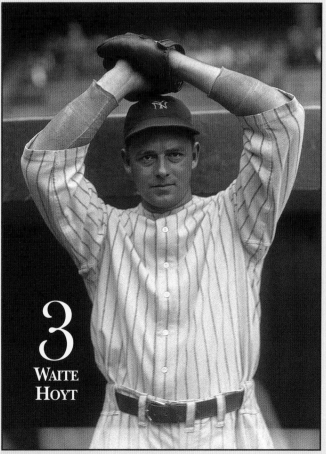

3
WAITE
HOYT

CLOSER

Mariano ◇1 Rivera

2

GOOSE GOSSAGE

Rivera, the unflappable Panamanian righthander, has emerged as the top closer for a franchise blessed with a long line of great relievers. Wilcy Moore, Johnny Murphy, Joe Page, Sparky Lyle, Goose Gossage, Dave Righetti ... the names roll easily off the tongues of New Yorkers. But Rivera, with his moving fastball and unshakeable poise, has claimed lofty status after six seasons as the team's full-time closer. He already has passed Righetti as the Yankees' saves leader and he owns the all-time postseason and World Series records for saves. His moving fastball continues to be a puzzle for American League hitters. After taking over as bullpen ace in 1997, Rivera posted 238 saves (an average of 40) over the next six seasons with a 2.25 ERA. He has been front and center in the postseason, pitching 33⅓ straight scoreless innings over one stretch and converting 23 consecutive save opportunities over another. Rivera, the full-time closer for three championship teams and the setup man for another, earned World Series MVP honors in 1999.

3

SPARKY LYLE

MOVERS and Shakers

Opening day 1923 holds special significance for Yankee fans. That's the day manager Miller Huggins (left), owner Jacob Ruppert (center) and Boston manager Frank Chance helped dedicate the spectacular new Yankee Stadium.

For Yankee haters, not much has changed over the last 70 or 80 years. They watch with gritted teeth as the pinstripe magic continues to unfold and they choke on the smug arrogance that hangs thickly over the franchise, smothering opponents with an endless succession of pennants, championships and unprecedented success.

It's a proud tradition, passed from generation to generation, and it is sustained the old-fashioned way—with an eye for talent and a bundle of cold, hard cash. The new-age Yankees, under the sometimes-stormy leadership of George Steinbrenner, still buy their success, just as they did in the 1920s when Colonel Jacob Ruppert began construction of the greatest sports machine ever conceived.

"I have told my scouts to go after every prospect," Ruppert once told New York World-Telegram reporter Dan Daniel. "I want to keep winning, and if I can take a pennant by 50 games, that's all right with me. The success of baseball depends on each club owner building up to the highest standard. ... I say quite frankly that I intend to keep every great player I can acquire."

The words could just as easily have come from Steinbrenner, who has followed the winning blueprint handed down by his predecessors. Ruppert set the bar high with his eye-opening $125,000 purchase of Babe Ruth in 1920 and Yankee owners have been leaping for the stars ever since.

Faces through the years: Colonel Tillinghast Huston (left photo), co-owner of the Yankees from 1915-22; Lou Gehrig, owner Ruppert and manager Joe McCarthy (center photo, 1938), and current owner George Steinbrenner (right).

"Men die, others come after them and the world carries on. It is said that in this cosmic scheme of ours, no human is indispensable. And so everybody feels that though Colonel Jacob Ruppert is gone, the greatness of the Yankees will be perpetuated, and others will keep the club at the high level it has achieved. Achieved because of his lavish hand, love for the game, intense pride in being first in everything he did and his eager riding of a hobby. ... Ruppert built the Yankees to a pinnacle and forced not only his own league, but the National as well, to build to keep up his hot pace."

—Dan Daniel, reporting on Ruppert's death in a 1939 issue of The Sporting News

Money and home runs were always topics of discussion when Ed Barrow (standing), Babe Ruth and Ruppert got together in the 1920s.

Ruppert never envisioned such extravagant spending when he handed over $225,000 in 1915 and became part owner of "an orphan ball club, without a home of its own, without players of outstanding ability, without prestige."

He was, simply, a New York beer baron looking for a diversion. What he found

was a passion for baseball, a zeal that would revitalize a franchise drifting aimlessly under the leadership of Frank Farrell and Big Bill Devery. When Ruppert joined hands with Colonel Tillinghast Huston, a former war hero, the franchise had never won an American League pennant, much less a championship.

The colonels formed an unlikely union. Ruppert had inherited the family-built brewery and the enormous wealth that went with it, but he also had picked up his father's business acumen, decisive nature and attention to detail. The Ruppert Brewery flourished under his stern direction. Huston was a veteran of the Spanish-American war, a former officer and leader of men who was accustomed to having his orders carried out.

Neither had any baseball experience, a costly barrier to their early efforts to turn things around. Neither would back down from their strong opinions, an inevitable source of conflict. When push came to shove, Huston was no match for

The diminutive Huggins was a big man in baseball circles, where he hobnobbed with the likes of Philadelphia Athletics manager Connie Mack (left).

the business and politically savvy Ruppert.

An eight-year New York congressman who later became an officer in the Seventh Regiment, Ruppert ran the Yankees with the same iron-fisted efficiency he demanded from his brewery workers. Winning no longer was an option under his demanding leadership. Baseball was Ruppert's competitive outlet and he hated to lose, a trait he would pass on to future Yankee owners.

The most celebrated Ruppert-Huston power struggle occurred in 1917, after Bill Donovan had led the Yankees to a 71-82 record and sixth-place finish in the American League. Both owners agreed a managerial change was in order, but neither liked the other's choice for a replacement. Ruppert wanted to hire 5-foot-6 dynamo Miller Huggins, manager of the St. Louis Cardinals; Huston favored Brooklyn manager Wilbert Robinson, a longtime drinking companion.

Huston, stationed in France at the time, cabled Ruppert with his recommendation. Ruppert gave Robinson the brushoff, telling him he was too old at 53, and hired Huggins. Huston was livid, but there was little he could do. His animosity was manifested in future dealings with Huggins, whom he openly detested, criticized and undermined through the remainder of his Yankees association.

It was clear that Ruppert intended to take center stage during reconstruction of the Yankees—and Huston was shoved into the background. He targeted Boston owner Harry Frazee as his immediate source for talent, noting that the would-be Broadway producer was struggling to finance numerous outside ventures. The Red Sox were loaded with talent and money was no object for the determined Ruppert.

The Ruppert-Frazee association started innocently enough in 1919, when the Yankees sent two mediocre players and $40,000 to Boston for pitcher Carl Mays. But that was merely an appetizer for 1920, a profitable year during which Ruppert would lay the cornerstones for future success. Taking a leap of faith at the recommendation of Huggins, the colonel purchased Ruth for $125,000 and a $350,000 loan against the mortgage of Fenway Park. Then he bought the services of Red Sox manager Ed Barrow, the man responsible for converting Ruth from successful pitcher to record-shattering slugger.

Barrow, a shrewd baseball mind, was installed as the team's business manager with the directive to build a championship machine. He was up to the challenge.

"For almost a quarter of a century, Barrow was the Yankees. This was his baby, his brainchild. Its success was his success, and the man and his product were virtually inseparable. When the MacPhail-Topping-Webb syndicate bought the team from the Ruppert heirs, it was written that the Yanks represented the mightiest of all baseball empires. Cousin Ed made them that."

—*New York Times columnist Arthur Daley*

Barrow pieced together an unprecedented scouting system and attacked his job with well-organized enthusiasm. Given carte blanche to purchase whatever talent he deemed necessary, he went back to Frazee, his former boss, and engineered an eight-player trade that secured pitcher Waite Hoyt, a future Hall of Famer. In quick succession, he tapped the Red Sox for pitchers Joe Bush, Sad Sam Jones, George Pipgras and Herb Pennock as well as shortstop Everett Scott and third baseman Joe Dugan.

The domineering, sometimes-blustery Barrow also provided a shield between Huggins and Huston, allowing the manager to maintain team discipline and make decisions without fear of second guessing. And having managed Ruth at Boston, he provided disciplinary support for Huggins in his dealing with the fun-loving but temperamental superstar. The reinforced Yankees responded by winning their first A.L. pennant in 1921, with the amazing Ruth contributing 59 home runs. They came back in 1922 with another, prompting Ruppert to look into his far-seeing crystal ball.

The visionary and the builder. Ruppert (left) laid out his vision of Yankee dominance and Barrow made it come true—beyond even Ruppert's wildest dream.

"The fans of New York will go where there is a first-class ballclub playing the sort of baseball the people want," he explained in 1922 as he began construction on a stadium in the Bronx, a showcase for his "new Yankees" and the fan-pleasing Bambino. "If the Yankees are bad, the fans will not go to the Polo Grounds to see them. If they are good, the people will go wherever the Yankees are."

Ruppert's vision was well-founded. The team that had played second fiddle as Polo Grounds tenants of the National League Giants for 10 seasons soon would be taking center stage, just across the Harlem River, in the grandest, most spacious ballpark in baseball history. Ruth was a major attraction. The promise of success was another. Ruppert's big investment soon would pay huge dividends.

But not for Huston. Unwilling to commit to the high-stakes financial game being played, he sold his half interest in the team to Ruppert before Yankee Stadium went on display on opening day of 1923. The show now belonged to Ruppert, Barrow and Huggins—and it was a good one.

The 1923 season, with the team playing in a sparkling-new facility, was a masterpiece. The Yankees stormed to 98 victories, captured their third straight pennant and capped it off by winning the World Series. The franchise's first championship came at the expense of the Giants, who had defeated the Yankees in the previous two fall classics.

The diminutive Huggins would guide the Yankees to three more pennants, including a 1927 triumph in which the Bronx Bombers, powered by Ruth's 60 home runs and a young first baseman named Lou Gehrig, rolled to 110 regular-season wins and a World Series sweep of the Pirates. The Yankees' powerful roster was filled with players procured by Ruppert's bottomless pocket book and the

McCarthy, hired under the Ruppert directive 'I do not like to finish second,' choreographed his pennant parade around major contributions from pitcher Red Ruffing (left, left photo) and young center fielder Joe DiMaggio (right, right photo).

unerring talent assessments and trading skills of Barrow and Huggins.

But that successful marriage was about to end. Huggins, always on the edge physically, fell ill and died suddenly from blood poisoning late in the 1929 season, a shocking emotional blow for the entire Yankees organization. An important transition period was at hand, both in terms of leadership and philosophy.

"Miller Huggins' life was a constant struggle by a little man, never too well fortified in health, against bigger men, physically. ... In his first five years as Yankee manager, he had to battle one of his bosses, Colonel Tillinghast L. Huston, who was openly anti-Huggins. Frequently Hug also had to battle a hostile clubhouse, especially such stars as Babe Ruth, Carl Mays and Joe Bush, to prove to them that he was boss. Constant conflict wore down the little man."
—*Frederick G. Lieb, reminiscing in a 1964 issue of* The Sporting News

The leadership problem was solved in October 1930 when former pitcher Bob Shawkey, a stopgap replacement for Huggins, was fired after a third-place finish. Ruppert hired former Chicago Cubs manager Joe McCarthy and gave him a simple directive: "I will stand for you finishing second this year," he said, "but remember, McCarthy, I do not like to finish second."

The philosophical transition was more complicated. Barrow had been remarkably successful in his player purchases from independent minor league teams, but his occasional mistakes were costly and more teams now were competing for top talent. Ruppert had long admired the Branch Rickey concept of a minor league farm system feeding players onto the major league roster and he finally decided to act.

Barrow, a baseball traditionalist, long had resisted the idea, much as he would

George Weiss (right) began his Yankees association as builder of the game's most prolific farm system and ended it as the franchise's chief strategist and business guru. Weiss hired Casey Stengel (left) as manager before the 1949 season.

fight the concept of night baseball throughout his Yankee years. But Ruppert was adamant in 1931 when he instructed Barrow to find someone to build him a farm system. The Yankee boss punctuated his order by purchasing the Newark franchise of the International League—a team that would send a steady stream of players to New York.

Given no choice, Barrow began a search that eventually would lead him to George Weiss, the quiet, reserved general manager of the International League's Baltimore Orioles. The longtime minor league owner and executive was a perfect fit. Weiss would become another Yankee pillar, a combination builder-strategist-talent scout and undeniable master of the game's elite minor league farm system. His far-reaching scouting tentacles, combined with Ruppert's willingness to spend, helped launch the greatest pennant run in baseball history.

McCarthy took the Yankees to a championship in 1932, the last the team would win with Ruth in the lineup. But the real fun started in 1936 when the Yankees won the first of an unprecedented four straight championships and six in an eight-year span. The spurt coincided with the arrival of center fielder Joe DiMaggio, a Weiss acquisition from the San Francisco Seals of the Pacific Coast League, and such farmhands as George Selkirk, Red Rolfe, Charlie Keller, Joe Gordon, Spud Chandler, Tiny Bonham and Phil Rizzuto.

The Yankee express was running full throttle and other teams couldn't keep up. Cries of "break up the Yankees" resounded throughout baseball, but Ruppert's crack team kept pouring it on. Even when Ruppert died in January 1939, the rampage continued with Barrow now acting as team president for his heirs.

Barrow's final Yankee years were plagued by the uncertainties of World War II and his 24-year New York association ended abruptly in 1945, when the tax-burdened Ruppert estate sold the team to a group organized by Larry MacPhail. For the bargain price of $2.8 million, the trio of MacPhail, Dan Topping and Del Webb took control with MacPhail replacing Barrow as team president.

McCarthy, whose record of excellence included eight A.L. pennants and seven World Series winners in 15 years as manager, followed Barrow out the door a year later, resigning for personal reasons early in the 1946 campaign. It was another shocking blow.

Dan Topping (left) and the blustery, innovative Larry MacPhail (right) formed two-thirds of the ownership group that took control of the Yankees franchise in 1945.

"Much more important than their scores was the way McCarthy's teams played baseball, their way of going on and off the field, the unmistakable stamp they bore which was unmistakably the McCarthy stamp. There have been more fiery teams than Joe's, more exciting ones, more appealing ones. But these eyes have not seen teams which played, as a unit, more nearly perfect baseball, whose members understood more clearly what they were about and what was expected of them, who showed evidence of a firmer command than McCarthy's."
—New York Herald Tribune columnist Red Smith

Four straight World Series winners triggered this impromptu 1952 celebration from (left to right) Weiss, Topping, Stengel, co-owner Del Webb and A.L. President Will Harridge.

It was a stormy three-year marriage for MacPhail, who was showy, dramatic and prone to temperamental outbursts—the virtual opposite of the arch-conservative Barrow. The dignity of the franchise, the championship aura of invincibility that Ruppert and Barrow had labored to build, was tested severely with the unpredictable MacPhail calling the shots.

After two interim failures, MacPhail eventually settled on Bucky Harris as McCarthy's replacement and the former "Boy Wonder" led the Yankees to another championship in 1947. But the dramatic seven-game World Series was followed by a stormy celebration that would rock the franchise.

Early in the festivities, MacPhail praised Weiss as the architect of the championship Yankees. Later in the evening, after a drink-induced heated argument, he fired him. That was the last straw. Tired of his tirades and inconsistent behavior, Topping and Webb forced MacPhail out and promoted Weiss to general manager.

It was a master stroke. The aloof and portly Weiss became the new-era Barrow, an outstanding strategist, businessman and talent scout who would restore the team's sagging championship aura. His first priority was to replace Harris, whom he felt lacked the disciplinary skills important in a manager. The opportunity arose when the Yanks struggled to a third-place finish in 1948.

Weiss quickly cut Harris loose, then stunned New Yorkers with his choice for a replacement—59-year-old Casey Stengel. Fans screamed in disbelief, pointing to the Old Professor's failed managerial stints in Brooklyn and Boston and his reputation as a "baseball clown."

"To the bulk of the baseball public, Stengel is a stoop-shouldered, arm-waving, pixie-like clown who specializes in droll stories and double talk. His players see him in an entirely different light. To them, he is sometimes a crotchety, self-centered martinet, sometimes a grumbling but kindly old Mr. Chips, always a genius at winning ball games."
—Milton Richmond, writing for This Week magazine in 1957

Some clown. The always-colorful Stengel, unorthodox in speech and manner, silenced critics by guiding the Yankees to a 1949 championship. Then he rubbed it in everyone's face by winning World Series in 1950, '51, '52 and '53—an unprecedented five in a row. Before he retired after the 1960 World Series, he had stretched his ledger to 10 pennants and seven championships in 12 years, surpassing even the amazing records of McCarthy and Huggins.

Much of Stengel's success could be attributed to the constant flow of players,

DiMaggio (left photo) retired on a happy note in 1951 after helping (left to right) Topping, Stengel and Webb celebrate a third straight championship. By 1961, Webb was basking in the glow of another title, courtesy of new manager Ralph Houk (right photo).

courtesy of Weiss. DiMaggio retired in 1951, the same year Mickey Mantle arrived. Trades and the farm system produced consistent winners like Hank Bauer, Gil McDougald, Bobby Richardson, Yogi Berra, Elston Howard, Roger Maris, Norm Siebern, Bill Skowron, Vic Raschi, Allie Reynolds, Ralph Terry, Bob Turley, Whitey Ford, Tony Kubek, Clete Boyer, Luis Arroyo and many others.

Not only did the crafty Stengel weld these talented players into a well-oiled baseball machine, he entertained New York fans with his special comedic flair and endearingly buffoonish behavior. The championship parade continued amid the outward appearance of fun and tranquility. But the illusion of calm would be shattered unexpectedly.

After watching the Yankees fall in a dramatic seven-game 1960 World Series that was decided by Pittsburgh second baseman Bill Mazeroski's walkoff home run, Topping and Webb implemented a front-office youth movement that resulted in the forced retirements of the 70-year-old Stengel and the 65-year-old Weiss. Roy Hamey was named general manager and Ralph Houk stepped in for Stengel.

If 1960 wasn't the end of another Yankee era, it was close to it. Still fueled by Weiss-produced talent, the Yanks continued their winning ways under Houk, capturing pennants in each of his three seasons and winning two championships. When Houk was promoted to general manager after the 1963 season, the Yankees stretched their consecutive-pennant streak to five under Yogi Berra before losing to St. Louis in a seven-game World Series. And, just like that, it was over.

"No other man, not even Babe Ruth or Ty Cobb, had a more profound and lasting influence on the game. None ever built as George Weiss built, defying time to obliterate his work. ... So soundly did he build that after his departure the team he left behind went right on winning for four years in a row."

—*New York Times columnist Red Smith*

By 1965, many of the Yankees' top players were nearing the end and the minor league talent supply was drying up. The team dropped to sixth place under Johnny Keane that season and all the way to the cellar in 1966. Not even Houk's

Another changing of the guard came in 1973 when team president Michael Burke, representing CBS, passed on the ownership mantle to a group headed by managing general partner Steinbrenner (center).

return to the dugout could re-energize the proud franchise, which would suffer through its most extended pennant drought since the beginning of the century.

The collapse traced to the end of the Topping-Webb regime, but CBS, the media conglomerate that had purchased 80 percent of the team in late 1964, took most of the grief. Webb and Topping each retained 10 percent interest and Topping stayed on as team president, but Webb sold out in 1965 and Topping finally departed after the disastrous 1966 campaign, handing over the leadership reins to CBS man Michael Burke.

The CBS years were a painful period for spoiled New Yorkers, who watched their once-proud Yankees wallow in mediocrity. After a difficult eight years of rebuilding and indecision, CBS got out of the baseball business, selling the team for $10 million to a limited partnership headed by the aggressive Steinbrenner, a shipbuilding tycoon who assumed the title Managing General Partner. Fans who had just about given up hope for the Yankees' return to championship form were unprepared for the storm that was about to hit the Big Apple.

The Steinbrenner reign, which would carry through the last quarter of the century and into the next, would be filled with success, controversy, craziness, intrigue and enough bizarre behavior to qualify as a real life soap opera. When former relief pitcher Sparky Lyle referred to the Yankees operation as the Bronx Zoo, he wasn't being facetious.

"Having found a stage to suit his ego, Steinbrenner became the very model of the ubiquitous, meddling, despotic genius of an owner. With his hands on every detail and around every throat, he has in 25 years jammed a century's worth of triumph, honor, folly and disgrace into his possession of baseball's Hope Diamond, the Yankees. In a baseball sense, Steinbrenner himself never much mattered. All that ever really mattered was that the Yankees be the Yankees. So if Steinbrenner's mad-genius operation helped raise the Yankees from their CBS deathbed to win five A.L. pennants and three World Series, then everyone in baseball owes him a nod of thanks, however grudgingly that nod may come."

—Dave Kindred in TSN's 1998 Yearbook entitled The Yankees

Steinbrenner experienced his first pennant-clinching celebration in 1976, delivering victory hugs to coach Yogi Berra (left) and manager Billy Martin (right).

The Steinbrenner era opened just in time for the March 1973 announcement that Yankee pitchers Fritz Peterson and Mike Kekich had swapped wives, families and even dogs in a strange story that drew national headlines. A year and a half later, Steinbrenner was suspended from baseball for two years by commissioner Bowie Kuhn after his conviction for illegal political campaign contributions.

During Steinbrenner's absence, the Yankees completed their two-year stint as tenants of the New York Mets at Shea Stadium while Yankee Stadium was being refurbished, landed prize free-agent pitcher Catfish Hunter, hired Billy Martin to replace 1974 Manager of the Year Bill Virdon and completed a magical 1976 regular season in which they captured their first A.L. East Division title, won their first pennant since 1964 on a spectacular A.L. Championship Series walkoff home run by Chris Chambliss and lost in the World Series to Cincinnati.

A few months after his return, Steinbrenner signed free-agent outfielder Reggie Jackson to a five-year, $2.9 million contract. Jackson immediately gave the rising Yankees, who already featured such stars as Thurman Munson, Graig Nettles, Willie Randolph, Roy White, Chambliss and Hunter, a championship look. But he also brought to New York a Steinbrenner-size ego that led to confrontations with the owner and manager, irritated teammates ("I'm the straw that stirs the drink") and delighted the New York media. Most importantly, his big bat won games and blazed new postseason trails.

While constantly bickering with each other, sniping at Steinbrenner and complaining to the media, the Yankees won championships in 1977 and '78, lost in

Martin (standing, arm raised) and Steinbrenner (sitting, gestering with his hand) were front and center again in 1977, when the Yankees celebrated their first championship since 1962 with a New York victory parade.

the 1980 ALCS and fell in the 1981 World Series. Jackson was hailed as Mr. October and Steinbrenner's huff-and-puff antics were tolerated. Even when the Yankees fell on hard times in the 1980s and early '90s, life was never dull as Steinbrenner spent lavishly on free agents, changed managers on a whim and feuded publicly with his players, especially outfielder Dave Winfield.

From his 1973 beginning with the Yankees through the 2002 season, Steinbrenner changed managers 20 times. The fiery Martin was hired and fired five times, Bob Lemon and Lou Piniella each had two stints in the hot seat and Dick Howser was forced to resign in 1980 after the team he had guided to 103 regular-season wins lost to Kansas City in the ALCS.

Steinbrenner was suspended again in 1983 for his bitter tirades against umpires and he was banned from baseball for life in 1990 after paying an admitted gambler $40,000 to dig up damaging information on Winfield. But the ban was lifted later and by the mid-1990s, Steinbrenner was back in good graces, the Yankees were building for another championship run and the team's payroll was hovering around the $100 million mark—a shocking figure for baseball's small-market franchises.

Anybody who believes that money can't buy happiness should consider this: The Yankees, under manager Joe Torre, won four World Series in five years with a high-priced roster featuring shortstop Derek Jeter, center fielder Bernie Williams, right fielder Paul O'Neill, first baseman Tino Martinez and pitchers David Cone, Andy Pettitte, Orlando Hernandez and Mariano Rivera.

Which brings this celebrated franchise full circle. Steinbrenner's pay-first-ask-questions-later approach is not all that different from the one used by Ruppert back in the 1920s, when he gave New York its first American League championship. In baseball, money talks.

And some things never change.

Steinbrenner added another trophy to his case in 1996, when new manager Joe Torre (left) guided the Yankees to the first of four World Series championships in a five-year span.

YANKEE *Stadium*

Babe Ruth, the Sultan of Swat: 714 lifetime home runs, .690 career slugging percentage, 60 home runs in '27, 177 runs scored in '21

Home of Triple Crown winners Gehrig, '34, and Mantle, '56

Joltin' Joe DiMaggio, center fielder for 9 World Series champions. He started 56-game hitting streak here, May 15, 1941

Where Dodger Al Gionfriddo made spectacular catch of DiMaggio's long drive in Game 6 of '47 World Series

Ruth christens sparkling new Yankee Stadium with three-run homer on opening day in 1923

Monuments to Miller Huggins (1932), Gehrig (1941) and Ruth (1949) stood on playing field, in fair territory, for many years

Where Dodger Sandy Amoros raced into the corner to rob Yogi Berra and save Game 7 of 1955 World Series

Whitey Ford: 25-4 in 1961 Cy Young season, 236-106 for career

June 13, 1948— Yankee Stadium celebrates 25th anniversary

Billy Martin ends '53 World Series with ninth-inning Game 6 single, his 12th hit of classic

Allie Reynolds tops Red Sox with record-tying second no-hitter of season, clinching tie for 1951 pennant

Home of catching greats Bill Dickey, three-time MVP Yogi Berra, Elston Howard

STADIUM Yankee 1923-73
PRE-RENOVATION

Casey Stengel managed 10 pennant winners: '49, '50, '51, '52, '53, '55, '56, '57, '58, '60

Joe McCarthy managed 8 pennant winners: '32, '36, '37, '38, '39, '41, '42, '43

Hank Bauer dooms Giants with bases-loaded triple, Series-saving catch in Game 6 of '51 fall classic

Mantle hits monster shot off Stadium facade, May 22, 1963

Landing point of Mantle's third-deck homer off Barney Schultz in Game 3 of '64 Series

Area where Roger Maris homer No. 61 landed, Oct. 1, 1961

Where Mickey Mantle, a.k.a. The Mick, drilled 500th career homer, May 14, 1967

Where Don Larsen shocked baseball world with his perfect game in 1956 World Series

Where Mantle tripped over drainage outlet in 1951 World Series, suffering serious knee injury

Babe Ruth Day, April 27, 1947—A cancer-stricken Bambino thanks Yankee fans

First baseman Lou Gehrig played many of his 2,130 consecutive games here, en route to career marks of 493 homers, 1,995 RBIs and .340 average

Lou Gehrig Appreciation Day, July 4, 1939—A farewell to the Iron Horse, the "luckiest man on the face of the Earth"

Billed as the grandest sports arena ever constructed, Yankee Stadium opened its gates April 18, 1923, to a reported crowd of 74,200—by far, the largest ever to attend a major league game. The three-tiered, $2.5-million facility with the majestic green facade and all the modern conveniences was huge, powerful and imposing, not unlike the city it served.

More than anything else, it was "home" for a rootless Yankees team that had spent its last 10 seasons as Polo Grounds tenants of the National League's Giants. The ballpark, constructed in the Bronx, just across the Harlem River from the Polo Grounds, signaled a new era of prosperity for a Yankees franchise that was coming off consecutive losses to the Giants in its first World Series.

The park featured a 296-foot right field porch that would take advantage of the booming bat of lefthanded slugger Babe Ruth. The left field foul pole measured only 301 feet, but the wall jutted out quickly to left-center, creating a 461-foot "death valley" for righthanded batters. For many years, monuments honoring Miller Huggins, Lou Gehrig and Ruth provided obstacles for fielders chasing balls to the distant center field fence.

Over the years, fans would come to cherish the distinctive facade, which hung regally from the rim of a third deck that wrapped behind home plate, extending beyond both foul poles into fair territory, and the green grandstand seats that blended with the lush, perfectly manicured grass. A scoreboard rose from ground level above the open right-center field wall, over which passengers on the elevated train could get tantalizing glimpses of action.

But more than anything else, Yankee Stadium became the enduring symbol for championship success. Before the grand old Lady was renovated in 1974 and '75, the Bronx Bombers won 27 American League pennants and 20 World Series championships—and created an almost mystical aura that still envelops the game's proudest franchise.

Shortstop Derek Jeter, the main cog in Yankees' 1996-2001 pennant and championship machine

Joe Torre has managed five pennant winners and four World Series champions— '96, '98, '99 and 2000

Monument Park

Tino Martinez, Scott Brosius hit two-out, two-run, game-tying home runs in ninth inning on consecutive nights to stun Diamondbacks in Games 4 and 5 of 2001 Series … Jeter, Alfonso Soriano provide game-winning hits

Opening day '78: Roger Maris returns to Stadium for first time since '66 trade to Cardinals

Thurman Munson hits ALCS-turning home run into bullpen vs. Royals in 1978 Game 3

Where fiery Billy Martin was hired and fired as manager five times by George Steinbrenner

Louisiana Lightning: Ron Guidry dominates with 25-3 record, 1.74 ERA in 1978 Cy Young season … strikes out 18 Angels June 17

Site of K.C. third baseman George Brett's Pine Tar tirade, July 24, 1983

Chicago's Tom Seaver wins 500th game, Aug. 4, 1985

David Wells fires first regular-season perfect game in Yankees history, May 17, 1998 … David Cone spices up "Yogi Berra Day" with another perfect game, July 18, 1999

STADIUM
Yankee
1976-Present
POST-RENOVATION

Home of George Steinbrenner's Bronx Zoo

Remodeled Yankee Stadium opens April 15, 1976

Landing area for Brett's third-deck homer off Goose Gossage—the deciding blow in Game 3 of '80 ALCS

Where 12-year-old Jeffrey Maier made the catch of his life on Jeter's home run in Game 1 of 1996 ALCS

Where Chris Chambliss hit ALCS-winning home run in 1976

Area patroled by '85 A.L. MVP Don Mattingly from 1980-95—one of most popular players in Yankees history

World Series playground for always-controversial Reggie Jackson, a.k.a. Mr. October

Jackson's three homers on consecutive pitches finish off Dodgers in Game 6 of '77 World Series

Where Roger Clemens threw broken piece of bat, narrowly missing Mets star Mike Piazza, during intense and confrontational Game 2 of 2000 Subway Series

May 14, 1996: Comeback-minded Doc Gooden no-hits Mariners

Wade Boggs gets victory ride on police horse after 1996 Series-clinching victory

Last game of century takes place at Stadium as Yanks complete sweep of Braves for 25th World Series championship, Oct. 27, 1999

Yankee Stadium got a facelift during the two-year renovation (1974-75) that forced the Yankees to share Shea Stadium facilities with the cross-town Mets. And almost on cue, the Yankees began adding to their impressive pennant collection when they returned to the Bronx in 1976, after an 11-year absence from the World Series spotlight.

History still oozes from every nook and cranny of remodeled Yankee Stadium, but differences are front and center. The distinctive facade now is represented by a white, concrete facsimile that spans the top of the scoreboard from the left field to right field grandstands, and Monument Park is open to visitors beyond the left-center field fence, where they can

view the Huggins, Gehrig, Ruth, Joe DiMaggio and Mickey Mantle monuments as well as plaques honoring other Yankee legends.

The inviting right field porch now measures 310 feet with the left field foul pole at 312 and a more friendly left center at 430. Blue grandstand seats (green is out) no longer are impeded by view-blocking supportive steel pillars and fans are entertained by a 560-foot-long, state-of-the-art scoreboard below the concrete facade. Everything is bright and clean without sacrificing the Yankee Stadium mystique.

The Yanks celebrated their return to the "new" Stadium by winning American League pennants in 1976, '77, '78 and '81 and adding two champi-

onships. Through the year 2001, Yankee Stadium had served as home for 26 World Series winners and 36 A.L. champions.

First game (pre-renovation): April 18, 1923. The House That Ruth Built was christened with a three-run homer by the Bambino and a 4-1 victory over Boston.

First game (post-renovation): April 15, 1976. Rebuilt Yankee Stadium opened with an 11-4 win over Minnesota that was witnessed by 52,613.

Site of 36 World Series: 1923, '26, '27, '28, '32, '36, '37, '38, '39, '41, '42, '43, '47, '49, '50, '51, '52, '53, '55, '56, '57, '58, '60, '61, '62, '63, '64, '76, '77, '78, '81, '96, '98, '99, 2000, '01.

Site of three All-Star Games: 1939, '60, '77.

The CHAMPIONS

The emotional Subway Series, which tested the loyalties of baseball-crazy New Yorkers (below), ended with a satisfying victory ride for Yankees manager Joe Torre (above).

F rom a baseball perspective, the 2000 World Series was a mismatch. But from the tunnel-vision vantage point of a city divided, it was a classic battle of teams, loyalties and emotions. It was New York, New York, the powerful Yankees vs. the upstart Mets and the first "Subway Series" since 1956—all wrapped in a tense, riveting and dramatic pinstriped package.

In the end, the Yankees prevailed in five games, thanks largely to the clutch contributions of unlikely heroes Jose Vizcaino, Mike Stanton and Luis Sojo. But it never was easy, much like a regular season that ended with a 2½-game margin over Boston in the A.L. East Division and hard-fought Division Series and ALCS wins over Oakland and Seattle.

The wild-card Mets, who finished second to Atlanta in the N.L. East, were eager and hungry after playoff wins over San Francisco and St. Louis. But the Yankees were experienced and poised, qualities that showed up quickly and frequently. They needed all the poise they could garner in a marathon Game 1 at Yankee Stadium—an emotionally charged battle decided after a Series-record 4 hours and 51 minutes by Vizcaino's fourth hit, a single in the 12th inning.

"I was thinking I would be going to the World Series, but I didn't think I'd be a hero in the first game," said Vizcaino, a surprise starter at second base. In a game that started as a pitching duel between lefthanders Andy Pettitte of the Yankees and Al Leiter of the Mets, Vizcaino delivered a ninth-inning single that set up

Chuck Knoblauch's score-tying sacrifice fly and his bases-loaded winner in the 12th.

What Game 2 lacked in longevity, it more than made up for with drama. The 56,059 fans at Yankee Stadium were barely settled into their seats when the main attraction—Yankee righthander Roger Clemens vs. Mets catcher Mike Piazza—took center stage.

Pregame talk had focused on a midseason interleague game during which Clemens hit Piazza on the head, drawing heated accusations from Mets players that the beaning had been intentional. Clemens dismissed such talk, but Piazza had seven hits and three home runs in 12 previous career at-bats against the five-time Cy Young winner.

As if on cue, hype turned to reality when Piazza swung at a first-inning Clemens pitch and fouled the ball, his bat

When Yankees starter Roger Clemens fired a piece of broken bat toward Mets runner Mike Piazza (left) in the first inning of Game 2, tempers flared and both benches emptied. Piazza walked toward Clemens (above), but cooler heads prevailed and the field finally was cleared for a resumption of action.

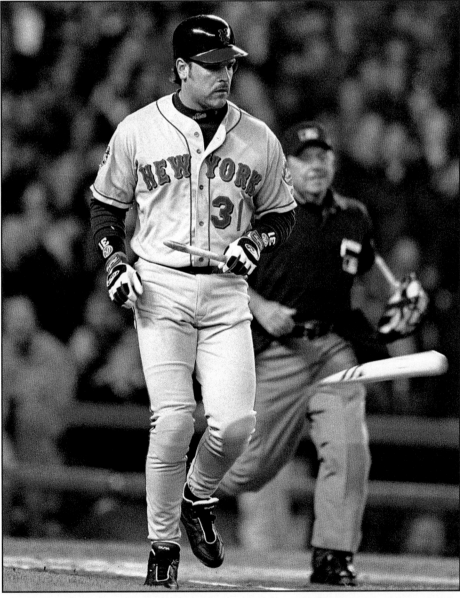

splintering into pieces. As the barrel sailed toward the mound, Piazza ran toward first, not knowing the ball's location. Clemens picked up the jagged piece of bat and flung it toward the first base dugout, just missing Piazza, who stopped and glared as both benches emptied.

"There was no intent," Clemens said after the game. "I was fired up and emotional and flung the bat toward the on-deck circle where the batboy was. I had no idea Mike was running."

"It was just so bizarre," said Piazza, apparently willing to give Clemens the benefit of the doubt. Other Mets players weren't so generous. "I think he knew what he was doing all along and is coming up with excuses," reliever John Franco said.

When the game resumed, Clemens mowed down the Mets on two hits over eight innings, striking out nine. The Mets trailed 6-0 in the ninth when they suddenly rallied for five runs off relievers Jeff Nelson and Mariano Rivera, all coming on homers by Piazza and Jay Payton. It was too little, too late as the Yankees posted their record 14th straight Series victory.

When the fall classic moved to Shea Stadium for Game 3, the Mets brought an

Game 4 belonged to Yankees shortstop Derek Jeter, who hit a home run and a triple (below) and scored two runs in a 3-2 win.

Jorge Posada slides into home with the winning run of Game 5, just as the throw arrives from center field. Posada scored on Luis Sojo's single and another run scored when the ball bounced away from Mets catcher Piazza.

end to that streak. They also posted their first Series win since 1986 while handing Yankees starter Orlando Hernandez his first Series defeat after eight straight wins. The 4-2 triumph was decided in the eighth inning when Benny Agbayani broke a 2-2 tie with an RBI double and Bubba Trammell added a sacrifice fly.

Any of the 55,290 fans who gathered at Shea thinking that victory would inspire the Mets in Game 4 were provided a cruel dose of reality. Yankees shortstop Derek Jeter hit the first pitch of the game from Bobby J. Jones over the left field wall, changing the momentum of the Series.

"Putting a run on the board was the difference in the game," Mets manager Bobby Valentine said. The Yankees added solo runs in the second and third and

It was not hard to tell Mets fans from Yankee fans over a passionate five-game test of loyalties and emotions.

withstood a two-run homer by Piazza to record a 3-2 victory. Rivera worked the final two innings for his 17th straight postseason save.

One win away from their third straight championship and fourth in five years, the Yankees turned matters over to Pettitte in Game 5. The reliable lefty worked seven innings and allowed two unearned runs before leaving with the score tied. True to form, the opportunistic Yankees scored twice in the ninth for a 4-2 knockout.

"I just wasn't able to close it out and finish the (ninth) inning," said Leiter, who carried a five-hitter into the ninth. He struck out Tino Martinez and Paul O'Neill to open the frame, but Jorge Posada walked and Scott Brosius singled, bringing up reserve second baseman Sojo. He slapped Leiter's 142nd pitch up the middle, driving home Posada with the winner. Brosius also scored when center fielder Payton's throw bounced into the dugout.

"This was super satisfying," said Yankees manager Joe Torre after watching Rivera retire Piazza on a long fly ball to seal the franchise's 26th World Series win. "It's never easy, but we had a lot of trouble putting things together this year."

Series MVP honors went to Jeter, who also homered in the fifth game off Leiter and batted .409 overall. Stanton, a lefthanded reliever, won Games 1 and 5 without allowing a run in 4⅓ innings.

"The Mets gave us everything we could want," said Yankees owner George Steinbrenner. "It was great for the city of New York. I hope we don't have to go through this again for another 44 years."

It was a frustrating World Series for Bubba Trammell (right) and his Mets teammates, who could not quite keep pace with the Yankees express.

The greatest championship run in sports history began, fittingly, in 1923, the same year the Yankees opened a baseball palace just across the Harlem River from the Polo Grounds—the home they had shared with the Giants since 1913. This World Series will be remembered as the Yankee Stadium showcase, complete with pomp, circumstance, the slugging exploits of Babe Ruth and sweet revenge against the Giants, who had defeated the Yankees in the previous two World Series.

Ruth, a .393 hitter with 41 home runs during the regular season, put on a fall classic show with a .368 average, three homers, a triple, a double and eight walks. His two home runs helped the Yankees and Herb Pennock post a 4-2 victory in Game 2 and he connected again in Game 6, a Series-clinching 6-4 win for Pennock.

Ironically, the first two Series games in Yankee Stadium history were won by the Giants and both were decided on late home runs by sore-legged outfielder Casey Stengel, who would gain lasting fame more than a quarter of a century later as manager of the Yankees. Stengel's ninth-inning inside-the-park blow disappointed 55,307 fans and gave the Giants a 5-4 win in Game 1 and his seventh-inning homer off Sad Sam Jones gave Art Nehf a 1-0 victory before 62,430 in Game 3.

Yankee Stadium was considered a baseball palace in 1923, when Babe Ruth led the New Yorkers to their first World Series championship.

With lefty Herb Pennock posting wins in Games 2 and 6, the Yankees claimed their first World Series title.

A pre-1927 Yankees-Pirates World Series get-together featured future Hall of Famers (left to right) Lloyd Waner, Babe Ruth, Paul Waner and Lou Gehrig.

Center fielder Earle Combs shows off his sweet swing in a Game 2 at-bat vs. the Pirates. Combs scored the Series-ending run in Game 4.

For pure, unadulterated, top-this-if-you-can legend, the 1927 Yankees have a special niche in baseball history. This was a championship express piloted by diminutive manager Miller Huggins and powered by heavy hitters Babe Ruth and Lou Gehrig. Murderer's Row (occupied by Ruth, Gehrig, Bob Meusel and Tony Lazzeri) was a section in first class. The home run was a typical destination.

If ever a team seemed destined to lose a World Series, it was the unfortunate Pittsburgh Pirates, the talented National League champions featuring the Waner brothers, Paul and Lloyd, Pie Traynor and Glenn Wright. They simply were in the wrong place at the wrong time. The Pirates had not witnessed Yankees devastation first-hand, but they had read and heard plenty about the Bronx Bombers' American League-record 110 wins, Ruth's single-season-record 60 home runs, Gehrig's 175 RBIs and the pitching of Waite Hoyt, Wilcy Moore, Herb Pennock and Urban Shocker.

True to expectations, the Yankees made quick work of the Pirates, thanks primarily to two Pittsburgh errors in Game 1 that helped them post a 5-4 victory at Forbes Field and the complete-game pitching efforts of George Pipgras and Pennock (a three-hitter) that gave them 6-2 and 8-1 wins in Games 2 and 3.

The Yankees, thanks to Ruth's two-run Game 4 homer, entered the bottom of the ninth locked in a 3-3 tie before 57,909 fans at Yankee Stadium. Earle Combs walked to open the inning, moved around on a bunt and wild pitch and raced home with the Series-ending run when reliever John Miljus threw a second wild pitch. Ironically, the powerful Yanks finished the Series with only two home runs—both by Ruth.

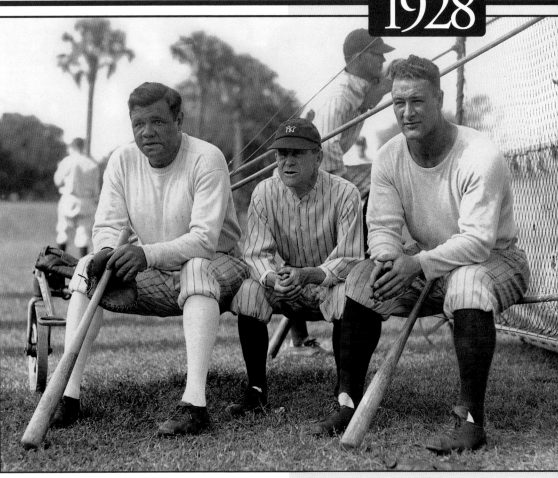

This was the Babe Ruth and Lou Gehrig show. While the rest of the Yankees batted .196 and hit two home runs in the four-game World Series sweep of St. Louis, the most prominent 1-2 punch in baseball burned the Cardinals for a .593 average (16-for-27), seven home runs and 13 RBIs. The dominating performance simply reaffirmed the greatness of the 1927-28 Bronx Bombers, who had slipped from 110 to 101 regular-season wins.

Ruth, who was playing on a bad ankle after his 54-homer, 142-RBI regular season, collected three of his Series-leading 10 hits in a 4-1 opening-game win and concluded his .625 postseason salvo with three Game 4 home runs in a 7-3 Series-ending victory. It was his second three-homer Series game against the Cardinals—both at Sportsman's Park—in three years.

Gehrig, who also drove in 142 regular-season runs, batted .545 and hit four Series home runs, two in a 7-3 third-game win. He finished the fall classic with a four-game-record nine RBIs.

Thanks to the lusty hitting of Ruth and Gehrig, the Yankees needed only three pitchers to shut down the Cardinals. Waite Hoyt went all the way in Games 1 and 4. George Pipgras allowed only four hits in a 9-3 Game 2 win and Tom Zachary spread out nine hits for a 7-3 win in Game 3.

Little Miller Huggins (above center) was the brains behind the 1928 World Series-champion Yankees while Babe Ruth and Lou Gehrig (right) supplied the brawn. Another beneficiary of the relentless Ruth-Gehrig offensive barrage was pitcher George Pipgras (far left), who beat the Cardinals in Game 2.

When Ruth and Gehrig didn't get you, second baseman Tony Lazzeri usually did. Lazzeri (left) greets Cardinals outfielder Ernie Orsatti before the 1928 Series.

Baseball hungry New York fans line up outside Yankee Stadium, hoping to purchase bleacher tickets for the 1932 Yankees-Chicago Cubs World Series.

Yankees first baseman Lou Gehrig devastated the Chicago Cubs with another outstanding World Series performance. But, as often happened throughout his Hall of Fame career, teammate Babe Ruth stole the spotlight.

"I didn't think I would ever see a ballplayer that good," said Cubs manager Charley Grimm after watching Gehrig bat .529, pound three homers, drive in eight runs and score nine times during a Yankees sweep that lifted their postseason winning streak to 12. But Gehrig had plenty of help. The Yankees manhandled Cubs pitching, scoring 37 runs and pounding out a team average of .313 as catcher Bill Dickey batted .438, center fielder Earle Combs .375 and third baseman Joe Sewell .333.

And then, of course, there was Ruth, the dynamic showman who put his indelible stamp on the 1932 World Series with a simple wave of his hand in the fifth inning of Game 3 at Chicago's Wrigley Field. Ruth, who had hit a three-run homer in the first, was batting against Chicago pitcher Charlie Root with the bases empty in a 4-4 game.

The Bambino also was taking a lot of abuse from the Cubs bench and charged-up fans, thanks primarily to his public criticism of Chicago players who had voted former Yankee Mark Koenig only a half share of their Series pot. Emotion also was running high among fans because of the return of Joe McCarthy, the New York manager who had been fired by the Cubs two years earlier.

Barraged by insults from every direction, Ruth took a called strike and raised his hand. Root missed with two pitches and then fired another strike, which the Babe acknowledged with another raised hand. With the taunting and invectives getting louder and more vindictive, Ruth suddenly made a gesture toward center field.

Whatever its meaning, Ruth swung viciously at Root's next pitch and connected, driving the ball over the center field wall at the base of the flagpole. Gehrig followed with another homer and the Yankees went on to post a 7-5 victory, all but sealing the championship they officially claimed the next day.

Debate started immediately. Some said Ruth was indicating where he would hit the next pitch with his sweeping gesture. Others said he simply was gesturing toward the Cubs bench. Ruth let the argument rage, content with the knowledge that his final World Series home run would forever be remembered as the "called shot."

The illustration (below left) by Robert Thom catches the spirit of Babe Ruth's "called-shot home run" in the 1932 Series. Ruth (above) is greeted by Lou Gehrig after the memorable Game 3 blow.

Giants top guns Mel Ott (left) and Jo-Jo Moore pose for a 1936 World Series photograph with Yankee sluggers Joe DiMaggio (second from right) and Lou Gehrig.

So far, the Yankees had merely been impressive—four World Series championships in 13 years. Now it was time to get serious. Shrugging off predictions they would never sustain World Series success without Babe Ruth and riding the crest of a 102-win regular season under manager Joe McCarthy, the Bronx Bombers began an unprecedented run that would net them four straight championships and six over an incredible eight-year stretch.

Appropriately, the Giants were back in the 1936 World Series spotlight and this time it took six games for the Yanks to dispatch their former postseason nemesis. After dropping a 6-1 opener to Giants ace Carl Hubbell (26-6 during the regular season), the Yankees did it with both power (18-4 in Game 2, 13-5 in Game 6) and finesse (2-1 in Game 3, 5-2 in Game 4). The fourth game featured a home run by old reliable, Lou Gehrig, and a rare defeat for Hubbell.

The Yankees' top guns were left fielder Jake Powell (.455) and third baseman Red Rolfe (.400), but contributions also were made by Tony Lazzeri, who hit a Game 2 grand slam, and Gehrig, who homered twice and drove in seven runs. Lefty Gomez, benefiting from the two Yankee explosions, recorded a pair of victories.

This World Series marked a passing of the torch for Yankee fans. Ruth was gone, but rookie center fielder Joe DiMaggio, who had batted .323 and driven in 125 runs during the season, made his World Series debut with nine hits and a .346 average.

Giants ace Carl Hubbell (left, right photo) and Yankee Lefty Gomez draw a big crowd at the pre-Series media gathering. Yankee Red Rolfe (left photo) slides safely into third after a Game 6 DiMaggio single as Giants third baseman Travis Jackson awaits the late throw.

As the Yankees express kicked up to full throttle, everybody stepped aside and admired its state-of-the-art efficiency. First American League rivals were overwhelmed as the Bronx Bombers rolled to 102 wins. Then the National League-champion Giants were run over in a five-game World Series as the Yanks notched consecutive championships for a second time.

A roster that featured future Hall of Famers Joe DiMaggio, Lou Gehrig, Bill Dickey, Tony Lazzeri, Lefty Gomez and Red Ruffing was simply too much. That became apparent to the Giants in consecutive Series-opening 8-1 losses at Yankee Stadium and a 5-1 loss at the Polo Grounds. The Giants managed only six hits in the opener against Gomez, seven hits in Game 2 against Ruffing and five hits in Game 3 against Monte Pearson, who needed last-out relief from Johnny Murphy.

The Giants' only victory (7-3) came courtesy of Carl Hubbell's talented left arm in Game 4, but the Yankees wrapped up the Series, 4-2, the next day behind Gomez as DiMaggio chipped in with his first Series home run.

Lazzeri, playing in his last season with the Yankees, went out on a high note with a home run and .400 average. Gehrig, who had driven in 159 runs during his last big regular season, managed a homer and three RBIs—his last in World Series play.

Giants rookie Cliff Melton shakes hands with Yankees righthander Red Ruffing (right) before a Game 2 matchup in the World Series. Ruffing posted an 8-1 victory, much to the dismay of food-munching Giants fans.

Hard-hitting second baseman Tony Lazzeri batted .400 and belted a home run in the last of his six World Series with the Yankees.

Memories from the 1938 World Series (left to right): managers Joe McCarthy and Gabby Hartnett conferring with commissioner Kenesaw Mountain Landis in Game 2; Cubs shortstop Billy Jurges firing to first over sliding Joe DiMaggio on a Game 3 double play attempt; Chicago catcher Ken O'Dea getting a warm greeting after a Game 4 home run, and McCarthy celebrating with friends and family after his team's Game 4 Series-clinching victory.

I t was a mismatch, much like the 1932 World Series that featured the same two teams. The Yankees, with 100-RBI men Joe DiMaggio (140), Bill Dickey (115) and Lou Gehrig (114) in the middle of a dangerous lineup, simply overpowered the light-hitting Chicago Cubs, whose top gun, outfielder Augie Galan, had driven in 69 runs.

With the sweep, the Yankees became seven-time World Series champions and the first team to win three straight fall classics. The Yankees' dominance, punctuated by four sweeps in their last six Series appearances, was beginning to inspire talk of a baseball dynasty.

Manager Joe McCarthy watched comfortably as ace Red Ruffing opened proceedings with a 3-1 victory at Chicago and then closed out the Series four days later with an 8-3 decision at Yankee Stadium. In between, the Cubs were shut down 6-3 and 5-2 by Lefty Gomez and Monte Pearson.

Dickey, who collected four hits in the opener, and second baseman Joe Gordon shared hitting honors with .400 averages. But normally light-hitting shortstop Frankie Crosetti was the difference-maker in Game 2, when he hit a momentum-shifting two-run homer off Dizzy Dean, and Game 4, when he drove in four runs with a double and triple.

The Series was the last for Lou Gehrig, whose career would be shut down by a fatal disease in 1939. Gehrig collected four singles in his final postseason appearance.

Game 3 starting pitchers Clay Bryant (left) and Monte Pearson pose for photographers. Pearson got the best of this matchup and a 5-2 victory.

The 1938 Yankees were in an autograph-signing mood, both before and after their World Series battle against the Cubs.

A Murderer's Row combination of Reds and Yankees: Left to right are Harry Craft, Bill Dickey, Ernie Lombardi, Joe DiMaggio, Frank McCormick and George Selkirk.

In a season that forever will be associated with the emotional demise of Lou Gehrig, the Yankee machine rolled to 106 victories, a 17-game advantage over second-place Boston in the American League and its record fourth straight World Series championship. The four-game win over Cincinnati was New York's fifth sweep in its last seven postseason appearances and lifted its record over that span to an unbelievable 28-3.

But unlike the Yankees' 1938 sweep of the Chicago Cubs, this one wasn't easy. Reds pitchers held the Yanks to a .206 average and really deserved a better fate. The

Series turned on the Bronx Bombers' ability to hit the ball out of the park and the pitching of Red Ruffing, Monte Pearson, Bump Hadley and reliever Johnny Murphy.

After Ruffing had outdueled Paul Derringer in a 2-1 opener at Yankee Stadium, Pearson recorded a two-hit, 4-0 shutout with Babe Dahlgren, Gehrig's first base replacement, supplying a key home run. Game 3 captured the tone of the Series with the Yankees managing only five hits but winning 7-3, thanks to two home runs by rookie Charlie Keller and one each by Joe DiMaggio and Bill Dickey.

The Yankees scored three runs on a memorable 10th-inning play and escaped with a 7-4 win in the finale. With runners on first and third, DiMaggio singled and circled the bases when first the ball was misplayed in the outfield and then Keller collided with Reds catcher Ernie Lombardi, who lay stunned near home plate—"Lombardi's Snooze."

Game 2 at Yankee Stadium produced crowded bleachers and a pitching matchup of Bucky Walters (left) and Monte Pearson. The most memorable play of the Series took place in the 10th inning of Game 4 when DiMaggio slid safely across the plate (left) as Reds catcher Lombardi (4) "snoozed."

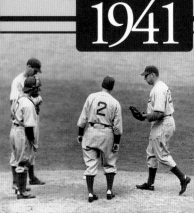

Scenes from the 1941 Series (left to right): Dodgers manager Leo Durocher (2) greeting reliever Hugh Casey (23) in Game 4; Durocher arguing his case in Game 5; the Yankee slugging trio of Joe DiMaggio, Charlie Keller and Bill Dickey; Keller scoring a Game 2 run on pitcher Spud Chandler's infield single.

Shortstop Pee Wee Reese (left), the heart of the Dodgers, poses with Yankees Joe Gordon (center) and Dickey.

Having taken one year off from their unprecedented championship run, the Yankees returned to the World Series seeking their fifth title in six years. The Brooklyn Dodgers, 100-game winners in capturing their first National League pennant since 1920, figured to provide a serious test to the Bronx Bombers' usual postseason dominance.

That certainly appeared to be the case as Yankees ace Red Ruffing and Brooklyn righthander Whitlow Wyatt traded 3-2 victories in the first two games. After the Yankees scored two eighth-inning runs to give Marius Russo a 2-1 win in Game 3, the Dodgers fought back in Game 4 as reliever Hugh Casey carried a 4-3 lead into the top of the ninth. With two out, nobody on base and two strikes on Tommy Henrich, 33,813 fans at Ebbets Field braced for a Series-knotting victory.

Casey's next pitch broke down and away, enticing Henrich to swing and miss. But instead of a game-ending strikeout, Brooklyn fans watched as the ball eluded Dodgers catcher Mickey Owen, allowing Henrich to reach first base. When Joe DiMaggio followed with a single and Charlie Keller and Joe Gordon ripped two-run doubles, the Yankees had a stunning 7-4 win.

"That was a tough break for poor Mickey to get," said Henrich, who homered the next day in the Yankees' Series-clinching 3-1 victory—their 32nd in 36 Series games. "I bet he feels like a nickel's worth of dog meat."

Tommy Henrich (left) started the Yankees' improbable Game 4, ninth-inning rally by reaching first base on a strikeout. Teammates (left to right) DiMaggio, Keller and Gordon all followed with key hits.

Cardinals runner Stan Musial is out at second as Yankee Joe Gordon completes a Game 3 double play.

Cardinals outfielder Danny Litwhiler is safe at first on a Game 3 infield single at dressed-up Yankee Stadium.

This was war-time baseball and the rosters for both the Yankees and St. Louis Cardinals were missing key players—Joe DiMaggio, Phil Rizzuto and Red Ruffing for the Yanks; Enos Slaughter, Terry Moore and Johnny Beazley for the Cards. Still, there was a strong desire to avenge a 1942 loss to the Cardinals that had snapped the Yankees' eight-Series winning streak.

This would be manager Joe McCarthy's seventh and last Series championship, and it would come with the Yankees' typical postseason efficiency—solid pitching plus timely hitting equals a five-game victory. The New Yorkers managed only a .220 average, but that was enough for a pitching staff that carved out a 1.40 ERA.

Spud Chandler got the Yankees off to a fast start with a seven-hit, 4-2 win in the opener and then provided the clincher six days later with a 10-hit, 2-0 shutout decided by catcher Bill Dickey's two-run homer. Hank Borowy worked eight innings in a 6-2 Game 3 win and Marius Russo was strong in a 2-1 Game 4 triumph that put the Yanks in control after St. Louis had evened things with a 4-3 second-game win behind Mort Cooper.

The Series turned in the eighth inning of Game 3. Rookie third baseman Billy Johnson provided the big blow, a bases-loaded triple, that wiped out a 2-1 Cardinals lead in a five-run outburst.

With Joe DiMaggio serving in the Army, Charlie Keller (left) became the center-piece of New York's lineup. Musial (right) handled that role for the Cardinals.

Game 7 hero Joe Page (center, top photo) gets a victory hug from Joe DiMaggio (left) and team president Larry MacPhail. Allie Reynolds (above right) outdueled Dodgers starter Vic Lombardi in a 10-3 Game 2 Yankees win.

It was a classic among the long line of grueling World Series that would be played between the rival Yankees and Brooklyn Dodgers—filled with drama, excitement and intensity. It also was the Yankees' 11th Series victory, their first in seven games and first under new manager Bucky Harris.

Most of the drama was packed into two of them—the fourth and sixth, both Dodger victories. All four New York wins were crafted with typical Yankee efficiency—outstanding pitching by Spec Shea and reliever Joe Page, timely hitting by outfielders Johnny Lindell, Tommy Henrich and Joe DiMaggio.

Shea and Page were especially prominent. They combined for a 5-3 Series-opening win and Shea returned in Game 5, after a gut-wrenching Yankees loss, and shut down the Dodgers 2-1 on four hits. Page stepped up in Game 7 to work five one-hit innings of relief as the Yankees, down 2-0 early, recorded a clinching 5-2 victory.

Game 4 was an Ebbets Field emotion-twister that spot-lighted Yankees journeyman righthander Floyd "Bill" Bevens, a 7-13 regular-season performer who was, literally, unhittable for most of the afternoon. Fighting only his control (he walked 10 and allowed a fifth-inning run), Bevens entered the ninth inning with a 2-1 lead and a chance to throw the first no-hitter in World Series history. But with two out and two men on base (via walks), pinch-hitter Cookie Lavagetto sent the crowd of 33,443 into hysterics by driving a pitch off the right field wall for a two-run, game-winning, no-hitter-ruining double.

While Game 6 might have fallen short of the fourth-game drama, it wasn't lacking for excitement. The Dodgers, on the brink of elimination, took a 4-0 lead, fell behind 5-4 and then scored four times in the top of the sixth for an 8-5 advantage. The outcome was decided in the bottom of the inning when DiMaggio, batting with two men on base, drove a pitch toward the 415-foot sign guarding the Yankee bullpen. But just as it appeared the ball might fall over the fence, Dodgers left fielder Al Gionfriddo made an incredible twisting, glove-extending catch that saved the Dodgers' eventual 8-6 victory.

The two key moments of the 1947 World Series: Dodgers left fielder Al Gionfriddo makes his spectacular catch in Game 6 (top photo) and Brooklyn pinch hitter Cookie Lavagetto breaks up Bill Bevens' no-hit attempt in the ninth inning of Game 4 (above).

Ecstatic fans swarm the field at Yankee Stadium after watching their Bronx Bombers post a 5-2 victory over the Dodgers in Game 7 of an exciting and eventful World Series.

Joe DiMaggio gets a big greeting from enthusiastic teammates after hitting a home run, his only one of the Series, in the Yankees' title-clinching Game 5 win over Brooklyn.

His name was Casey Stengel and his clown reputation had preceded him to New York. But seven other American League teams and various National League champions would find nothing funny about the new Yankees manager over the next 12 seasons. Stengel directed the first of his 10 pennant winners in 1949 and capped that success with the first of his seven World Series championships, a five-game romp past the outmanned Brooklyn Dodgers.

Pitching dominated early as the teams traded 1-0 Series-opening victories. Brooklyn ace Don Newcombe and Yankees righthander Allie Reynolds dueled masterfully into the ninth inning of Game 1, which was decided by Tommy Henrich's walkoff home run. Brooklyn's Preacher Roe outpitched Vic Raschi in the second game with Jackie Robinson scoring the only run in the second inning on a Gil Hodges single.

It was all Yankees after that. A two-run, ninth-inning single by Johnny Mize broke a 1-1 deadlock and keyed a 4-3 third-game win and right fielder Cliff Mapes and third baseman Bobby Brown were unlikely Yankees heroes in Game 4, combining for five RBIs in a 6-4 victory.

Second baseman Jerry Coleman drove in three runs the next day as the Yanks closed out their 12th World Series championship with a 10-6 win.

Tommy Henrich (above) supplied the only run in Game 1 with a ninth-inning homer and Bobby Brown earned a victory kiss from Phil Rizzuto (right) with three hits and two RBIs in the Game 5 finale.

Joe DiMaggio steps on the plate after hitting a 10th-inning home run— the decisive blow in New York's 2-1 Game 2 win over the Phillies.

The 1950 World Series had a little old—those relentless Yankees—and a little new—the long-suffering Philadelphia Phillies, who had gone pennantless for 35 years before edging out the Brooklyn Dodgers on Dick Sisler's final-day home run. But there would be nothing new or unexpected about the result—the Yankees' sixth sweep and 13th championship over the last 28 years.

The powerful Yanks, who had been known to bludgeon Series opponents into submission, eased past the Phillies while batting only .222 and scoring 11 runs. The pattern was set in the Game 1 opener at Philadelphia when Vic Raschi fired a two-hit shutout and outdueled Phillies emergency starter Jim Konstanty, 1-0. The only run scored on Jerry Coleman's fourth-inning sacrifice fly.

It was more of the same in the second and third games. Allie Reynolds and Phillies ace Robin Roberts were locked in a 1-1 battle through nine innings of Game 2, but Joe DiMaggio decided matters in the 10th with a solo home run. Eddie Lopat and Tom Ferrick held the Whiz Kids to two runs in Game 3 and Coleman's ninth-inning single delivered a 3-2 victory.

Yankees lefthander Whitey Ford was one out away from a shutout in the finale when left fielder Gene Woodling dropped a fly ball, allowing two runs to score. But Reynolds recorded the final out and preserved a 5-2 victory.

Manager Casey Stengel celebrates the Yankees' 13th championship with co-owners Dan Topping (left) and Del Webb (right).

Monte Irvin got the Giants off to a flying start with four Game 1 hits and a steal of home, during which he eluded the late tag of New York catcher Yogi Berra (above). One of the top guns in the Yankees' come-from-behind victory was infielder Gil McDougald, who delivered a third-inning grand slam home run (above right) in a Series-turning 13-1 Game 5 romp.

Starring roles in the Yankees' critical Game 5 win belonged to (left to right) Phil Rizzuto, pitcher Eddie Lopat and McDougald.

The Yankees knew this one wouldn't be easy. The New York Giants were on a roll, having won 37 of their last 44 regular-season games to catch the Brooklyn Dodgers and two of three pennant-playoff games to claim the National League championship. The wildest pennant race in baseball history had been decided only a day earlier by the most dramatic home run in baseball history—Bobby Thomson's "Shot Heard 'Round the World."

So it didn't come as a shock when the Giants parlayed that momentum into a 5-1 World Series-opening victory at Yankee Stadium, thanks in large part to the seven-hit pitching of Dave Koslo and the heroics of left fielder Monte Irvin, who collected four hits and recorded the first Series steal of home since 1928.

The Yankees needed a momentum-shifter and they got it from lefthander Eddie Lopat, who pitched a five hitter in a clutch 3-1 victory. After the Giants fought back for a 6-2 third-game win, the rest of the Series belonged to the Bronx Bombers.

Allie Reynolds went all the way in a 6-2 Game 4 victory that featured a home run by Joe DiMaggio and the Yankees pulled out the big offensive guns in Game 5, a 13-1 win that featured rookie Gil McDougald's grand slam and a home run by shortstop Phil Rizzuto. The finale belonged to veteran outfielder Hank Bauer, who tripled home three runs and made a sensational Series-ending catch with the Yankees leading 4-3 and the tying run in scoring position.

Bauer, who had struggled mightily in past Series, was one of several interest-

ing sidescripts. The 1951 Series is remembered as the last for the great DiMaggio and the first for two other great center fielders—the Giants' Willie Mays and the Yankees' Mickey Mantle. It also is remembered for a Game 2 accident in which Mantle tripped on the cover of a Yankee Stadium drainage outlet, ending his season and signaling the start of knee problems that would dog him his entire career.

The Yankees' third straight Series win also was their fourth in a row over the cross-river Giants.

Yankee home run hitters Mickey Mantle (left) and Gene Woodling (right) flank Game 7 savior Bob Kuzava.

By 1952, it had become painfully obvious the road to World Series success ran through the middle of Yankee Stadium. That might have been only a few miles on the map for frustrated Brooklyn fans, but it was a universe away from reality.

The Yankees, under manager Casey Stengel, were looking for a record-tying fourth consecutive championship and 15th overall. The Dodgers were at the opposite end of the spectrum, looking for their first title after five World Series setbacks, including 1941, 1947 and 1949 losses to the dreaded Yanks. This battle would pit supreme confidence against desperation.

The teams split the first four games, the Dodgers winning behind Joe Black and Preacher Roe and the Yankees answering behind Vic Raschi and Allie Reynolds. It appeared the Yankee jinx might end when the Dodgers, aided by an 11th-inning RBI double by Duke Snider and Carl Furillo's home run-saving catch against Johnny Mize, claimed a 6-5 fifth-game victory that put them in the driver's seat with the final two contests scheduled for Ebbets Field.

Dodger righthander Billy Loes carried a 1-0 lead into the seventh inning of Game 6, thanks to Snider's sixth-inning home run off Raschi. But the relentless Yankees took the lead on Yogi Berra's homer and Raschi's RBI single. Mickey Mantle's first World Series home run in the eighth offset Snider's second blast in the bottom of the inning and the Yankees held on for a Series-extending 3-2 win.

Game 7 was decided in a strange seventh inning. Mantle, who had homered in the sixth, singled home another run to give the Yankees a 4-2 lead. But the Dodgers loaded the bases in the bottom of the inning and Snider, who had already hit four Series homers, stood at the plate with one out. Yankee lefthander Bob Kuzava entered the game and retired Snider on a popup.

With two out, Kuzava worked the count to 3-2 on Jackie Robinson, who hit an apparent rally-killing popup near the mound. But as the ball descended, first baseman Joe Collins lost it in the lights and nobody took control. Realizing what was happening with all three runners racing around the bases, second baseman Billy Martin sprinted forward and made a lunging, shoetop catch, saving a 4-2 victory—and the Series.

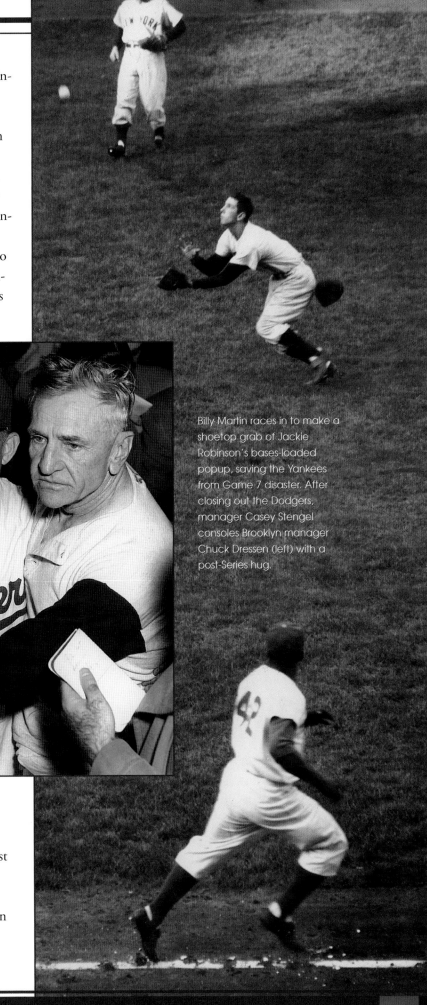

Billy Martin races in to make a shoetop grab of Jackie Robinson's bases-loaded popup, saving the Yankees from Game 7 disaster. After closing out the Dodgers, manager Casey Stengel consoles Brooklyn manager Chuck Dressen (left) with a post-Series hug.

Call this the Billy Martin Show. As if inspired by his World Series-saving catch against Brooklyn in Game 7 of the 1952 fall classic, the feisty Yankees second baseman performed surgery on the 1953 Dodgers with his bat. The first of his record 12 hits, a bases-loaded first-inning triple, set the tone in the opener; his Game 6 ninth-inning RBI single concluded the Yankees' unprecedented fifth consecutive World Series championship.

Yankees left fielder Gene Woodling not only homered in Game 5, he also cut down Dodgers first baseman Gil Hodges at the plate with a perfect throw to catcher Yogi Berra.

Martin's heriocs added insult to injury for the frustrated Dodgers, who had lost all six of their previous World Series ventures, including four to the hated Yankees. The Dodgers had stormed through the National League with 105 wins and they boasted the league MVP (catcher Roy Campanella), batting champion (Carl Furillo) and rookie of the year (Jim Gilliam). Five .300 hitters were complemented by two 40-homer men (Campanella and Duke Snider), three 100-RBI men (Campanella, Snider and Gil Hodges) and a 20-game winner (Carl Erskine).

On paper, this team had the makings of a champion. But that didn't matter to the Yankees, who roughed up Erskine for four runs in the first inning of the Yankee Stadium opener and went on to a 9-5 victory. Eddie Lopat came back the next day to scatter nine hits and home runs by Martin and Mickey Mantle produced a 4-2 win.

Down two-games-to-none, the Dodgers needed a fix and got it from Erskine, who struck out 14 Yankees in a 3-2 victory decided by Campanella's eighth-

Yankees (below, left to right) Hank Bauer, Berra, Billy Martin and Joe Collins had reason to celebrate after Game 1. Carl Furillo evaded Berra's tag to score a Game 2 run for the Dodgers (right photo), but the Yankees still won,

Game 5 pitcher Jim
McDonald (with towel) got
home run support from
teammates (left to right)
Gil McDougald, Billy Martin,
Mickey Mantle and Gene
Woodling in an 11-7 win.

inning home run. Snider stepped front and center in
Game 4 with two doubles, a homer and four RBIs as the
Dodgers evened matters with a 7-3 win.

But that's as good as it would get for the Dodgers.
Game 5 homers by Martin, Mantle, Gil McDougald and
Gene Woodling buried Brooklyn in an 11-7 Yankee vic-
tory at Ebbets Field. And the Bombers wrapped things
up the next afternoon, 4-3 at Yankee Stadium, on
Martin's ninth-inning single after Furillo had given the
Dodgers temporary life in the top of the inning with a
dramatic two-run homer.

The championship also was the fifth in a row for Casey
Stengel in as many seasons as Yankees manager, surpassing the four straight titles Joe McCarthy won as Yankees
boss from 1936-39.

Mantle's Game 5 homer,
a grand slam, earned
him a welcome home
greeting from Yogi Berra
(8), Joe Collins (15) and
Hank Bauer (9).

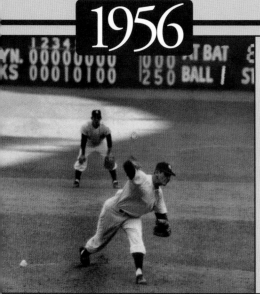

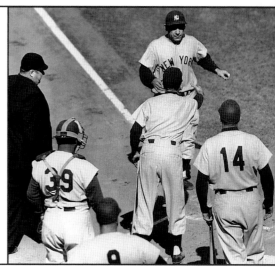

Don Larsen (above) finishes his Game 5 perfecto and receives congratulations (center) from Dodgers starter Sal Maglie. Game 7 belonged to Yogi Berra, who heads for home (right photo) on the first of two home runs.

Having won 16 of 20 World Series appearances and 16 of their last 18, it must have come as a major shock to the Yankees when they fell to Brooklyn in a seven-game 1955 fall classic—those same Dodgers who had failed to win in five previous battles against their Bronx neighbors. Shock turned to concern as the Yankees lost the first two games of the 1956 Series to the Dodgers with 11 pitchers surrendering 19 runs and 21 hits.

Hank Bauer (left) and Mickey Mantle (right) hit Game 4 homers and Tom Sturdivant (center) pitched the Yankees to a 6-2 victory over the Dodgers.

Had baseball's balance of power shifted to the Dodgers and the National League? For anybody who had reached that conclusion, a reality check was close at hand.

Whitey Ford, a 19-game winner, got the Yankees back on track with a 5-3 third-game win that featured home runs by Enos Slaughter and Billy Martin. Then Tom Sturdivant checked the Dodgers on six hits in a 6-2 win as Mickey Mantle and Hank Bauer contributed homers. With the Series knotted at two games, manager Casey Stengel trotted out his secret weapon for the pivotal fifth contest.

Don Larsen had been shelled for four runs in his Game 2 start. But using his new no-windup delivery, the journeyman righthander began mowing down Dodger hitters without incident. As 64,519 fans at Yankee Stadium watched in wonder, Larsen moved through eight innings without surrendering a hit or a walk and stood only three outs away from the first no-hitter—the first perfect game—in World Series history.

Larsen, protecting a 2-0 lead supplied by Mantle's homer and Hank Bauer's single against tough-luck Brooklyn starter Sal Maglie, opened the ninth by retiring Carl Furillo on a fly ball and Roy Campanella on a grounder. Yankee fans exploded in ecstacy moments later when Larsen slipped a called third strike past pinch hitter Dale Mitchell to complete his 97-pitch, 2-0 masterpiece.

The Dodgers fought back in Game 6 when Clem Labine outdueled Bob Turley in a 1-0 battle that was decided by Jackie Robinson's 10th-inning single. But hopes for a second straight championship were dashed the next day when Bill Skowron hit a grand slam and Yogi Berra homered twice to support the three-hit pitching of Johnny Kucks in the Yankees' Series-ending 9-0 victory.

New York pitchers, dreadful early, had held the Dodgers to one run and seven hits over the last three games.

Johnny Kucks (center) stopped the Dodgers on three hits in a Game 7 shutout that featured a home run by first baseman Bill Skowron (left) and two by catcher Yogi Berra (right).

Down three games to one, the Yankees got Game 5 heroics from (left to right) Elston Howard, Bob Turley and Gil McDougald. Turley pitched a five-hitter, McDougald hit a homer and left fielder Howard made a great catch.

Braves lefty Warren Spahn (left) and batterymate Del Crandall celebrate Spahn's two-hit shutout of the Yankees in Game 4.

The Braves were confident. A seven-game victory over the Yankees in the 1957 World Series had lifted them to their first Milwaukee championship and a pitching staff that featured Warren Spahn and Lew Burdette was certainly capable of repeating that accomplishment. Nothing in the early going of the 1958 fall classic suggested they wouldn't.

Spahn outlasted the Whitey Ford-Ryne Duren tandem in the opener and was rewarded when center fielder Billy Bruton singled home a 10th-inning run for a 4-3 win. Spahn was even better in Game 4, holding the Yanks to two hits—a Mickey Mantle triple and Bill Skowron single—and silencing a capacity Yankee Stadium crowd with a 3-0 victory.

Sandwiched between the Spahn wins were a 13-5 victory in which Burdette helped his own cause with a three-run homer and a 4-0 Yankee win on a combined six-hitter by Don Larsen and Duren. Only one team, the 1925 Pittsburgh Pirates, had recovered from a three-games-to-one deficit to win a World Series—the daunting task that now faced the Bronx Bombers.

Bob Turley, a 21-game winner, steadied the Yankees with a five-hit, 7-0 shutout that featured a home run, double and three RBIs by second baseman Gil McDougald. But the real momentum-shifter came two days later at Milwaukee's

County Stadium. The Yankees got to Spahn for two 10th-inning runs, one on McDougald's home run and the other on Skowron's single, for a 4-2 lead. Then Turley was called in the bottom of the inning to squelch a Braves rally that cut the final margin to 4-3.

The Braves scored on a first-inning groundout in Game 7, but the Yankees nicked Burdette for two runs in the second. Turley was called for the third straight game, this time to replace Larsen with two on base in the third, and he responded with 6⅔ clutch innings that lifted the Yankees to their 18th Series victory.

Turley surrendered only a sixth-inning homer to Milwaukee catcher Del Crandall that tied the game. The Yankees rewarded him with four runs in the eighth, three on a Skowron homer, and a 6-2 victory.

Skowron and Hank Bauer supplied much of the Yankee punch in the Series with a combined six homers and 15 RBIs.

The happy Yankees, the second team in history to recover from a three-games-to-one World Series deficit, dash off the field after their Game 7 win at Milwaukee's County Stadium.

Game 7 moments: Second baseman Gil McDougald forces out Milwaukee's Joe Torre (left); manager Casey Stengel replaces pitcher Don Larsen (18) with Bob Turley (right, center photo), and managers Stengel and Fred Haney exchange post-Series pleasantries (right).

Game 3 home run hitters Roger Maris (left) and John Blanchard (right) sandwich winning reliever Luis Arroyo.

I f ever a Yankees team fit the long-accepted moniker "Bronx Bombers," it was the 1961 pennant machine driven by new manager Ralph Houk and powered by outfielders Roger Maris and Mickey Mantle. The '61 Yankees, 109-game winners after a devastating seven-game loss to Pittsburgh in the 1960 World Series, literally clubbed opponents into submission, a game plan that did not change in a five-game fall classic victory over the Cincinnati Reds.

One thing, however, did change. Maris and Mantle, who had combined for 115 of the Yankees' record 240 home runs, disappeared from the postseason spotlight, leaving players like Bill Skowron, Johnny Blanchard, Elston Howard and Hector Lopez to fill the void. Maris, baseball's new single-season home run king with 61, contributed only two Series hits and one homer, and Mantle, who hit 54, was homerless in six Series at-bats while battling a hip injury.

Game 1 at Yankee Stadium gave the Reds a disturbing preview. Whitey Ford, 25-4 during the regular season, blanked Cincinnati on two singles and both New York runs were supplied by homers—catcher Howard in the fourth, first baseman Skowron in the sixth. The Reds' only victory came the next day when Joey Jay stopped the Yankees 6-2 on four hits.

Bobby Richardson (left) collected three hits in Game 1 and shared the Yankees spotlight with (right photo, left to right) Bill Skowron, Whitey Ford and Elston Howard. Skowron greets Howard (center photo) after his fourth-inning homer.

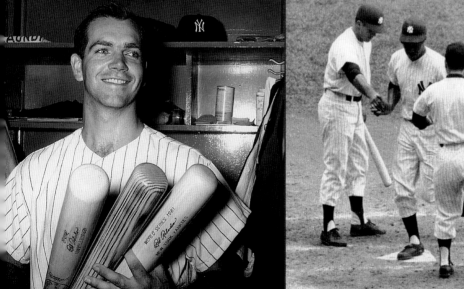

Any hope the Reds had of beating the powerful Yanks disappeared in a cloud of home runs that decided Game 3 at Crosley Field—the first World Series contest at Cincinnati since 1940. Reds starter Bob Purkey carried a 2-1 lead and a four-hitter into the eighth inning and retired the first two Yankees. But Blanchard, pinch hitting for pitcher Bud Daley, drove a pitch into the right field bleachers to tie the game. After relief ace Luis Arroyo had shut down the Reds in the bottom of the inning, Maris led off the ninth with his first Series hit—a game-deciding homer to right.

The final two games were a mere formality. Ford and Jim Coates combined for a 7-0 shutout in Game 4 and Daley, working in relief of Ralph Terry, got offensive help from Lopez (a homer, 5 RBIs) and Blanchard (a homer, 2 RBIs) in a 13-5 clincher.

Lopez finished the Series with seven RBIs in nine at-bats and Ford lifted his Series record for consecutive scoreless innings to 32.

Crosley Field's scoreboard tells the story of Game 4 as right fielder Hector Lopez catches a fly ball for the final out and a three-games-to-one Yankees advantage.

Rookie Yankees manager Ralph Houk celebrates his first World Series win with a victory cigar and a hearty cheer.

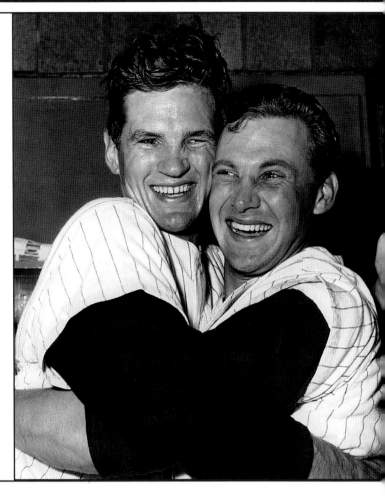

Ralph Terry, who got a victory ride after his Game 7 shutout (left), also shared the Game 5 spotlight (left, right photo) with Tom Tresh, who crashed a three-run homer.

It was a classic baseball moment. World Series Game 7 ... bottom of the ninth ... two out ... Yankees lead 1-0 ... Ralph Terry, the victim of Bill Mazeroski's Series-ending home run in 1960, facing San Francisco slugger Willie McCovey with runners at second and third ... a 1-1 count. This was a script that could have been written only by the baseball gods, and the ending was even better.

The record shows that McCovey blistered a line drive toward right field that Yankees second baseman Bobby Richardson reached up and snared for the Series-ending out. But it doesn't show how close the Giants came—an excruciating inch or two in any direction—to winning the franchise's first West Coast championship.

Terry had been rescued moments earlier when Matty Alou, who reached on a leadoff ninth-inning bunt single, was forced to stop at third by right fielder Roger Maris' outstanding defensive effort on Willie Mays' slashing double. Lost also in the glare of Richardson's catch was the pitching of Jack Sanford and Billy O'Dell, who had allowed the

Whitey Ford (center) pitched the Yankees to a 6-2 win in Game 1, getting offensive help from Elston Howard (left) and Clete Boyer.

Yankees only a fifth-inning run that scored on a double-play grounder.

The entire Series had been back and forth—and drawn out. It was played over a 13-day period, thanks to four rainouts and two travel days. But it was worth the wait.

Whitey Ford, with home run help from third baseman Clete Boyer, pitched the Yankees to a 6-2 win in the first Series game ever played at Candlestick Park. McCovey homered and Sanford was outstanding in Game 2, limiting the Bombers to three hits in a 2-0 shutout. The win-one-lose-one pattern continued with the Yankees prevailing 3-2 in Game 3 and San Francisco winning Game 4, 7-3, on light-hitting second baseman Chuck Hiller's grand slam.

After the Yankees posted a 5-3 win behind Terry in Game 5 at Yankee Stadium, the Giants had to wait five days to even the count on Billy Pierce's three-hit, 5-2 win at Candlestick. That set up one of the grandest finales in baseball history.

It was especially grand for the Yankees, who became World Series champions for the 20th time in 40 seasons—and the 20th time in 27 overall appearances.

Yankees third baseman Clete Boyer couldn't stop the rain, which forced four cancellations in the 13-day Series. When Game 5 was played, Giants right fielder Matty Alou couldn't stop an eighth-inning homer by Tom Tresh (left).

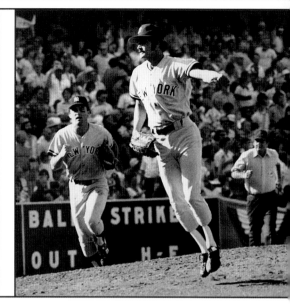

Mike Torrez (left) and Ron Guidry (right) celebrate after recording the final out of Games 3 and 4 under the watchful eye of manager Billy Martin (center).

For long-spoiled Yankee fans, it had been a nightmare. Fourteen excruciating seasons had passed since their last World Series championship and an 11-year gap had separated the 1964 and 1976 American League pennant winners. What the team needed was a DiMaggio or Gehrig-like postseason performer to carry the banner into a new era of prosperity.

Enter Reginald Martinez Jackson, a lefthanded slugger who could generate controversy and excitement with both his powerful bat and outspoken personality. He was a free-agent recruit who spent his first New York season feuding with teammates, battling manager Billy Martin and lifting the hopes of fans with his 32 home runs and 110 RBIs.

The Yankees bickered their way to 100 wins, a second straight East Division title and a tough League Championship Series victory over Kansas City in which Jackson managed only two hits and one RBI. But he would more than make up for that in a memorable six-game World Series against the Los Angeles Dodgers.

The Yankees raised hopes for their 21st championship by winning three of the first four games. Paul Blair singled home Willie Randolph in the 12th inning to secure an opening-game 4-3 win and complete-game performances by Mike Torrez and Ron Guidry doomed the Dodgers in Games 3 and 4. Guidry's 4-2 win featured a solo home run by Jackson, who connected again on the first pitch of his final at-bat in a 10-4 Game 5 loss.

Paul Blair (losing helmet) was the center of attention after his 12th-inning single gave the Yankees a 4-3 victory in Game 1.

Game 6 at Yankee Stadium is remembered as the "Reggie, Reggie, Reggie" game. That's one "Reggie" for each of the three home runs Jackson hit in a show-stopping 8-4 Series-clinching victory. Jackson, who had created an early season storm with his "I'm the straw that stirs the drink" magazine quote, silenced critics, hostile teammates and skeptical fans by drilling first-pitch homers in the fourth and fifth innings after a first at-bat walk and capped the third three-homer Series game in history (Babe Ruth had the other two) with an eighth-inning shot over the center field fence..

As the crowd of 56,407 chanted his name, Jackson basked in the glow of his achievement—first-pitch home runs on four straight official at-bats and a record five homers in the Series. Mr. October had arrived.

Reggie Jackson (44), who left an indelible stamp on the 1977 World Series with his home run exploits, gets a warm greeting from Martin and his Yankee teammates after scoring a Game 3 run on a Lou Piniella single.

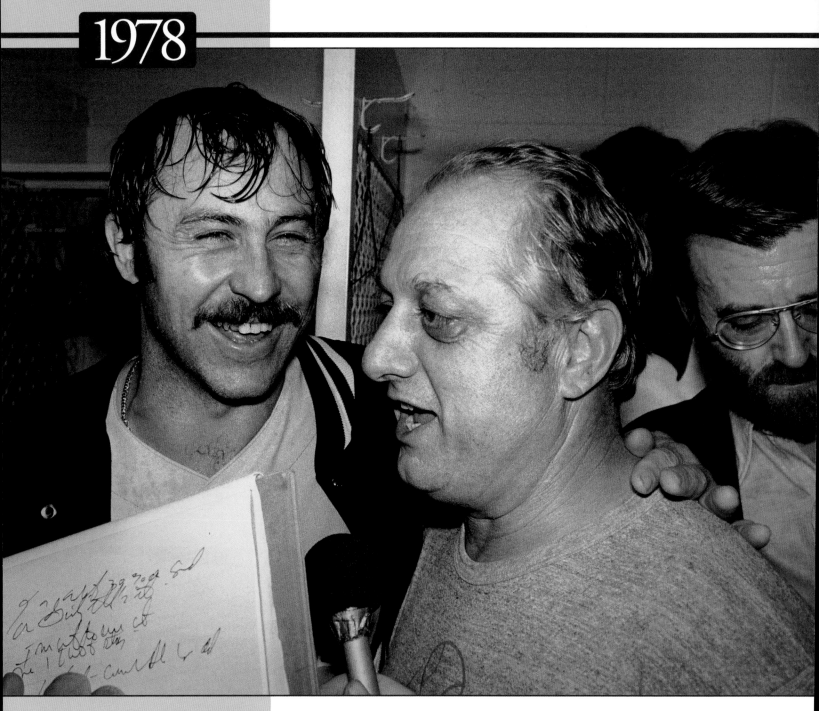

Game 6 winner Catfish Hunter (left) shares a post-Series moment with Tom Lasorda, who watched his Dodgers lose to the Yankees for a second straight season.

It was a crazy, gut-wrenching, heart-stopping kind of season. First the Yankees dropped 14 games behind the Boston Red Sox in the American League East Division race before roaring back to force a season-ending tie. Then they fell behind the Red Sox 2-0 after six innings of a one-game division playoff at Fenway Park before roaring back for a 5-4 victory, keyed by an unlikely three-run homer by light-hitting shortstop Bucky Dent.

So it was not an unfamiliar situation when the Yankees, four-game A.L. Championship Series winners over Kansas City, entered Game 3 of the World Series staring at a two-games-to-none deficit to National League-champion Los Angeles. A two-home run, five-RBI performance by second baseman Dave Lopes helped the Dodgers post an 11-5 win in the opener and a four-RBI Game 2 barrage by third baseman Ron Cey powered a 4-3 win—a victory saved by 21-year-old reliever Bob Welch with a thrilling mano-a-mano strikeout of Reggie Jackson.

But the Dodger success only seemed to inspire the slumbering New Yorkers.

With their backs planted firmly against the wall and hopes for a glorious end to a long, controversial season fading fast, Bob Lemon's Yanks roared back one more time and cemented their second straight championship with four consecutive wins.

Two of the top guns were fired by unlikely sources—second baseman Brian Doyle, a .192 regular-season hitter subbing for injured Willie Randolph, batted .438, and Dent, a .243 hitter, batted .417 with 10 hits. But more serious damage was done by the lightning-quick glove of third baseman Graig Nettles and the October-empowered bat of Jackson, which produced two homers and eight RBIs.

Ace Ron Guidry, 25-3 during a spectacular regular season, steadied the Yankee ship

Reggie Jackson, New York's Mr. October, watches the flight of a Game 6 homer that helped the Yankees wrap up their 22nd World Series win.

in Game 3, but not without a struggle. Pitching without his best stuff, the hard-throwing lefty was saved by the fielding wizardry of Nettles, who made four sensational plays, two with the bases loaded, to thwart big Dodger innings and help the Yanks get on the board with a 5-1 victory. Lou Piniella's 10th-inning single ended Game 4, a 4-3 Series-squaring win.

The Yankees took control as catcher Thurman Munson and left fielder Roy White combined for eight RBIs in a 12-2 fifth-game romp and they closed out their 22nd World Series victory two days later at Los Angeles behind the combined seven-hit pitching of Catfish Hunter and Goose Gossage and the combined seven-hit, seven-RBI barrage of the Doyle-Dent-Jackson trio.

The 7-2 finale allowed the Yankees to become the first team to overcome a 2-0 Series deficit with four straight wins.

Manager Bob Lemon (center) had reason to smile after watching Thurman Munson (left) key a Game 5 win with three hits and five RBIs and Goose Gossage retire the final batter of Game 6, prompting another Yankees championship celebration (right).

Pounded by the Braves in Game 1,
21-game regular-season winner
Andy Pettitte (above) pitched the
Yanks to a crucial 1-0 Game 5 win.

David Cone (above) changed the
World Series momentum with a victory
in Game 3 and reserve catcher Jim
Leyritz (opposite page, top) received
an enthusiastic greeting from third
base coach Willie Randolph (30) after
hitting a dramatic game-tying homer
in Game 4. Closer John Wetteland
signaled the feelings of all Yankee
fans and players (opposite page,
below) after recording his fourth save
in the Game 6 clincher.

Missing from World Series action since 1981, the Yankees stormed back into the spotlight with a six-game victory over the defending-champion Atlanta Braves. The franchise's 34th pennant and 23rd championship provided a nostalgic reminder of glories past and an ominous preview of success to come.

Unlike the "Bronx Bombers" of old, this team was built around pitching, defense and timely hitting, all of which were demonstrated after the Braves had jumped to a two-games-to-none advantage. The Yankees needed only two homers and 18 runs to give manager Joe Torre an emotional championship as his brother, Frank, lay in the hospital after undergoing a heart transplant.

It appeared Torre would have to wait for that title when John Smoltz and Greg

Maddux pitched the Braves to Series-opening 12-1 and 4-0 wins at Yankee Stadium. In the first game, 19-year-old center fielder Andruw Jones became the youngest player to hit a World Series home run and joined Gene Tenace as the only players to homer in their first two Series at-bats. In the second, first baseman Fred McGriff drove in three runs.

But the momentum would shift dramatically. After David Cone, Mariano Rivera, Graeme Lloyd and John Wetteland combined to check the Braves on six hits in a 5-2 victory at Atlanta, the Yankees pulled even in a Series-turning Game 4.

The Braves jumped to a 6-0 lead after five innings and had the Yankees on the ropes. But they fought back with three runs in the sixth and tied the score in the eighth on a shocking three-run homer by backup catcher Jim Leyritz off Mark Wohlers. When the Yanks scored two 10th-inning runs, one on a bases-loaded walk to Wade Boggs, to decide an 8-6 victory, the momentum shift could be felt throughout the baseball world.

Game 5 was a 1-0 thriller in which Andy Pettitte outdueled Smoltz with Wetteland earning his third straight save. The game ended when right fielder Paul O'Neill, with Braves runners at first and third, raced into right-center field and made an outstanding glove-extending catch to rob Luis Polonia.

The clincher, a 3-2 win carved out by Jimmy Key and four relievers, came, fittingly, at Yankee Stadium. The outcome was decided in a three-run third inning that featured RBI hits by Joe Girardi, Derek Jeter and Bernie Williams. The championship was sealed by Wetteland's fourth Series save, which became official when third baseman Charlie Hayes pulled in Mark Lemke's foul popup and triggered a wild celebration.

The kind of championship celebration that had been missing from Yankee Stadium for 18 years.

David Wells got the Yankees off to a positive start with a victory in Game 1—his first career World Series win.

The 1927 Yankees they were not. But there's no denying the 1998 Yankees at least equal billing as the greatest team in baseball history. Not only did they win an American League-record 114 games, they cruised through the Division Series (against Texas), Championship Series (Cleveland) and World Series (San Diego) with 11 wins in 13 outings for an overall 125-50 record and the franchise's 24th World Series crown.

They almost made it look too easy. The 1998 champions were built around a pitching staff featuring starters David Cone, David Wells, Orlando Hernandez and Andy Pettitte and one of the deepest bullpens in the game. Shortstop

Yankees closer Mariano Rivera (42) gets a victory hug from catcher Joe Girardi after recording the final out of a clinching 3-0 win over San Diego. The save was Rivera's third in the impressive four-game sweep.

Derek Jeter, outfielders Paul O'Neill and Bernie Williams and first baseman Tino Martinez headed a workmanlike cast of position players.

Any hope for the Padres to upset the powerful A.L. champions slipped away with a discouraging Series-opening loss at Yankee Stadium. San Diego held a 5-2 lead after six innings with ace Kevin Brown in control. But Brown, who was pitching in pain after being hit on the shin by a second-inning line drive, finally gave way to Donne Wall with one out and two runners on base in the seventh— and the roof caved in.

Wall surrendered a three-run homer to second baseman Chuck Knoblauch that tied the game and Mark Langston came on to give up a gut-wrenching two-out grand slam to Martinez. Before the dust had cleared, the Yankees owned a 9-5 advantage that Jeff Nelson and Mariano Rivera converted into a 9-6 victory.

Williams and catcher Jorge Posada homered to support the pitching of Hernandez, Mike Stanton and Nelson in a 9-3 second-game win and third-game heroics belonged to Scott Brosius. The third baseman hit a three-run, eighth-inning home run, his second homer of the game, and drove in four runs to give the Yankees a 5-4 victory.

The Yanks, showing their killer instinct, wrapped up their second championship in three years behind the combined seven-hit pitching of Pettitte, Nelson and Rivera. One of the Yankee runs in a 3-0 victory was driven home by Brosius, who finished with eight hits and a .471 average, and another by Ricky Ledee, who managed six hits and four RBIs in 10 Series at-bats.

Scott Brosius connects with a Trevor Hoffman pitch (left) and gets a warm welcome at the plate (right) from Paul O'Neill after a decisive Game 3 home run—his second of the day. Ricky Ledee (below) led the Yankees with six Series hits and a .600 average.

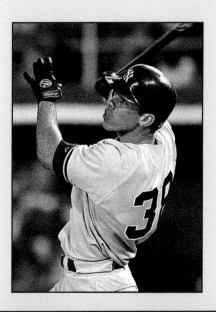

Orlando Hernandez (above) pitched seven innings in his Game 1 start, allowing only one hit—a fourth-inning home run by Braves third baseman Chipper Jones.

The Yankees steamrolled their way through the 1999 Series, thanks to the Game 3 home run heroics of Chad Curtis (center, right photos) and the Game 4 work of Roger Clemens (left). Clemens triggered a victory celebration (right) by recording his first career World Series win.

I t was just like old times. Another season, another championship for the Yankees. Even the dominance factor was front and center, much as it had been during those Miller Huggins, Joe McCarthy and Casey Stengel eras of yesteryear.

This team formed an unmistakable link with the past. In 1928, the Yankees of Ruth and Gehrig completed the legacy of 1927, when the so-called "greatest team in history" coasted through a 110-44 season and a four-game World Series sweep of Pittsburgh. In 1999, the Yankees of Jeter, O'Neill and Williams did the same for a 1998 squad that had rolled through a record-setting 114-48 season and an 11-2 playoff run that concluded with a Series sweep of San Diego.

While the Yankees were unable to match their 1998 regular-season success

(98 wins), they actually were more dominant through the postseason. They swept Texas in the Division Series, handled Boston in a five-game A.L. Championship Series and copped their second straight title and third in four seasons with a sweep of Atlanta in the fall classic.

Game 1 at Atlanta was a microcosm of the entire Series. Through seven innings, the Braves had managed only one hit (Chipper Jones' fourth-inning home run) off Orlando Hernandez; the Yankees had touched Greg Maddux for only three singles and trailed 1-0. But the Yanks exploded for four eighth-inning runs off Maddux—one coming on shortstop Derek Jeter's single and two more on right fielder Paul O'Neill's single—and a 4-1 victory.

After the Yankees rolled to a 7-2 second-game win behind the combined five-hit pitching of David Cone, Ramiro Mendoza and Jeff Nelson, Game 3 took on special importance for Atlanta. The Braves responded by building a quick 5-1 lead, but the Yankees' powerful bullpen shut them down. The Yanks chipped away and caught the Braves on Chuck Knoblauch's two-run, eighth-inning home run off Tom Glavine. They won in the 10th on a homer by unlikely hero Chad Curtis—his second of the game and seventh of the 1999 season.

Game 4 was a Yankee Stadium celebration with 37-year-old Roger Clemens at center stage. A 247-game career winner, the Rocket earned his first World Series victory with 7⅔ four-hit innings in a 4-1 victory that extended the Yankees' World Series record-tying winning streak to 12 games.

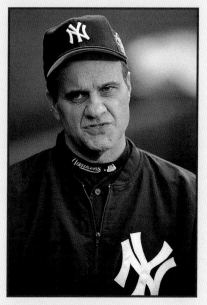

The Series sweep, the Yankees' second straight and third title in four years, put manager Joe Torre in select company.

Luis Gonzalez had reason to celebrate after bringing the 2001 World Series to a dramatic end with a ninth-inning, Game 7-ending single off Yankees closer Mariano Rivera.

When the Arizona Diamondbacks closed out their first championship with a two-run, ninth-inning rally in Game 7 of the 2001 World Series, they handed the Yankees only their 12th loss in 38 fall classics. The 3-2 victory, decided by Luis Gonzalez' one-out single, also ended the phenomenal streak of 23 straight postseason saves by closer Mariano Rivera and the Yankees' run of four Series wins in a five-year span.

The Arizona pitching tandem of Randy Johnson and Curt Schilling was too much in one of the most exciting World Series ever played. Johnson became the first three-game Series winner since 1968, posting his final victory in a Game 7 relief role, and Schilling won once while posting a 1.69 ERA.

The Diamondbacks needed the Johnson-Schilling magic to overcome some powerful Yankee voodoo that turned a two-games-to-one deficit into a shocking three-games-to-two advantage. On consecutive nights at Yankee Stadium, the Bronx Bombers avoided defeat with two-out, two-run homers in the ninth off young Arizona reliever Byung-Hyun Kim and went on to win both games in extra innings. Tino Martinez' shot tied Game 4 at 3-3 and Derek Jeter won it with a solo homer in the 10th; Scott Brosius tied Game 5 at 2-2 and Alfonso Soriano won it with an RBI single in the 12th.

But Arizona staged its own comeback by winning Games 6 and 7, a not-unfamiliar scenario in Yankees history. Of their 12 Series losses, six have come in heart-breaking seventh games.

Following are the 11 other Yankee World Series losses:

1921 The first "All-New York World Series" opened with consecutive 3-0 Yankee victories—the first postseason wins in franchise history—but ended badly with the Giants prevailing, five-games-to-three. Babe Ruth, a veteran of three previous Series as a Red Sox pitcher, batted .313 and hit his first fall classic home run.

1922 John McGraw's Giants were too strong in a Series sweep that included a 10-inning tie. The Yankees scored only 11 runs in the all-Polo Grounds rematch and hit two homers—both by second baseman Aaron Ward. Giants pitchers carved out a 1.57 ERA and held slumping Ruth to two hits and a .118 average.

1926 The classic moment of this Series was provided in the seventh inning of Game 7 by aging Cardinals righthander Grover Alexander, who struck out Yankees rookie Tony Lazzeri with the bases loaded, preserving a 3-2 victory. Ruth, who hit three homers in Game 4 at Sportsman's Park, made the final out of the Series when he was cut down trying to steal second base.

Managers Miller Huggins (left) of the Yankees and John McGraw of the Giants were front and center in the 1921 and '22 World Series, both won by the National League champions.

1942 The Yankees, winners in their last eight Series, won the opener against the Cardinals before losing four straight. The Game 5 clincher was provided by St. Louis third baseman Whitey Kurowski, who hit a two-run, ninth-inning homer off Red Ruffing to give rookie Johnny Beazley a 4-2 victory.

1955 The Dodgers, losers in each of their seven previous Series, finally brought a championship to Brooklyn and ended their frustrating Yankees losing streak at five. Game 7 was classic—a 2-0 Johnny Podres shutout that was saved by left fielder Sandy Amoros' spectacular sixth-inning catch of a Yogi Berra drive.

Sandy Amoros robs Yogi Berra of extra bases and dims the Yankees' hopes in Game 7 of the 1955 World Series with a spectacular sixth-inning catch (above). Winning pitcher Johnny Podres (below right) celebrates the Dodgers' first championship with ecstatic teammates Don Hoak and Roy Campanella (39).

1957 The Yankees lost their third seven-game Series, this one to the resurgent Braves. Milwaukee got three wins from righthander Lew Burdette, including a 5-0 shutout in Game 7, and a key two-run, Series-squaring homer by Eddie Mathews in the 10th inning of Game 4.

1960 Outscored 55-27 and outhit 91-60 by the Yankees, Pittsburgh prevailed when second baseman Bill Mazeroski hit a Series-ending home run in the ninth inning of Game 7 at Forbes Field. Mazeroski's dramatic blast off Ralph Terry gave the Pirates a 10-9 win after the Yanks had scored twice to tie the game in the top of the inning. The Yankees' three wins were by scores of 16-3, 10-0 and 12-0.

1963 In one of the most dominating pitching performances in Series history, the Dodgers held the Yankees to four runs and 22 hits while posting a shocking four-game sweep. Sandy Koufax won twice for Los Angeles, but Don Drysdale captured single-game honors with his three-hit 1-0 shutout in Game 3.

1964 Mickey Mantle ended Game 3 with his Series-record 16th homer and Bobby Richardson set a single-Series record with 13 hits, but the Cardinals still prevailed in seven games. The key blow for St. Louis was delivered by Ken Boyer, who hit a sixth-inning grand slam off Al Downing to turn a 3-0 Game 4 deficit into a Series-turning 4-3 win.

1976 With Johnny Bench (.533, two homers) leading a relentless Cincinnati assault, the Yankees, playing in their first fall classic since 1964, were swept by the powerful Big Red Machine. The only positive for a Yankees team that was outscored 22-8 was catcher Thurman Munson, who batted .529.

1981 Turnabout was fair play in this Series as the Dodgers recovered from a two-games-to-none deficit with four straight victories, matching the winning formula the Yankees had used against them in 1978. Reliever George Frazier was a three-time loser, tying a Series record.

Braves catcher Del Crandall and third baseman Eddie Mathews (41) mob winning pitcher Lew Burdette after Game 7 of the 1957 fall classic.

The Yankees lost dramatically to Pittsburgh in the 1960 World Series when Bill Mazeroski hit a ninth-inning home run and made a memorable run (below) around the bases.

GREATEST
Feats/Moments

1. DiMaggio Compiles 56-Game Streak

It started May 15 at New York and ended 63 days later at Cleveland, a two-month siege that will forever be etched in baseball lore. During a torrid 56-game hitting streak that obliterated existing records and established Joe DiMaggio as an official American icon, the Yankees center fielder batted .408 in 223 at-bats with 91 hits, 16 doubles, four triples, 15 home runs and 55 RBIs while literally carrying the Bronx Bombers from fourth place to first in the American League standings. The mysterious and graceful DiMaggio built the streak methodically, game by game, with determination and dramatic flair, starting with a May 15 single off Chicago's Edgar Smith. He reached 41 games on June 29, tying the 1922 modern-era record of St. Louis Browns star George Sisler, and passed Willie Keeler's all-time mark of 44 (1897) three days later in a game against Boston. The streak reached 56 when DiMaggio enjoyed a three-hit game at Cleveland, but it ended the next afternoon when he failed to hit in three at-bats against Indians pitchers Al Smith and Jim Bagby Jr.

1

July 1, 1941, marked a key moment in DiMaggio's 56-game hitting streak. The Yankees slugger had reason to smile (right) after matching Willie Keeler's 44-game record of 1897.

Gehrig (center), in a ceremony preceding his record-setting 1,308th consecutive game, receives a cup from newspaperman Edgar G. Brands and A.L. president Will Harridge (left). Standing next to Gehrig is teammate Joe Sewell.

2

2. Ironman Gehrig Plays 2,130 Straight Games

He was the unflappable Iron Horse, a pillar of the Yankees championship dynasty from June 1, 1925, until May 1, 1939—a 2,130-game span in which Lou Gehrig never failed to play in a regular-season game. While performing an ironman feat that would stand as a cherished record for more than five decades, Gehrig played through injuries, illnesses and fatigue over 15 seasons while ranking as one of the most feared hitters in the game. Gehrig's streak, which started when he pinch hit for Pee Wee Wanninger in 1925, ended in 1939 when the big first baseman, suffering from a mysterious ailment, removed himself from the lineup for a game against Detroit. He never played again. Eventually diagnosed with amyotrophic lateral sclerosis, an incurable disease, Gehrig died in 1941 at age 37.

3. Ruth Pounds Out 60 Home Runs

In a performance that set the standard by which home run hitters would forever be judged, Babe Ruth scaled the 60 plateau while leading the 1927 Yankees to 110 wins, a World Series victory over Pittsburgh and accolades as the greatest team ever assembled. Ruth, breaking his own 1921 record of 59 homers, concluded a wild September rush with 17, No. 60 coming in the season's second-to-last game at Yankee Stadium. The final blast off Washington lefthander Tom Zachary, an eighth-inning shot into the right field bleachers, highlighted a season in which Ruth batted .356, scored 158 runs and drove in 164 while combining with Lou Gehrig for 107 homers and 339 RBIs in the heart of a "Murderer's Row" lineup. Ruth played in 151 of the Yankees' 155 games.

Ruth watches the flight of homer No. 60, a record-setting blast in the second-to-last game of the 1927 season off Washington lefty Tom Zachary.

4. Maris Passes the Bambino

Roger Maris, the quiet man from Fargo, N.D., made history in 1961 by claiming Babe Ruth's 34-year-old home run record and outdueling teammate Mickey

Mantle in a riveting assault that highlighted another Yankees run to a World Series championship. Maris, a 27-year-old lefthanded batter, hit 61 homers, one more than the great Bambino managed in 1927 and seven more than Mantle managed before a September injury kept him from also challenging the record. Maris, who finished August with a 51-48 lead over Mantle, hit his 59th home run as New York clinched the American League pennant in its 155th game, connected for No. 60 on September 26 against Baltimore and hit the record-breaker in the fourth inning of the October 1 season finale off Boston rookie righthander Tracy Stallard at Yankee Stadium.

Maris is greeted at the plate (left) by Yogi Berra (8) and the Yankees batboy after hitting his record 61st homer on the final day of the 1961 season off Boston rookie Tracy Stallard.

5. Gehrig Sets A.L. RBI Mark

While his Yankees were finishing a disappointing second to Philadelphia in the 1931 standings, first baseman Lou Gehrig was driving in 184 runs—a still-standing American League record and a figure topped only by Hack Wilson's 1930 National League mark of 191. Gehrig was a run-producing machine, batting .341 with 211 hits, 163 runs and 46 homers, a total that tied teammate Babe Ruth for league honors. He was most prolific from August 28 to September 1, homering in six straight games (three of them grand slams) and driving in 21 runs. Gehrig drove in four runs in a September 20 doubleheader sweep of Cleveland to top his previous A.L. RBI mark of 175 in 1927.

The 1956 season was a smile-producing breakthrough for Mantle (right), who powered his way to an American League Triple Crown.

6. Mantle Shows Right Stuff

Inconsistent and unable to meet unfair fan expectations over his first five New York seasons, Mickey Mantle enjoyed a breakthrough 1956 campaign that few players have matched. The Mick, still playing in the shadow of center field predecessor Joe DiMaggio, powered his way to a Triple Crown, topping the American League in average (.353), home runs (52) and RBIs (130) while leading the Yankees to a World Series championship. The powerful switch-hitter, who also led A.L. batters in total bases (376) and runs scored (132), became only the eighth player to reach the 50-homer plateau in a season. Mantle was an easy choice for the first of three MVP citations he would win.

7. Guidry Posts 25-3 Record

In a 1978 season of managerial controversy, comeback magic and high drama, Ron Guidry never wavered. The Yankees' Louisiana Lightning used his 96-mph fastball to carve out a pitching legacy—25-3, an American League-leading 1.74 ERA, nine shutouts and 248 strikeouts. Guidry's 25th victory came at Boston's Fenway Park in the special one-game playoff to decide the East Division championship and raised his winning percentage to .893, the highest in history for a 20-game winner. He capped his big season with wins in the ALCS and World Series and unanimous selection as A.L. Cy Young winner.

Guidry was in his top Louisiana Lightning form in 1978 when he posted a 25-3 record and 1.74 ERA while helping the Yankees win a World Series championship.

8. Ironman Chesbro Wins 41 Games

Numbers define the 1904 heroics of Highlanders righthander Jack Chesbro, not the final-day mistake that haunted the proud spitballer the rest of his life. Those numbers begin with his incredible 41-12 record (the most single-season wins in the 20th century) and include six shutouts, a one-hitter, a two-hitter, a three-hitter, eight four-hitters, an amazing 454⅔ innings and 48 complete games in 51 starts. But Chesbro's ironman effort and 1.82 ERA became lost in the shadow of one errant pitch that allowed Boston to break a 2-2 ninth-inning tie and clinch a pennant. The wild pitch came in the opening game of a doubleheader on the season's final day at Hilltop Park. A win in that game and the nightcap would have given the New Yorkers their first American League flag.

9. Gehrig Triples His Pleasure

He had set and reset the American League RBI record, hit four home runs in a single game and performed numerous other hitting feats, both in regular-season and World Series play. So it wasn't shocking to see Yankees first baseman Lou Gehrig reach new offensive heights in 1934 when he captured a Triple Crown—leading the league with a .363 average, 49 home runs and 165 RBIs. Gehrig, who had always played in the shadow of teammate Babe Ruth, performed his "triple" magic in the Bambino's final New York season, yielding the spotlight only when Ruth hit his 700th career home run. Despite Gehrig's offensive heroics, the Yanks finished in second place (94-60), seven games behind first-place Detroit.

10. Mattingly Enjoys Power Surge

Yankees fans light up when talking about a Don Mattingly line drive or sparkling defensive play at first base. But over an eight-game, 11-day stretch in 1987, he was the game's most prolific power hitter. Mattingly's record-tying homer streak started July 8 when he connected twice against Minnesota and he homered in each of New York's next seven games. His July 18 shot off Texas righthander Jose Guzman over the left-center field fence at Arlington Stadium tied the 31-year-old record of Pittsburgh's Dale Long and gave him 10 homers in his eight-game surge. Mattingly received a curtain-call ovation from 41,871 Rangers fans after his 18th homer of the season.

Mattingly (below) watches the flight of his home run off Texas righthander Jose Guzman—a shot that gave him record status with former Pittsburgh first baseman Dale Long. It was the eighth straight game in which Mattingly had homered.

1

Dent (right) and Reggie Jackson celebrate the Yankees' 1978 division-clinching playoff victory over the Boston Red Sox. Both hit home runs in the dramatic game at Fenway Park.

1. Dent's Homer Ruins Red Sox

If shortstop Bucky Dent wasn't the most unlikely of Yankee heroes in an improbable 1978 season, he certainly was close. But in the one-game playoff between the Yankees and Boston to decide the East Division title, Dent drove a three-run homer over the left field wall at Fenway Park and a dagger into the hearts of Red Sox fans everywhere. Dent, a little righthanded hitter who had homered only four times through the previous 162 games, connected in the seventh inning off Mike Torrez, wiping out a 2-0 Boston advantage and sending shock waves through the crowd of 32,925. The Yankees went on to win 5-4, completing their amazing comeback from a 14-game division deficit in mid-July.

2

Manager Joe McCarthy gives Gehrig a silver trophy inscribed with names of his teammates and a special poem written in his honor during ceremonies on Lou Gehrig Appreciation Day at Yankee Stadium.

2. A Farewell to Gehrig

It has been called the "Gettysburg Address of Baseball." And who has not seen the picture of Lou Gehrig, the one-time Yankees Iron Horse, standing with head bowed near microphones positioned at home plate as former teammates, team officials and players from the Washington Senators and Yankees form a semicircle around him? It was one of the most dramatic and moving moments ever experienced on a baseball field and it happened on Lou Gehrig Appreciation Day at Yankee Stadium between games of a July 4, 1939, doubleheader. After listening to tributes and receiving numerous gifts as 61,808 fans roared their approval, a disease-stricken Gehrig delivered the emotional speech that included the now-immortal line, "I consider myself the luckiest man on the face of the earth. ..."

3. Wells Shows Perfect Form

For more than four decades, Don Larsen enjoyed status as the only Yankee to pitch a perfect game. So David Wells, who had attended the same San Diego high school as Larsen, was understandably giddy on May 17, 1998, after retiring all 27 Minnesota hitters he faced in a 4-0 victory before 49,820 roaring fans at Yankee Stadium. The free-spirited and portly lefthander struck out 11 in a brilliant performance that brought back memories of Larsen's perfecto in the 1956 World Series. Few Twins hit the ball hard and only one, Paul Molitor in the seventh inning, came close to a walk—he struck out after going to a 3-1 count. After Wells retired Pat Meares on a fly to right fielder Paul O'Neill for the final out, he was carried off the field by ecstatic teammates.

Wells (left) was on top of the world May 17, 1998, after retiring 27 straight Twins en route to pitching the second perfect game in Yankees history. Cone (below) followed his lead a year later against the Expos, a perfectly uplifting experience that cemented his place in Yankees lore.

4. Cone Matches Wells' Perfecto

The Yankees' second perfect game in as many seasons was pitched by righthander David Cone on July 18, 1999, at Yankee Stadium—"Yogi Berra Day"—after Don Larsen had thrown out the ceremonial first pitch. Cone, who wasn't born when Larsen fired his 1956 World Series perfect game, retired all 27 Montreal hitters he faced en route to a 6-0 victory—one year, two months and a day after David Wells had fired a perfecto at Minnesota. With 41,930 fans cheering him on, Cone dominated the young Expos, throwing only 20 balls in his 88-pitch masterpiece. Cone, who struck out 10, most with his nasty slider, fell to his knees, grabbed his head and was quickly mobbed by teammates after retiring Orlando Cabrera for the final out on a pop to third baseman Scott Brosius.

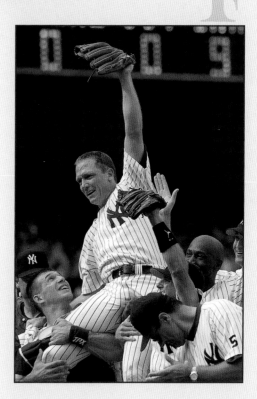

5. Babe Ruth Has His Day

He was thin, slumped in the shoulders and obviously weak from a series of operations to combat throat cancer. But there was no mistaking the room-lighting smile and indomitable spirit when Babe Ruth, wearing a long overcoat, stepped to a field microphone at Yankee Stadium before a game against Washington on April 27, 1947. In a speech piped in to ballparks around the major leagues on "Babe Ruth Day," the Bambino spoke elegantly, in a raspy and subdued voice. "The only real game in the world, I think, is baseball," he said. "There's been so many lovely things said about me, I'm just glad I had the opportunity to thank everybody." As the crowd of 58,339 roared, the 52-year-old Ruth waved his approval and walked off the field.

Ruth, far removed from the athletic form that had vaulted him to the top of the baseball world, posed with manager Bucky Harris (left) at Yankee Stadium on Babe Ruth Day in 1947.

A young Mantle (right) looks over the display put together in honor of his 565-foot home run.

6. *Mantle Has Deep Thoughts*

It is a baseball legend, a 565-foot blast that soared out of Washington's Griffith Stadium and lifted 21-year-old Mickey Mantle to legendary status. Batting righthanded in a game played April 17, 1953, Mantle belted a fifth-inning pitch from Chuck Stobbs toward left-center field. The rising drive cleared the fence at the 391-foot mark, glanced off a football scoreboard perched atop the 50-foot outer wall and bounded out of sight, finally stopping in the back yard of a nearby house. The ball, the first to clear the outer left field wall on the fly, traveled 460 feet in the air, a distance that would have been considerably more if not for the scoreboard. Mantle's two-run homer helped the Yankees beat the Senators, 7-3.

Reynolds holds up two fingers after pitching his second no-hitter of 1951—an 8-0 win over the Red Sox. The big righthander became only the second pitcher to accomplish the double no-hit feat.

7. *Reynolds Fires Second No-Hitter*

Vic Raschi and Eddie Lopat won more games (21 apiece) for the 1951 Yankees, but neither could match Allie Reynolds for special effects. The Chief won 17 and became the second pitcher to throw two no-hitters in a season—the first to fire one in a pennant-clinching situation. After holding the Indians hitless July 12 in a 1-0 victory, Reynolds stopped Boston, 8-0, in the opener of a September 28 doubleheader at Yankee Stadium, securing at least a tie for the Yankees in the A.L. pennant race. Reynolds completed his second gem in style, retiring Red Sox slugger Ted Williams on a foul pop to catcher Yogi Berra—after Berra had dropped a Williams popup earlier in the at-bat. Reynolds watched the nightcap from the bench as Raschi pitched a pennant-clinching victory.

8. Ruth Christens Yankee Stadium

Festive, colorful and historically significant, Yankee Stadium opened its gates for the first time on April 18, 1923, as baseball's grandest and most modern facility. Among the more than 70,000 fans were generals, governors, colonels and politicians, all of whom soaked up the atmosphere and participated in the celebratory spectacle of the Yankees' new Bronx home. But nothing could top the roar that shook the triple-decked stadium in the fourth inning of the Yankees game against Boston when Babe Ruth, ever the showman, drove a pitch from Howard Ehmke into the right field bleachers for a three-run homer—the key blow in a 4-1 win over the Red Sox. The home run, and victory, provided a fitting and memorable debut for "The House That Ruth Built."

9. Homer Raises Sticky Issue

Nothing before or since a July 24, 1983, game at Yankee Stadium has ever rivaled the "Pine Tar" controversy. First Kansas City star George Brett had an apparent game-deciding home run off Goose Gossage taken away by umpires after Yankees manager Billy Martin protested that his bat violated a rule limiting how high the sticky substance can extend up from its handle. Then he had it restored by American League president Lee MacPhail, who ruled that the substance, illegally applied or not, did not enhance Brett's hitting ability. The game was later played to an uneventful finish from the point of controversy with the Royals winning, 5-4. But the videotape of Brett darting out of the dugout in a rage and being restrained by umpire Joe Brinkman remains a baseball classic.

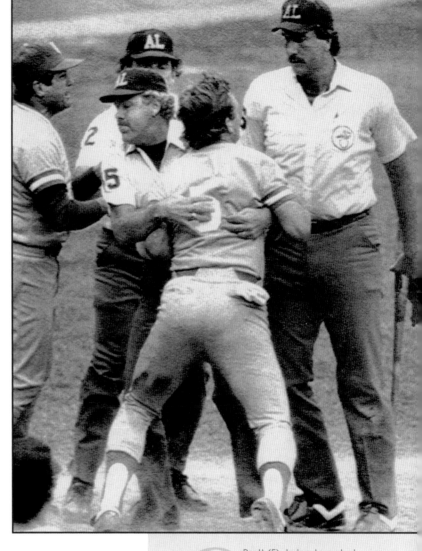

Brett (5), trying to get at umpire Tim McClelland, is restrained by umpire Joe Brinkman after McClelland disallowed his "Pine Tar" homer during a July 24, 1983 game at Yankee Stadium.

10. Fired-Up Guidry Strikes Out 18

It was a scene that would be replayed throughout an incredible 1978 season: Ron Guidry, stepping out of the dugout to acknowledge 33,162 cheering, chanting fans after another outstanding performance. In this case, on the night of June 17, 1978 at Yankee Stadium, Guidry posted a team-record 18 strikeouts and raised his mark to 11-0. The overpowering lefthander fanned every California hitter at least once and had a ninth-inning chance to join Nolan Ryan, Steve Carlton and Tom Seaver as the only pitchers to strike out 19 in a regulation game. With the crowd roaring every time he reached two strikes on a hitter, Guidry fanned Dave Chalk and Joe Rudi to open the inning. But he fell short of the record when Don Baylor singled and Ron Jackson grounded into a force, ending a four-hit, 4-0 shutout that lowered Guidry's ERA to 1.45.

1

The enduring image of Larsen hugging Berra (8) provides a perfect exclamation point for Game 5 of the 1956 World Series.

Jackson connects off Dodgers righthander Charlie Hough—his memorable third home run in the Yankees' Game 6 World Series clincher in 1977.

2

1. Larsen Fires Perfect Game

The picture is enduring: Yogi Berra, wearing uniform No. 8, held aloft by Don Larsen in that ecstatic moment following Game 5 of the 1956 World Series at Yankee Stadium. A 2-0 New York victory was only a sidescript to the drama of baseball's first postseason no-hitter—and perfect game. For journeyman Larsen, it was a ticket to baseball immortality. Using his new no-windup delivery, the big righthander set down all 27 Brooklyn hitters he faced on 97 pitches, getting pinch hitter Dale Mitchell for the final out on a called third strike. Unable to get through the second inning of a Game 2 loss, Larsen came back to record baseball's first perfecto in 34 years while giving the Yanks a three-games-to-two Series edge in an eventual seven-game victory.

2. Three's a Charm for Mr. October

Three home runs on three pitches—a Reggie Jackson production worthy of his "Mr. October" reputation. The enigmatic right fielder muscled up in Game 6 of the 1977 World Series and treated 56,407 fans at Yankee Stadium to one of the great performances in postseason history. With the Yankees needing one win to wrap up their first championship since 1962, Jackson hit a two-run homer off Burt Hooton in the fourth inning, a two-run shot off Elias Sosa in the fifth and a solo blast off Charlie Hough in the eighth—all on first pitches. His final homer, a monster shot to center that insured an 8-4 victory, sent the Stadium into pandemonium. It also gave Jackson four home runs on consecutive swings (he had homered in his final at-bat of Game 5) and a record five for the Series.

3. Chambliss Homer Ends Drought

With one big swing and a madcap dash around the bases, first baseman Chris Chambliss took his place in Yankees lore. Chambliss' moment came October 14, 1976, when he drilled a leadoff home run in the bottom of the ninth inning off Kansas City reliever Mark Littell, giving the Yankees a 7-6 Game 5 victory in the A.L. Championship Series and their first pennant since 1964. As the ball cleared the right-center field fence, thousands of fans rushed the field. By the time Chambliss reached first, he was surrounded by souvenir hunters who already had removed the second and third base bags. As he circled near shortstop, he was jostled and bumped. He came nowhere near home plate, finally retreating to the New York clubhouse for his own safety.

4. High Drama at Yankee Stadium

For ninth-inning dramatics, nothing can match the stunning home runs hit by Yankees Tino Martinez and Scott Brosius in consecutive games of the 2001 World Series at Yankee Stadium. Both wiped away two-out, two-run Arizona leads and both tested the fortitude of young Diamondbacks closer Byung-Hyun Kim—devastating game-tying blasts that eventually produced Yankee wins. Martinez brought the Yankees back from the edge of a 3-1 defeat with his Game 4 blow,

setting the stage for Derek Jeter's winning home run in the 10th. The next night, as if on cue, Brosius erased a 2-0 deficit with a shot over the left field wall, setting up Alfonso Soriano's game-ending single in the 12th. Despite the heroics, the Yankees lost the Series in seven games.

5. A Line Drive Into Posterity

The vicious line drive is suspended in time, a perfect reminder of the fine line that separates baseball success from failure. A few inches higher ... to the left ... to the right ... and San Francisco slugger Willie McCovey becomes a 1962 World Series hero. Instead, Yankees second baseman Bobby Richardson, in the right spot at the right time, snares the drive, which is headed for right field with the potential tying and winning runs stationed at second and third base with two out in the ninth inning of Game 7. The Giants, so close to winning their first West Coast title, watch the Yankees walk away with their second straight crown and 20th overall. And Ralph Terry, who had served up Bill Mazeroski's championship-securing home run two years earlier, walks away a World Series winner.

On consecutive nights during the 2001 World Series, Martinez (above center) and Brosius (left) hit dramatic ninth-inning home runs to help the Yankees secure comeback victories over the stunned Diamondbacks.

Leyritz (13) is mobbed by happy teammates after hitting a game-tying Game 4 homer off Atlanta reliever Mark Wohlers in the 1996 World Series.

6. Babe Ruth Calls His Shot

Did he or didn't he? More than seven decades later, nobody knows for sure whether Babe Ruth really "called" one of the most legendary home runs in baseball history. In the fifth inning of Game 3 of the 1932 World Series at Chicago's Wrigley Field, Ruth reacted to the taunting of Cubs players with a sweeping gesture, seemingly toward center field. When he hit Charlie Root's next pitch into the center field seats to break a 4-4 tie, a legend was born. Teammates and opponents had differing opinions whether Ruth, who also had homered in the first inning of that eventual 7-5 victory, really was calling his shot or simply sweeping aside taunts. Ruth never explained his action, letting fans and media come to their own conclusions.

7. Leyritz Homer Rocks Braves

He was a sixth-inning defensive replacement, a journeyman catcher who had hit seven home runs during the 1996 regular season. But Jim Leyritz took on a Ruthian-type aura in Game 4 of the World Series when he brought the Yankees back from the dead and put them on course to win their first championship since 1978. Down two-games-to-one and trailing 6-0 after five innings at Atlanta's Fulton County Stadium, the Yanks appeared doomed. But they cut their deficit to 6-3 in the sixth and put two men on in the eighth for Leyritz, an unlikely hero who drove a two-out Mark Wohlers pitch over the left field fence for an electrifying game-tying homer. The Yankees posted an 8-6 win in 10 innings and won Games 5 and 6 to claim the franchise's 23rd championship.

8. Mantle Needs Just One Swing

For pure dramatic impact, it's hard to beat the home run Mickey Mantle shot into Yankee Stadium's right field stands in Game 3 of the 1964 World Series—a drive that forever linked him with St. Louis reliever Barney Schultz. With the Series knotted at a game apiece and the score tied 1-1 in the top of the ninth inning, Cardinals manager Johnny Keane pinch hit for starting pitcher Curt Simmons. When St. Louis failed to score, Keane turned to Schultz, who had surrendered only one homer in 30 regular-season appearances. Mantle, batting left-handed, pounded Schultz's first pitch for his record-setting 16th World Series homer and an electrifying Yankees victory. Mantle hit two more homers in his final fall classic, but the Cardinals won in seven games.

9. Billy Martin to the Rescue

With the bases loaded and two out in the Dodgers' half of the seventh inning, all three runners took off as Yankees lefty Bob Kuzava, trying to protect a 4-2 lead, delivered a 3-2 pitch to Jackie Robinson—the moment of truth in Game 7 of the 1952 World Series. Kuzava's spirits soared when Robinson swung and lifted a high, rally-killing popup to the first base side of the mound. But it suddenly became apparent to 33,195 fans at Ebbets Field that Yankees first baseman Joe Collins, the man who should make the catch, was having trouble finding the ball. Having sized up an increasingly desperate situation, second baseman Billy Martin darted forward and made a lunging knee-high grab of the ball—preserving a 4-2 win and the Yankees' 15th World Series championship.

10. Owen's Mistake Lifts Yankees

It was a swing and a miss, a Tommy Henrich strikeout that signaled a 4-3 Dodgers victory in Game 4 of the 1941 World Series at Ebbets Field. But 33,813 fans watched in disbelief as reliever Hugh Casey's sharp-breaking curve eluded catcher Mickey Owen and bounded to the backstop as Henrich hustled to first base. Owen's misplay turned into instant disaster for the N.L.-champion Dodgers. Joe DiMaggio's single and Charlie Keller's two-run double gave the Yanks a 5-4 lead. Joe Gordon followed a walk to Bill Dickey with another two-run double to complete the scoring in a stunning 7-4 New York victory. The Yankees, handed a three-games-to-one Series advantage, closed out the devastated Dodgers the next day with a 3-1 Game 5 win.

9 Dodger Jackie Robinson watches as Martin makes his shoestring catch, saving Game 7 of the 1952 World Series for the Yankees.

10 Yankee Henrich heads for first as Dodgers catcher Owen chases the ball that got away in Game 4 of the 1941 World Series.

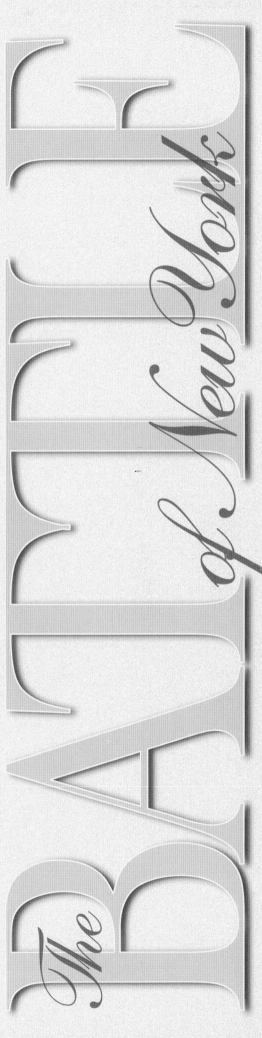

The BANK of New York

I t is all-out war, a territorial conflict waged on multiple fronts by hundreds of thousands of people. The battle for baseball and public relations supremacy has been going on for the better part of a century, not restricted to New York but carried on there with more determination, conviction and passion than anywhere else in a sports-hungry nation.

Blame John J. McGraw, baseball's Little Napoleon and the iron-fisted baron of Big Apple baseball over the century's first three decades. Blame Babe Ruth. ... or Yankee arrogance. ... or Bill Terry. ... or Leo Durocher and Eddie Stanky. ... or Dodgers frustration. ... or George Steinbrenner and Billy Martin. ... or the bumbling Mets. Blame the very nature of this huge metropolitan melting pot, where people, ideals, lifestyles and competitive fires are stoked by intense regional allegiances.

The spotlight is everything in the media capital of the sports world and it has been since the beginning of baseball time—or at least since the American and National leagues joined hands in 1901. It's all about bragging rights, public awareness and winning, both on the field and off.

"It was a contest among the boroughs. It was a pitting of New York City baseball teams against each other and against the rest of the world. Whom you rooted for provided an identity. It usually began when parents brought a child to a game and created a new Dodger or Giant or Yankee fan. Loyalty to the team became virtue. Hatred of the opposition was expected. Whole families rooted for one club. A non-conformist who switched allegiance provoked family rifts and worse.

"Brooklyn fueled the rivalry. A borough of neighborhoods with strange-sounding names—Canarsie, Gowanus, Red Hook, Flatbush—Brooklyn was a land and a lifestyle removed from the mainstream of metropolitan ways. Some people who lived in Brooklyn had never ventured across the river to Manhattan. ... The Giants and the Yankees were franchises of stars—the glamour teams. Brooklyn inspired among the players the phrase: 'If at first you don't succeed— try the Dodgers.' "

—*Harvey Frommer, from his book "New York City Baseball"*

No individual is more responsible for this three-headed rivalry than McGraw, the stocky, quick-fisted Irishman who brought respect to New York City sports just after the turn of the century. The man they called Mugsy forever will be linked with the Giants and National League baseball, but you can't escape the irony of his early contributions to the Yankees. It was McGraw who brought the Baltimore Orioles to life in the American League as manager and part owner in 1901. It was McGraw who defected to the Giants with several prominent players in 1902, incurring the wrath of A.L. president Ban Johnson and triggering a shift of the player-depleted Orioles franchise to New York.

It also was McGraw who, comfortable in his role as king of New York baseball and one of the city's most powerful social figures, unwittingly allowed the Yankees to escape his enormous shadow and claim the spotlight that once belonged only to him. McGraw's first mistake was overestimating his hold on New York and allowing the homeless, plodding, insignificant Yankees to become co-tenants of the Polo Grounds with his Giants in 1913. His second was the steering of prospective team owners Jacob Ruppert and Tillinghast Huston, an off-field drinking crony, to the Yankees in 1915.

Ruppert and Huston, unwilling to settle for the second-class status Yankee teams had been accorded through their first decade and a half, slowly began building a

From the top-of-the-world presence of John McGraw (opposite page) in the early century to the divided loyalties of fans rooting for the Mets and Yankees during the 2000 Subway Series, New York baseball has come a long way. One thing that has remained constant is the city's passion for the game.

Leo Durocher, a former Yankees infielder, kept things stirred up for Dodgers fans from 1939-48, managing the team to one N.L. pennant and battling umpires with unrestrained fury. When his Brooklyn magic faded, he took over for the hated Giants.

winner with a spending spree that caught the attention of McGraw and every New York fan. But the first chink in McGraw's previously unchallenged dynasty didn't show up until January 1920, when Ruppert purchased the contract of Boston Red Sox pitcher/slugger Babe Ruth for the then-incredible price of $125,000. Ruth, creator of the long, majestic home run, could never be lost in anybody's shadow.

"New York fans, who never dreamed of going to the Polo Grounds except when the Giants were in town, stormed the gates to see Ruth. ... As (the Yankees) rose in prestige, it soon became a case of the tenants at the Polo Grounds overshadowing—and outdrawing—their landlords. McGraw couldn't take it. 'Get 'em out of here. Make 'em build their own ballpark. They'll have to move so far away, maybe to Long Island City, that everyone will forget them,' McGraw ordered (Giants owner) Charlie Stoneham. ... The Yankees were tossed out, but they didn't move to Long Island City. Ruppert found a perfect plot of ground just on the other side of the Harlem River and built Yankee Stadium."

—*New York Times columnist Arthur Daley*

Ironically, the Yankees became the centerpiece of New York baseball during the Giants' most successful stretch under McGraw—four consecutive N.L. pennants and two championships from 1921-24. The two World Series wins came in 1921 and '22 at the expense of Ruth and his Yankees, but the Bronx Bombers just kept coming. They avenged those losses by beating the Giants in 1923 and marched on relentlessly, shielding themselves with an aura of invincibility that would carry, amazingly, into the mid-1960s.

McGraw could not penetrate that aura; neither could his still-successful Giants. New York fans watched in amazement as the Yankees spent freely for top-notch talent, built the most efficient farm system in the game and looked down, almost arrogantly, at their New York competition— the way McGraw had done years earlier.

When McGraw ended his three-decade reign as Giants manager during the 1932 season, the Yankees were en route to their seventh pennant and fourth World Series championship in 12 years. They clearly were the toast of New York, an organization feared on the field, admired for its aloof efficiency off it. The power and the spotlight that once belonged to McGraw's Giants were recalled in 1952 by *New York World Telegram* columnist Dan Daniel:

"No flags flew atop the Polo Grounds stands today. No martial strains of festival echoed across the Harlem. The 62-year-old arena appeared to be deserted, deep in a July apathy.

"Actually, the Polo Grounds was far from unpeopled. The park housed a glorious gathering of wraiths of diamond heroes of long ago, who evoked memories of a day when John Joseph McGraw was the Giants, and the Giants were New York baseball.

"For this was McGraw's golden anniversary as manager of the Giants. Fifty years ago today, he unveiled his reconstructed ball club before a skeptical 5,000 on this same Polo Grounds diamond. That was the day of the game's rebirth here. Fans hoped against hope that the fighting little Irishman who had been a Baltimore Oriole would revive the glories of Jim Mutrie's regime.

"Little did they dream that McGraw, soon to be called the Little Napoleon and, of course, a lot less refined names, would bring the Giants pennants and world championships."

In retrospect, the real battle of New York from 1925 to 1957 was fought between the Giants and Dodgers—not by the haughty Yankees. While the teams of Ruth, Lou Gehrig, Joe DiMaggio and Mickey Mantle played—and existed—on a different baseball plane, the National League rivals waged an intimate war that could never be reflected by mere records or standings.

The Dodgers had trembled in the Giants shadow through the McGraw era, winning only two pennants—in 1916 and 1920 under former McGraw pal Wilbert Robinson. Most of the time, they were weak; often they were lovably inefficient—not a serious threat to Giants superiority.

It was McGraw's successor who poured gasoline on the rivalry in 1934. Bill Terry, when asked how he thought the Dodgers might fare in the coming season, quipped: "Are the Dodgers still in the league?" That first punch was a haymaker.

Brooklyn fans declared war, turning every game against the hated Giants into a personal crusade. Ebbets Field became a loud,

Former Giants first baseman and manager Bill Terry (left, with Yankees great Joe DiMaggio in the late 1940s) poured gasoline on the Brooklyn-Giants rivalry in 1934 with the tongue-in-cheek question, 'Are the Dodgers still in the league?'

The 1951 World Series was an all-New York affair, orchestrated by managers Casey Stengel (left) of the Yankees and Durocher of the Giants. The Yankees prevailed in six games.

The Dodgers featuring (left to right) Duke Snider, Jackie Robinson and Pee Wee Reese were regular World Series participants, but the Yankees always blocked their championship path.

raucous, zany battleground every time the Giants set foot in Brooklyn; games at the Polo Grounds were enlivened by Brooklyn-accented jeers, cowbells and whistles, all of which helped the Dodgers play above their sixth-place form. The 1934 Giants were tied for first place with the Cardinals when they entered their final two-game series against the Dodgers at the Polo Grounds—and they lost both contests and the pennant, much to the delight of the Brooklyn faithful.

"Well, Brooklyn got sore," Daniel wrote in *The Sporting News* about Terry's comment. "It took umbrage. When Brooklyn takes umbrage, it takes it heavier than any other center in baseball."

That umbrage would become a part of every Brooklynite's daily life. Baseball was wound intricately into the borough's social fiber and every Dodger was embraced with loving fervor. "Brooklyn was a town that lived and died with the Dodgers," says former Yankee shortstop Phil Rizzuto, who grew up in the Borough of Churches. "When the Dodgers were playing, you could walk up and down the streets of Brooklyn and never miss a pitch. Everybody had the game on the radio. It meant so much."

And every Dodger game against the Giants, said former Brooklyn shortstop Pee Wee Reese, "was the most important game of your life." Quality of the teams did not matter—it was all about inspiration, hatred and kill-or-be-killed intensity.

"How I hated (the Dodgers) then," recalled former Giants star Bobby Thomson, referring to the late 1940s and early '50s. "Really hated them. Leo Durocher instilled that in us. But I must say the papers played their part, too, in drumming up the rivalry. If you played for Leo, the whole world was right if you beat the Dodgers. Nothing else mattered."

Durocher was a special case. A former Yankee shortstop, he played for and managed the Dodgers from 1939 through 1946, generating a tunnel-vision hatred against the Giants. Then, after sitting out a year under suspension, he returned to manage the Dodgers in 1948, only to be released on July 16. He signed that same day to replace Giants manager Mel Ott. Not only did that make him the most hated man in Brooklyn, he was a suspicious interloper on the Giants scene. But he won over Giants fans by delivering two pennants and one World Series championship in seven-plus years, including the incredible 1951 flag at the expense of Chuck Dressen's Dodgers—a pennant race decided by Thomson's playoff home run.

"When you had Dressen and Leo managing against each other, it was dog eat dog," says former Giants right fielder Don Mueller. "It was kind of mean."

It also was vital and kind of fun, as described by Frommer in his book *New York City Baseball*:

"Intimate, dramatic, personal, unpredictable baseball in New York City season after season was one of the most important things in the lives of many who lived in the Big Apple. And in the last weeks of September and the early days of October, baseball in New York City became for some the most important thing in their lives."

The late 1940s and '50s were a special time in New York. Not only were the Dodgers, Giants and Yankees powerful and exciting, the star quality of their players was at unprecedented heights. The New York flame was enhanced by the pio-

The incredible 1951 pennant race ended with Bobby Thomson's pennant-securing home run (left) for the Giants. The Dodgers finally captured their first World Series title in 1955 with a victory over the Yankees, prompting a victory hug between owner Walter O'Malley (below left) and manager Walter Alston.

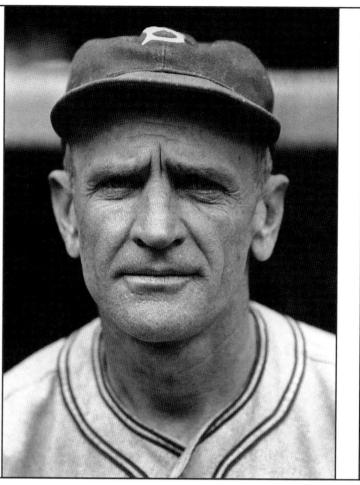

Nobody wore more hats on the New York baseball scene than Stengel, who (left to right) played for the Giants and managed the Dodgers, Yankees and Mets.

neering presence of Jackie Robinson, who broke baseball's color barrier with the Dodgers in 1947.

In the 10-year span from 1947 through 1956, the Dodgers and Giants combined to win eight N.L. pennants. But, inevitably, they would find the Yankees waiting for them in a World Series that would end in pride-sapping frustration. The Bronx Bombers, who won eight A.L. pennants and seven championships over that same span, were not viewed as rivals in the Dodger-Giants tradition—just a huge, insurmountable obstacle that blocked their road to success.

The Yankee pain was felt most acutely by the Dodgers and their long-suffering fans. The Bums won pennants in 1941, '47, '49, '52 and '53, but lost World Series battles to the Yankees each year. Two of the fall classics were decided in a seventh game; another in Game 6. Always, it seemed, the Dodgers were on the verge of delivering Brooklyn's first championship, only to fall to the Yankee mystique. When at last they broke through by winning Game 7 of an emotional 1955 World Series, the Yankees quickly cut them down to size in 1956.

The Dodgers lineup featuring Reese, Carl Furillo, Duke Snider, Robinson, Gil Hodges, Roy Campanella and Billy Cox could match up against the Yankees or any other team. But that wasn't enough.

"The Dodgers had good pitching in the National League, but the Yankees with (Allie) Reynolds, Whitey Ford and Vic Raschi just had stronger pitching," says New York-born sportswriter Jack Lang, who covered the Yankee-Dodger wars for the *Long Island News*. "Both teams had good hitting—there were

sluggers on both teams. I think it basically came down to the Yankees having better pitching in that era.

"But, really, the rivalry between the Dodgers and Yankees in those days was nonexistent. The only rivalry with the Yankees was when October rolled around and they played them in the World Series. That was the only team they ever played in the World Series."

If there was a three-team rivalry in New York during the marvelous and exciting 1950s, it existed more off the field, in the minds and emotions of fans for the Giants, Dodgers and Yankees. The swirling debate, never settled, revolved around the relative merits of the teams' center fielders (Willie Mays for the Giants, Snider for the Dodgers and Mickey Mantle for the Yankees) their shortstops (Alvin Dark, Giants, Reese, Dodgers, Rizzuto, Yankees) or their catchers (Campanella, Dodgers, Yogi Berra, Yankees). But there was never any doubt about the relative merits of the three teams—nobody could beat the Yankees.

Snider (left) and Giants great Willie Mays were two-thirds of New York's center field triumvirate that generated comparisons in the 1950s. The third player: Yankees star Mickey Mantle.

"On the one hand, the very real Yankee mystique was at work; on the other, the Dodgers were spooked. ... The Yankee mystique was formidable. The Brooklyn Eagle's editorial writer described it well for the faithful before the 1952 Series. 'Maybe the Yankees are professional World Series players. Perhaps . . . they cast a spell over the opponents and give them the jitters before the battle gets fairly under way. But there comes a day. ...' "
—*Carl E. Prince in his book Brooklyn's Dodgers*

Billy Martin (right) and Yankees owner George Steinbrenner (center) were on the best of terms during the Yankees' 1977 championship run. The third member of the celebration is coach Yogi Berra (left).

That "day" didn't arrive until the mid-1960s, when the Yankees finally fell on hard times. The front-office genius of Ed Barrow, George Weiss and Larry MacPhail had been pushed aside and there was no one to duplicate the managerial wizardry of Miller Huggins, Joe McCarthy and Casey Stengel. The Yankees, for the first time since 1919, were a team without a legendary aura in its clubhouse or the means to replenish a talent base that had become thin and diluted.

The entire complexion of New York baseball had changed by that time. The Dodgers and Giants shocked the baseball world after the 1957 season when they bolted for the greener pastures of California, a move that drove a stake into the heart of loyal fans. New York, the longtime mecca of major league baseball, was suddenly stripped of its National League identity. For four seasons, the Yankees had the New York market all to themselves, a prosperity that would change dramatically—and unexpectedly—with the arrival of a fresh-faced interloper in the N.L.'s 1962 expansion.

The New York Mets were everything the Yankees were not. They were inept, bumbling, unpredictable and fun—a striking contrast to the Bronx Bombers, who would continue their pennant and championship-winning rampage through the 1964 season. Stengel, the maestro of Yankee efficiency from 1949-60, was now the

clown prince of the zany Mets, who lost 452 games over their first four seasons. Casey called them "amazin'," but the enchanted New York media dubbed them "loveable" and fans flocked to see them lift the art of losing to a new level.

The Mets became an immediate public relations nightmare for the Yankees. That nightmare escalated in 1965, when the Yankees dropped from elite to mediocre status, and exploded in 1969, when the once-lowly Mets shocked the baseball world by winning the World Series while the 80-81 Yankees were finishing 28½ games behind Baltimore in the A.L. East Division.

That was the challenge that faced shipbuilding tycoon Steinbrenner in 1973 when, as the Mets were winning another pennant, he headed a limited partnership that purchased the staggering Yankees from the conservative ownership of CBS. The aggressive, impulsive, demanding, win-at-all-costs Steinbrenner quickly opened his deep pocketbook, declared war on the Mets and began playing a bizarre game of musical managers, whom he cast aside without hesitation when they fell short of his winning standards. The battle for New York media headlines became an obsession.

"As familiar with the demands of owner George Steinbrenner as any Yankees employee, (Lou) Piniella understood what was important and what was IMPORTANT. Steinbrenner annually had imposed certain demands on his managers—clinch the American League East championship by Flag Day, be in the hotel room for 2 p.m. telephone calls, win all games against college teams and never, under any circumstances, lose to the Mets." —Marty Noble, writing for The Sporting News in 1988

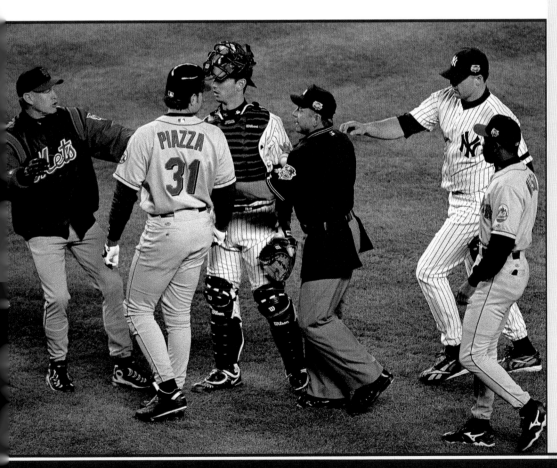

Center stage for new-era Mets-Yankees animosity belongs to Mike Piazza and Roger Clemens. Hard feelings reached their peak during Game 2 of the 2000 Subway Series when Mets catcher Piazza shattered his bat while fouling off a Clemens pitch (far left) and the Yankees big righthander picked up the jagged barrel and fired it toward the first base dugout (center), just missing Piazza, who had to be restrained (near left).

Steinbrenner, empowered by the advent of free agency, got his Yankees back into the title spotlight in 1976, the season his team returned to refurbished Yankee Stadium after sharing Shea Stadium for two years with the Mets. The Yankees regained championship momentum by winning five division titles, four pennants and two World Series from 1976-81. When they fell off in the standings, they made different kinds of headlines with strange managerial maneuvers (Martin was hired and fired five times in 14 years), owner-player rifts, clubhouse bickering, Steinbrenner tirades and front-office shake-ups that justified the public's image of a "Bronx Zoo."

There were no divided loyalties during the 2000 Subway Series for New York Mayor Rudy Giuliani, an avowed Yankees fan and seating companion of Steinbrenner.

Publicly, the volatile Yankees and more reserved Mets have chosen to ignore each other over the years. But behind the scenes, both organizations have remained perilously on edge. During most of the 1980s, any exhibition match between the Yankees and Mets was played with championship zest, an unwritten directive from the Boss. Winning was critical, so much so that the annual Mayor's Trophy battle was suspended briefly in the early '80s and Steinbrenner even outlawed spring meetings for a while at mid-decade.

Things have changed in recent years, however, as both teams realize they can benefit from a more reserved rivalry. "Yes, there is detente between our clubs," Steinbrenner said in 1988, two years after watching the Mets win their second World Series championship. "We're still competitors, but we've agreed we're neighbors and both playing for the good of New York. I pull for them, now that we're good friends."

Not that the 1997 introduction of interleague play has been taken lightly. Steinbrenner and the Mets ownership take every game very seriously; the fans fill the stadium, screaming, yelling and chanting for a bragging-rights victory. The players understand the minor ripple winning or losing to each other will make in the standings, but they are energized by the electric atmosphere.

Never moreso than during a 2000 regular season in which the Mets and Yankees played six times, with more than the usual emotional edge. The Yankees won four of those games and tension mounted when Yankees ace Roger Clemens beaned Mets catcher Mike Piazza, forcing him from the lineup for several days.

The Yankees denied accusations by the Mets that Clemens was intentionally throwing at Piazza, who had collected seven hits and three home runs in 12 career at-bats against the big righthander. But the undercurrent carried into a postseason that played out dramatically with the Yankees and Mets both winning pennants to set up the first all-New York World Series since the last Brooklyn-Yankees matchup in 1956.

The Subway Series was deja vu for longtime New Yorkers, who recalled the electricity of a city divided by its baseball loyalties. This was an Uncivil War and the pre-Series spotlight, naturally, centered on the Clemens-Piazza feud. Everybody wondered what might happen when the players faced each other for the first time in the fall classic and they didn't have to wait long to find out.

After the Yankees posted a 4-3 victory in the opener, Piazza stepped to the plate to face Clemens in the first inning of Game 2. Piazza swung at a Clemens pitch and shattered his bat, the ball going foul and the barrel of the bat ending up near Clemens. As Piazza ran toward first base, Clemens picked up the jagged piece of bat and flung it toward the first base dugout, narrowly missing the runner. Piazza stopped and glared at Clemens and both benches emptied. Clemens, who claimed he didn't realize Piazza was running on a foul ball, went on to shut out the Mets for eight innings in another Yankees victory.

The Yankees went on to win their third straight World Series in five games, but every contest was bitterly contested, every pitch delivered with a win-at-all-costs intensity. Emotion ran high, especially on the streets of New York and in the packed stands of Yankee Stadium and Shea Stadium.

Which is what a rivalry is all about—electricity, atmosphere, bragging rights and pride. In New York, it doesn't get more important than that.

There were feelings of deja vu for longtime New Yorkers when the Mets and Yankees lined up during introductions prior to Game 1 of the 2000 World Series at Yankee Stadium—the first Subway Series since 1956.

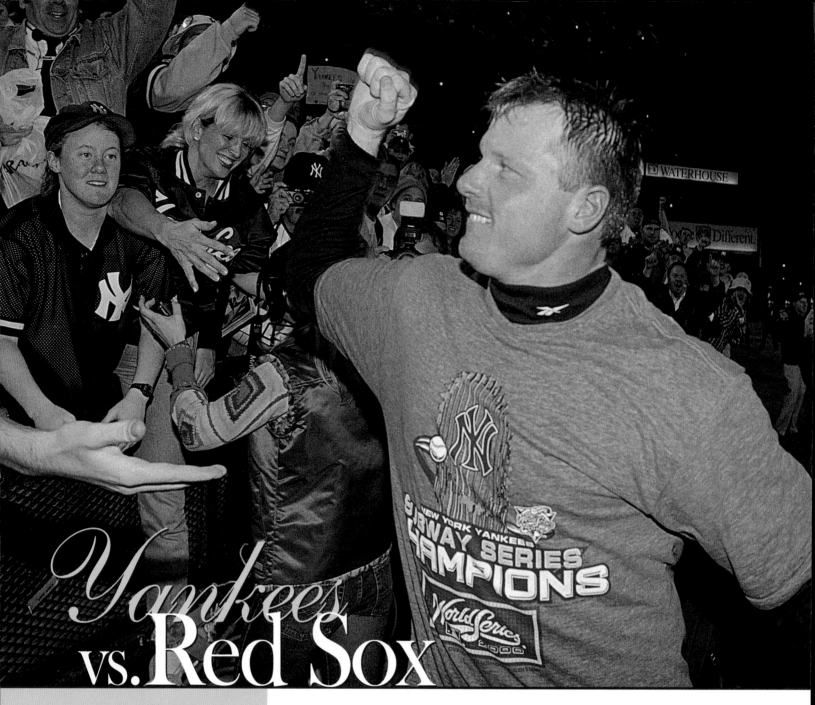

Yankees vs. Red Sox

The passion boils over, even though since 1918, when the Red Sox won their fifth and last World Series championship, the Yankees have won 34 more pennants, 26 more World Series and 7 more East Division titles than their Boston rivals while finishing ahead of them in the standings in 66 of 84 seasons— a plus 1,049½ games.

Yankees vs. Red Sox. It's a major league rivalry, an in-your-face, fist-flying, beer-drenching, unforgiving kind of battle between fans— and cities—that truly despise each other. Anyone sporting pinstripes or that confounded "NY" logo risks life and limb at Boston's Fenway Park. Pity the brave but foolhardy Red Sox fan who even hints his allegiance at Yankee Stadium.

If war is hell, then, by simple logic, a Yankees-Red Sox game gets excessively hot. This is as much about pride, respect and dignity as it is wins and losses. It's historic, old-society Boston vs. huge, cosmopolitan New York; Boston's Irish temper vs. New York arrogance; a blue-chip, corporate Goliath vs. an underfed David; massive, intimidating Yankee Stadium vs. cozy, quaint Fenway.

When these teams get together, pitches are thrown with extra force, balls are hit harder, defenders are more alert and fans are more impatient, less tolerant of failure. Untimely mistakes can be magnified.

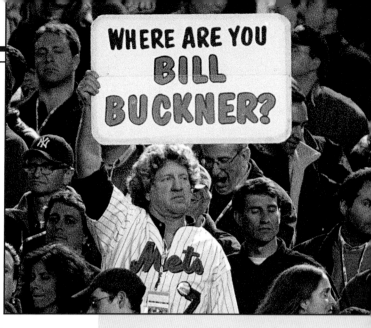

It says a lot when an avid Yankees fan, asked to divulge his favorite baseball moment, answers without hesitation, "Watching the ball roll through Bill Buckner's legs." Every Red Sox failure, like the memorable 1986 Buckner World Series misplay that cost the team its first championship since 1918, is cause celebre in New York.

Conversely, every Yankees success is like a dagger to the heart of Boston fans, who have lived in the shadow of the great Bronx machine and existed on a different competitive plane since that 1918 championship—seldom able to match victories, disturbingly incapable of grasping opportunity when it does present itself.

New Yorkers are greeted by chants of "Yankees Suck" at Fenway Park; Bostonians endure chants of "Nineteen-Eighteen" at Yankee Stadium—an all-too-legitimate reflection of the teams' fortunes for more than eight decades. While the Yankees have won 38 American League pennants and 26 World Series since 1918, the Red Sox have reached the fall classic only four times, losing each in heart-breaking seventh games.

If that's not grounds for an inferiority complex, consider this: It was the Red Sox ownership that set the Yankees juggernaut in motion. Following are a few of the more memorable factors that have fueled one of the most enduring rivalries in sports.

Yankees success cuts into Boston's baseball psyche like a dagger, especially when Red Sox fans are forced to endure images of such former favorites as Roger Clemens (opposite page) and Wade Boggs (below) celebrating New York championships. It's also difficult to stomach New York reminders of 1986 and Bill Buckner's infamous World Series misplay (above).

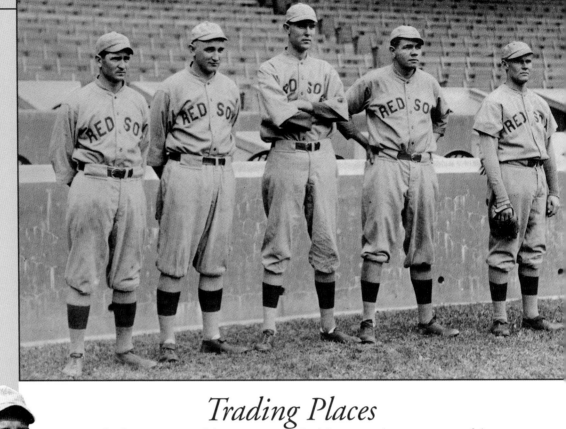

Three-fifths of Boston's 1916 pitching staff later helped fuel the Yankees' championship drive. Of (left to right) Rube Foster, Carl Mays, Ernie Shore, Babe Ruth and Dutch Leonard, only Foster and Leonard never played for the Yankees.

Ruth (below left) was an outstanding Red Sox pitcher before starting life anew as the Yankees' slugging right fielder. Lefty Herb Pennock (below right) also pitched for the Red Sox before becoming a key figure in the Yankees' rise to championship heights.

Trading Places

Over the first 20 years of the century, the Red Sox were the most successful team in baseball. Not only did they win the first World Series from Pittsburgh in 1903, they captured five of the first 15 and four in a seven-year span from 1912-18.

They also defeated the Highlanders on the final day of the 1904 season to claim a pennant, only to be snubbed by another New York team—John McGraw's National League Giants, who refused to play the "inferior American League" champs in a World Series. And so it began.

But it wasn't until 1919 that life as a Red Sox fan started to unravel. By then, Jacob Ruppert was in control of Yankee fortunes and Boston owner Harry Frazee was struggling to finance his costly theatrical pursuits. Ruppert started slowly by acquiring such players as Carl Mays, Ernie Shore and Duffy Lewis from Frazee in deals that typically were punctuated by cash outlays. Then he picked up steam with the January 1920 purchase of Babe Ruth—a big contributor to Boston World Series championships as a lefthanded pitcher in 1916 and '18—for $125,000.

Over the next three years, the Yankees would grab Hall of Fame pitchers Waite Hoyt and Herb Pennock off the rich Red Sox roster as well as such pennant contributors as Wally Schang, Joe Bush, Sad Sam Jones, Everett Scott, Joe Dugan and George Pipgras. Ruppert's accurate talent appraisals came courtesy of former Red Sox manager Ed Barrow, who was hired in late 1920 to build the colonel's baseball empire.

And build he did, initially at the expense of a Red Sox team that sank quickly into mediocrity as the Yankees were rising to championship heights. It was a gap, widened by deep pockets and aggressive New York owners, that would only frustrate Boston players and fans who struggled to escape the shadow of their huge East Coast rival.

The 1949 Factor

The Red Sox had the hated Yankees right where they wanted them—at last. Clinging to a one-game lead in the American League pennant race with two games to go, Boston was set up to throw 25-game winner Mel Parnell and 23-game winner Ellis Kinder at the Bronx Bombers, needing only one victory to secure the team's second pennant since 1918. And they could deliver the knockout blow, fittingly, before a packed house at Yankee Stadium.

How sweet would it be? Consider: From 1921-47, a 27-year span, the Yankees had won 15 pennants and finished ahead of the Red Sox in the American League standings 26 times. Over that stretch, the Yankees finished a whopping 652½ games ahead of Boston, even though the 1946 Red Sox captured a pennant of their own, topping the Yankees by 17 games. The teams had not battled head-to-head in a tight pennant race since 1904.

Red Sox fans, forced to endure interminable Yankee success, needed this one bad. What made 1949 even more special was a stirring Red Sox comeback from 12 games behind the first-place Yanks. Boston won 20 of 24 games in one sizzling stretch after the All-Star Game and 23 of 31 in August. By Labor Day, they trailed by 1½ games; on September 25,

they pulled into a first-place tie when Parnell beat the Yankees, 4-1.

In the opener of the final two-game series on Joe DiMaggio Day, Boston rushed out to a 4-0 lead, only to watch the Yankees rally against Parnell. Joe Page's superb relief work and Johnny Lindell's solo home run in the eighth inning gave the Yankees a season-saving 5-4 victory.

With the pennant at stake the next day, the Yankees, behind Vic Raschi, held a 1-0 lead in the eighth inning when Tommy Henrich homered and Jerry Coleman doubled with the bases loaded, breaking the game open. The Yankees withstood a three-run ninth-inning Boston rally to post a pennant-clinching 5-3 victory.

Recalling 1978

It was one game, a showdown at Fenway Park to decide the 1978 A.L. East Division champion. Everything was on the line after a crazy regular season that ended in a first-place tie, necessitating the playoff. This was Yankees-Red Sox in its highest form.

"As far as the pressure, the World Series pales in comparison," said former Yankees closer Goose Gossage. "It's by far the biggest game I ever pitched in. When you play 162 games and it comes down to identical records and you have to play one game for all the marbles, it just doesn't seem fair."

Especially to the Red Sox, who enjoyed a 14-game lead on July 19—five days before Yankees manager Billy Martin resigned, turning the struggling team over to laid-back Bob Lemon. The Yankees, under typical Bronx Zoo conditions, battled through distractions, egos, suspensions and clubhouse bickering to pull off the biggest comeback in A.L. history. As the Red Sox sputtered, the Yanks won 52 of 73 games down the stretch.

Mike Torrez delivers and Bucky Dent connects for a three-run homer that sparked the Yankees to a dramatic victory over Boston in the 1978 division playoff game at Fenway Park.

Four of those wins came over a memorable September weekend at Fenway during which the Yankees outhit the Red Sox, 67-21, and outscored them, 42-9. The Boston Massacre was fresh on everybody's mind when the teams finished with identical 99-63 records.

The playoff pitted Mike Torrez against Yankees 24-game winner Ron Guidry and Torrez carried a 2-0 lead into the seventh inning. That's when lightning struck in the form of light-hitting Yankees shortstop Bucky Dent, who crashed a three-run homer over the left field Green Monster, setting the stage for a 5-4 division-clinching victory. The win wasn't secured until Gossage retired Red Sox slugger Carl Yastrzemski on a ninth-inning popup with runners on first and third.

"It was one of those things where the night before, I went to bed and I can see myself tomorrow facing Yaz for the final out," Gossage said. "And here it is: ninth inning, two out and who's up? Yaz ... My legs were shaking, I was shaking all over. I was just trembling. It was like nothing I had ever faced to that point. I never faced another game like that in my career."

And the Beat Goes On

The rivalry has manifested itself in many other ways. Ted Williams vs. Joe DiMaggio was the great debate in the 1940s. Carlton Fisk and Thurman Munson

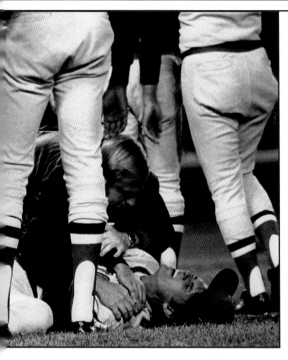

Boston lefty Bill Lee, who helped stoke anti-New York sentiment in the mid-1970s, is attended by the Red Sox trainer (left) after suffering a shoulder injury during a 1976 brawl with the Yankees.

carried on a personal feud in the 1970s. That was the decade of discontent for Red Sox and Yankees fans who were revved up by players who obviously did not like each other and teams that, for one of the few stretches in history, were competitive.

You can't talk about the '70s without mentioning Boston's Bill Lee, the flaky lefthander who was injured by a Graig Nettles body slam in a 1976 brawl. Lee, whose tongue was quicker than his fastball, directed his best verbal shots at Martin and owner George Steinbrenner.

"I don't like the man," Lee said of Martin in a 1977 issue of *The Sporting News*. "I don't like his neo-Nazi tactics. I was jumped a year ago by Billy Martin's Brown Shirts. Herman Goering the Second. They've got a convicted felon running the club.

"They're a team of robots owned by George Steinbrenner, who buys meat on the hoof. My hatred of the Yankees doesn't lie in individuals. They've been programmed and taught and brainwashed by Billy Martin."

Martin fired back: "What's the matter with Lee? He'd better learn how to fight if he wants to talk like that. ... My mother is 76 years old and she can whip him. Graig Nettles beat him, and he can't even fight." Martin punctuated his feelings by having a dead mackerel delivered to Lee's locker before a game at Fenway Park.

And so it goes. Boston's Wade Boggs edged New York's Don Mattingly for a hotly contested 1986 A.L. batting title as the Red Sox held off the Yankees in the A.L. East. Boston fans bristled in the '90s as Boggs, Roger Clemens and former manager Don Zimmer won championship rings while wearing pinstripes. Pedro vs. Roger, Nomar vs. Derek and Mo vs. Tino became worthy topics of debate.

But some things never change. The Red Sox continue to win battles while the Yankees win wars. When the teams met in the 1999 A.L. Championship Series—a postseason first—the Yankees won in five games. And, having taken care of that business, they went on to capture their 25th championship with a quick-and-easy World Series sweep of the Atlanta Braves.

The Ted Williams (left) vs. Joe DiMaggio debate raged in both Boston and New York during the 1940s.

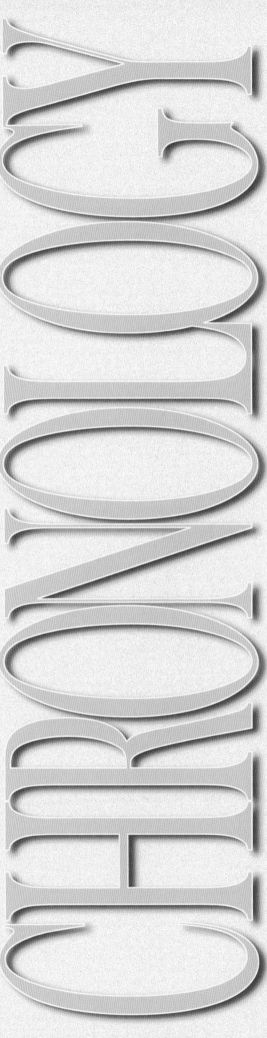

CHRONOLOGY

1901

Jan. 28—The American League formally organizes as a rival major league. The Baltimore Orioles, who will relocate to New York after two seasons, begin play under manager and part owner John McGraw.

April 26—Oriole Park is the site of the franchise's first game, a 10-6 win over Boston.

April 29—The Orioles help the Senators introduce baseball to the nation's capital. Many prominent guests enjoy watching Washington post a 5-2 victory.

Sept. 3—Iron man pitcher **Joe McGinnity** works both ends of a doubleheader for the Orioles, posting 10-0 and 6-1 complete-game wins over Milwaukee.

Sept. 29—The Orioles' inaugural season ends with a 68-65 record and fifth-place finish. McGinnity finishes 26-20 with an A.L.-leading 39 complete games and 382 innings.

1902

July 7—**McGraw** negotiates his release from the Orioles to sign as Giants manager. McGraw, conspiring with N.L. owners, then manipulates the sale of the Orioles to Giants owner Andrew Freedman, who releases the team's best players and signs most of them to Giants contracts.

July 17—The A.L. takes over operation of the Orioles franchise, which has only a handful of players remaining under the managerial guidance of Wilbert Robinson. League president Ban Johnson borrows players from other teams to get through the balance of the season.

Aug. 25—A.L. president Johnson announces his intention to field a New York team with Clark Griffith as manager in 1903. That team will be the remnants of the Baltimore franchise.

Sept. 28—The Orioles finish their final Baltimore season in last place with a 50-88 record.

1903

Jan. 9—The Orioles franchise is purchased for the bargain price of $18,000 by Frank Farrell and Bill Devery, who move it to Manhattan.

March 12—The A.L. approves membership of the New York franchise. Games will be played at Hilltop Park, a hastily constructed wooden facility located at 168th Street and Broadway—one of the highest points in Manhattan. The team will be known as the Highlanders.

April 22—The Senators hand pitcher **Jack Chesbro** a 3-1 loss at Washington in the franchise's first game under New York ownership.

April 23—The Highlanders' first win goes to Harry Howell—a 7-2 decision at Washington.

April 30—A crowd of 16,293 watches the Highlanders post a 6-2 win over Washington in the **Hilltop Park** inaugural.

Sept. 29—The Highlanders finish fourth, 72-62, in their first New York season.

1904

July 4—Spitballer Chesbro defeats Philadelphia for his 14th straight victory—an A.L. record that will stand until 1912.

Oct. 7—Chesbro claims his 41st victory with a 3-2 decision over Boston. The 41 wins will stand as a 20th century single-season record.

Oct. 10—Needing a final-day sweep of Boston to win their first pennant, the Highlanders lose the Hilltop Park opener 3-2 on a ninth-inning wild pitch by Chesbro. The Highlanders finish 92-59, a game and a half behind Boston, and Chesbro finishes 41-12 with 48 complete games and $454\frac{2}{3}$ innings.

1905

Aug. 30—Chesbro gains distinction as the pitcher who surrendered Ty Cobb's first big-league hit. The Detroit rookie doubles in his Tigers debut, a 5-3 win over the Highlanders at Bennett Park.

Sept. 16—Short of infielders because of injuries, lefthanded-throwing Highlanders outfielder Willie Keeler plays second base in both ends of a doubleheader against Washington.

Oct. 8—The Highlanders close their third New York season in sixth place, 71-78.

1906

Aug. 30—Slow Joe Doyle stops Washington 5-0 and becomes the first pitcher to throw shutouts in each of his first two big-league starts.

Sept. 1—The Highlanders sweep their third straight doubleheader from the Senators—six wins in three days.

Sept. 3—The Highlanders move into first place, thanks to a 9-0 forfeit victory over the Philadelphia Athletics at packed Hilltop Park. With the game tied 3-3 in the ninth, the A's march off the field and refuse to return because of a disputed umpire's decision regarding a baserunning collision between Keeler and the Philadelphia shortstop.

Oct. 3—The Highlanders lose 3-0 to Philadelphia, allowing Chicago's "Hitless Wonders" to clinch the pennant during a rainout. The New Yorkers will finish 90-61, three games back.

1907

June 28—Washington steals 13 bases off Highlanders catcher Branch Rickey, who will go on to big-league fame for contributions in other areas of the game.

Oct. 6—The Highlanders drop from second to fifth, 70-78 and 21 games behind first-place Detroit.

1908

June 24—Griffith, the team's only manager in New York, steps aside and is replaced by **Kid Elberfeld**.

June 30—Boston's **Cy Young**, still going strong at age 41, records his third career no-hitter and an 8-0 win over the Highlanders at Hilltop Park.

Sept. 7—Young Senators righthander Walter Johnson shuts out the Highlanders for the third time in four days, 4-0. Johnson will add a 1-0 whitewashing of New York on the final day of the season.

Oct. 7—A season-closing doubleheader loss to Washington drops the last-place Highlanders to 51-103, 39½ games behind first-place Detroit.

 **1909**

Sept. 11—The Highlanders sell the contract of Chesbro, the team's first great pitcher, to the Red Sox. Chesbro's departure will be followed by the postseason release of Keeler, the last remaining starter from the franchise's first New York game in 1903.

Oct. 4—Under new manager George Stallings, the Highlanders rise to 74-77 and a fifth-place finish, 23½ games behind first-place Detroit.

Dec. 14—Fiery shortstop Elberfeld, a key member of the Highlanders since mid-1903, is sold to the Senators for $5,000.

 **1910**

April 21—Righthanded spitballer Russ Ford shuts out Philadelphia 1-0, striking out nine. He will go on to post an eye-opening 26-6 record in his rookie season for the Highlanders.

Aug. 30—Tom Hughes makes it through 9⅓ innings with a no-hitter, but he loses that in the 10th and the game in the 11th when Cleveland scores five runs.

Sept. 23—Stallings is replaced as manager by first baseman **Hal Chase**, who guides the team to a final 88-63 record and second-place finish behind Philadelphia.

 **1911**

April 13—Part of the Polo Grounds grandstands and bleachers burn down, forcing the Giants to find temporary accommodations. At the Highlanders' invitation, the team plays a big chunk of its schedule at Hilltop Park. That generosity will be reciprocated two years later.

July 12—Third baseman Roy Hartzell drives in an A.L.-record eight runs—four on a grand slam, three on a bases-loaded double and one on a sacrifice fly in a 12-2 win over the Browns.

Nov. 21—Chase, coming off a 76-76, sixth-place finish, resigns as manager and is replaced by Harry Wolverton.

 **1912**

April 11—The Highlanders unveil their new pinstriped uniforms, a look that will come to represent the most successful franchise in sports. The pinstripes will not become permanent until 1915.

May 3—The Highlanders lose to the A's 18-15, despite scoring 10 runs in the ninth inning.

May 15—Detroit star **Cobb** charges into the Hilltop Park stands to fight a heckler and is suspended indefinitely by A.L. president Johnson. The suspension triggers a brief strike by Cobb's teammates and the Tigers play a game against the A's with replacement players.

Oct. 5—The Highlanders get a three-run homer from Chase and beat the Senators 8-6 in their final game at Hilltop Park, but the season ends with a 50-102 record and a last-place finish. The team finishes a whopping 55 games behind first-place Boston.

1913

Jan. 8—Frank Chance is named manager, replacing Wolverton.

Jan. 22—With the lease on Hilltop Park ready to expire, the N.L. Giants give the Highlanders permission to share the Polo Grounds for the 1913 season. They will remain tenants through 1922.

April—No longer "Highlanders," the team is officially renamed "Yankees."

April 10—The team's debut as Yankees is ruined by Senators fireballer Walter Johnson, who records a 2-1 victory at Washington.

Oct. 4—The first "Yankees" season is a bust—57-94, seventh place, 38 games behind first-place Philadelphia.

1914

Sept. 12—Roger Peckinpaugh replaces Chance as manager—the team's seventh over the last seven years. The 23-year-old shortstop is the youngest manager in history.

Oct. 7—A tie for sixth place is an improvement for the Yankees, who finish with a 70-84 record.

1915

Jan. 11—Col. Jacob Ruppert and Col. Tillinghast Huston purchase the Yankees for $460,000.

May 6—Boston pitcher **Babe Ruth** hits his first career home run against the Yankees and pitcher Jack Warhop at the Polo Grounds.

June 13—Philadelphia lefty Bruno Haas makes his big-league debut and issues 16 walks. The Yankees roll to a 15-7 victory.

June 28—The Yankees purchase the contract of pitcher **Bob Shawkey** from the A's for $18,000.

Oct. 6—Despite a season-ending doubleheader loss to Boston, the Yankees, under first-year manager Bill Donovan, finish at 69-83 and move up to fifth place.

1916

Feb. 15—The Yankees purchase the contract of future Hall of Fame third baseman Home Run Baker from Philadelphia for $37,500.

June 20—Boston shortstop **Everett Scott** begins a streak of 1,307 consecutive games, a milestone he will reach as a member of the Yankees.

Sept. 29—Ruth closes out his 23-12, 1.75-ERA season with a 3-0 shutout of the Yankees.

Oct. 4—An 80-74 record is good for fourth place, 11 games behind first-place Boston.

1917

April 11—Boston's Ruth, en route to a 24-13 record, gets off to a good start with a three-hit, 10-3 victory over the Yankees in the season opener for both teams.

April 24—Lefthander George Mogridge throws the first no-hitter in Yankees history, earning a 2-1 decision over the Red Sox at Fenway Park.

June 17—The first Sunday game in New York, a war charity exhibition, pits the Yankees against the Giants at the Polo Grounds.

Oct. 26—Owners **Ruppert** and Huston, unhappy over their team's 71-82 record and sixth-place finish, replace manager Donovan with diminutive **Miller Huggins** (left), who will bring success to the franchise.

1918

June 1—Leading Detroit 5-4 in the ninth inning and facing a bases-loaded, no-out jam, Yankees third baseman Baker snares Chick Gandil's line drive and turns it into a game-ending triple play.

Sept. 2—With the schedule reduced because of U.S. involvement in World War I, the Yankees limp home with a 60-63 record and fourth-place finish in Huggins' first season.

Dec. 18—The Yankees sign outfielder George Halas, who will go on to greater fame as co-founder of the NFL and longtime owner and coach of the Chicago Bears.

1919

July 30—The Yankees acquire pitcher **Carl Mays** from Boston for two players and $40,000.

Sept. 10—Ray Caldwell, traded to Cleveland before the season, no-hits his former teammates and posts a 3-0 victory in the opener of a doubleheader at the Polo Grounds.

Sept. 29—The improving Yankees finish 7½ games behind Chicago in third place at 80-59.

1920

Jan. 3—For $125,000 and a $350,000 loan against the mortgage of Fenway Park, the Yankees acquire Ruth from cash-strapped Red Sox owner Harry Frazee.

May 1—Ruth, playing strictly in the outfield, hits his first Yankees home run in a 6-0 win over Boston at the Polo Grounds.

July 6—The Yankees score a record 14 runs in the fifth inning, beat Washington 17-0.

July 19—Ruth breaks his own single-season home run record when he hits Nos. 30 and 31 in a victory over the White Sox.

Aug. 16—Cleveland shortstop Ray Chapman is beaned by a Mays pitch. He will die the next day at a New York hospital.

Sept. 29—Ruth, whose .847 slugging average is a big reason behind the Yankees' 95-59 record and third-place finish, connects for his 54th home run in the opener of a season-ending doubleheader sweep of the A's.

Oct. 28—A huge piece is added to the Yankees puzzle when former Boston manager **Ed Barrow** signs on as business manager.

Dec. 15—Barrow gets future Hall of Fame pitcher Waite Hoyt from Boston in an eight-player trade.

1921

July 12—Ruth hits career home run Nos. 137 and 138, passing former 19th-century star Roger Connor for the all-time record.

Sept. 15—Ruth tops his own single-season home run record when he hits No. 55 in a 10-6 win over St. Louis.

Oct. 1—The Yankees sweep a doubleheader from the A's, clinch their first A.L. pennant.

Oct. 2—The Yankees close out their 98-55 season with a 7-6 win over Boston and a 4½-game margin over second-place Cleveland. Ruth pounds his 59th home run and raises his total bases to 457 and slugging percentage to .846.

Oct. 5—Mays pitches a five-hitter and the Yankees beat the Giants 3-0 in the first game of an all-New York, all-Polo Grounds World Series—the first fall classic victory in team history.

Oct. 13—The Giants, having recovered from a two-games-to-none deficit, beat the Yankees 1-0 and close out a five-games-to-three World Series win.

Oct. 16—Ruth, Bob Meusel and pitcher Bill Piercy launch a post-season tour, defying the barnstorming ban of commissioner Kenesaw Mountain Landis. They will have to forfeit their World Series shares and sit out until May 20 of 1922 under suspension.

Dec. 20—The Yanks get Joe Bush, Everett Scott and Sad Sam Jones from Boston for four players.

1922

March 5—Ruth signs a three-year contract at $52,000 per year.

May 5—Construction begins on Yankee Stadium.

May 20—Ruth and Meusel return from their 1921 suspensions, one of several the Bambino would have to serve throughout this stormy season.

May 21—An ownership change: Ruppert buys out Huston for $1.5 million.

July 23—The Yankees acquire third baseman **Joe Dugan** in a six-player deal with Boston.

Sept. 10—The final A.L. regular-season games at the Polo Grounds draw more than 40,000 fans as the Yanks sweep the A's behind Bush and Hoyt.

Sept. 30—The Yankees beat Boston 3-1 and clinch their second straight pennant. Their final 94-60 record will be one game better than second-place St. Louis.

Oct. 8—The Giants, behind Art Nehf, complete a World Series sweep with a 5-3 victory at the Polo Grounds.

1923

Jan. 3—The Yankees acquire two rookies from the Red Sox, one a righthanded pitcher named George Pipgras.

Jan. 30—Another piece to the puzzle: The Yanks get pitcher Herb Pennock from Boston for three players and $50,000.

April 18—The grand opening of beautiful, spacious Yankee Stadium, located just across the Harlem River from the Polo Grounds, features a three-run homer by Ruth and a 4-1 win over the Red Sox.

May 2—Shortstop Scott plays in his 1,000th straight game, but the Yanks fall to Washington and Walter Johnson 3-0.

Sept. 4—Sad Sam Jones pitches a no-hitter and the Yankees claim a 2-0 victory over Philadelphia at Shibe Park.

Sept. 20—A 4-3 win over St. Louis gives the Yankees their third straight A.L. pennant. They will finish the season with a 98-54 record and 16-game lead over second-place Detroit.

Sept. 21—Ruth, a .393 hitter with 41 home runs, is a unanimous choice for the League MVP award.

Sept. 27—A recent callup from Hartford of the Eastern League, young Lou Gehrig hits his first major league home run in an 8-3 win over the Red Sox.

Oct. 10—The first World Series game at Yankee Stadium ends dramatically when sore-legged outfielder Casey Stengel labors around the bases with a ninth-inning, inside-the-park home run that gives the Giants a 5-4 victory.

Oct. 15—The Yankees, avenging two World Series losses to the Giants, claim the first of their 26 championships when Meusel delivers a Series-deciding eighth-inning single in Game 6.

1924

June 13—With the Yankees leading the Tigers 10-6 in the top of the ninth inning, Meusel hurls his bat at pitcher Bert Cole after being hit by a pitch, triggering a brawl. The Yankees win by forfeit when umpire Billy Evans cannot clear Detroit fans from the field.

Sept. 30—The three-year pennant run ends as the Yankees finish 89-63, two games behind Washington in second place.

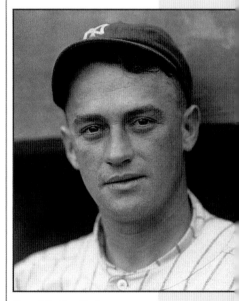

Dec. 17—The Yankees acquire four-time 20-game winner **Urban Shocker** from St. Louis for three pitchers.

1925

April 5—Ruth collapses in a North Carolina railroad station and undergoes an operation for an ulcer.

May 6—Huggins, upset with his team's poor play, benches Scott in favor of **Pee Wee Wanninger** and ends his record consecutive-games streak at 1,307.

June 1—Gehrig pinch hits for Wanninger, beginning his record consecutive-games streak. Ruth, finally healthy, plays his first game of the season.

June 2—Regular first baseman **Wally Pipp** sits out a game because of a headache. Gehrig takes his place and remains in the lineup for the next 14 years.

July 23—Gehrig hits the first of his record 23 grand slams in an 11-7 win over Washington.

Aug. 1—The Yanks buy the contract of second baseman Tony Lazzeri, who will finish the Pacific Coast League season for Salt Lake City with 60 home runs and 222 RBIs.

Oct. 4—The 69-85 Yankees finish in seventh place, 28½ games behind first-place Washington.

1926

May 28—Philadelphia ends the Yankees' 16-game winning streak with a 2-1 and 6-5 doubleheader sweep at Yankee Stadium.

Sept. 25—The Yankees clinch their fourth pennant and first since 1923 with a doubleheader sweep of the Browns. They will finish the next day with a 91-63 record and a three-game advantage over second-place Cleveland.

Oct. 2—Gehrig drives in the winning run and Pennock posts a 2-1 victory over the Cardinals in the World Series opener at Yankee Stadium.

Oct. 6—Ruth hits a World Series-record three home runs in a 10-5 Game 4 win over the Cardinals at Sportsman's Park.

Oct. 10—Aging Grover Alexander, pitching in relief, strikes out Lazzeri with the bases loaded in the seventh inning and then preserves the Cardinals' 3-2 Game 7 win. The Series ends with Ruth getting thrown out trying to steal second base.

1927

March 3—Ruth signs a three-year contract for $70,000 per year.

April 12—The Yankees batter the A's and pitcher Lefty Grove 8-3 in the season opener. They will never fall from first place.

Aug. 22—The Yankees lose their fourth straight game and Detroit wins its 13th straight, but the second-place Tigers still trail by 12 ½ games. Ruth hits his 40th homer in a 9-4 loss to Cleveland.

Sept. 11—The Browns beat the Yankees 6-2 in their final meeting, preventing the Bombers from posting a 22-game season sweep.

Sept. 13—Home runs 51 and 52 by Ruth key a sweep of the Indians and help the Yankees clinch their fifth pennant. They will finish two weeks later with an A.L.-record 110 wins, a 19-game advantage over the second-place A's and a team batting average of .307.

Sept. 29—Ruth hits his 58 and 59, tying his single-season record, in a 15-4 win over the Senators.

Sept. 30—Ruth hits his historic 60th home run to give the Yankees a 4-2 win over the Senators. He will finish the next day with 164 RBIs and a .356 average.

Oct. 8—Ruth's home run and a ninth-inning wild pitch secure a 4-3 win and a four-game World Series sweep of the Pirates. This Yankees team generally will be acknowledged as the greatest in baseball history.

Oct. 11—Gehrig is named League MVP. He finishes with 47 homers, a .373 average and a major league-record 175 RBIs.

1928

April 20—The team opens its sixth season at Yankee Stadium with the left field stands enlarged to three decks.

Sept. 7—Philadelphia sweeps two from the Red Sox while the Yankees lose twice to the Senators. The Yanks, once 11½ games in the lead, are now tied with the A's for first place.

Sept. 9—Shocker, released only two months earlier because of poor health, dies of pneumonia at age 38—the same day the Yankees take a big step toward another pennant with a doubleheader sweep of the Philadelphia Athletics.

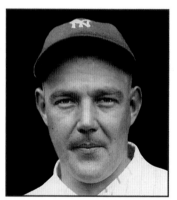

Sept. 28—**Pipgras** pitches the Yankees to a pennant-clinching 11-6 win over the Tigers. The Bronx Bombers will finish 101-53 with Ruth contributing 54 home runs.

Oct. 4—Gehrig and Ruth lead the way offensively as Hoyt posts a 4-1 win over the Cardinals in the World Series opener at Yankee Stadium.

Oct. 9—Ruth duplicates his 1926 performance by hitting three home runs in a World Series game against the Cardinals. The Yankees' 7-3 win completes a four-game sweep and secures their third championship.

1929

April 16—The Yankees open the season with an innovation: permanent numbers, corresponding to their position in the batting order, affixed to their uniforms.

Aug. 11—Indians pitcher Willis Hudlin surrenders home run No. 500 to Ruth in a game at Cleveland.

Aug. 17—The Yankees purchase the contract of pitcher **Lefty Gomez** from San Francisco of the Pacific Coast League.

Sept. 25—Manager Huggins, who guided the Yankees to six pennants and three championships, dies from blood poisoning at age 49.

Oct. 6—The Yankees close with a 5-2 loss to Philadelphia. The championship express is derailed by an 88-66 record and second-place finish behind the A's.

Oct. 17—Former pitcher Shawkey is hired to replace interim manager Art Fletcher.

1930

March 8—Ruth signs for two years at $80,000 per year, the biggest player contract ever.

May 6—The Yankees acquire pitcher Red Ruffing from Boston for Cedric Durst and $50,000.

May 24—Ruth homers in both ends of a doubleheader sweep of Philadelphia, giving him eight in a three-day, six-game stretch against the A's. The Babe hit three homers in doubleheaders against the Athletics on May 21 and 22.

Aug. 23—The Yanks purchase the contract of infielder **Frankie Crosetti** from San Francisco of the Pacific Coast League.

Sept. 28—Ruth pitches a complete-game 9-3 win over the Red Sox in the season finale. The Yankees finish 86-68, third behind the A's and Senators.

Oct. 14—Shawkey is out as manager and Joe McCarthy is in, a move that will reap big dividends.

1931

Aug. 18—Gehrig plays in his 1,000th straight game.

Aug. 21—Ruth connects for home run No. 600 off George Blaeholder in an 11-7 Yankees win at St. Louis.

Sept. 20—Gehrig drives in four runs in a doubleheader sweep of Cleveland, breaking his old A.L. RBI record of 175. He will finish with a still-standing record of 184.

Sept. 27—Gehrig hits his 46th home run, tying Ruth for the A.L. lead, and the Yankees beat the first-place A's and 31-game winner Lefty Grove to finish at 94-59.

Nov. 13—Ruppert buys the Newark franchise in the International League. Newark will send a steady stream of outstanding players to New York.

1932

Feb. 12—Another front-office piece falls into place: George Weiss, general manager of the Baltimore Orioles, joins the Yankees.

May 30—A monument in memory of Huggins is dedicated at Yankee Stadium. It begins a stately tradition.

June 3—Gehrig becomes the first player in the 20th century to hit four home runs in a game. He just misses a fifth as the Yankees crush the A's 20-13.

July 4—Catcher Bill Dickey, upset about a home plate collision, punches Washington's Carl Reynolds and breaks his jaw. Dickey will be suspended for 30 days and fined $1,000.

Sept. 13—The Yankees clinch their seventh pennant at Cleveland with their 100th win. They will finish two weeks later with a 107-47 record.

Oct. 1—Game 3 of the World Series, a 7-5 Yankees win over the Cubs, spotlights Ruth's called-shot home run in the fifth inning off Charlie Root.

Oct. 2—Lazzeri hits two homers and Earle Combs adds one in a 13-6 World Series clincher. The fall classic sweep is the third straight for the Yankees, dating back to 1927.

1933

March 24—In a Depression-era concession, Ruth signs for $52,000, down from his previous year's pay of $75,000.

July 6—Ruth steals the show at baseball's first All-Star Game with a two-run homer. The A.L. wins the Chicago classic 4-2.

July 26—Joe DiMaggio, an 18-year-old playing for San Francisco of the Pacific Coast League, goes hitless in five at-bats against Oakland pitcher Ed Walsh Jr. and sees his amazing 61-game hitting streak come to an end.

Aug. 17—Gehrig breaks Scott's consecutive-games record when he stretches his streak to 1,308 during a loss to the Browns.

Oct. 1—**Ruth** pitches a 6-5 complete-game, season-ending win over the Red Sox and adds a home run for good measure. The Yankees finish 91-59 in second place.

1934

July 13—Detroit's Tommy Bridges serves up Ruth's historic 700th home run in a game at Navin Field.

July 17—Ruth draws his 2,000th career walk in a game at Cleveland. He will end his career with a staggering record total of 2,062.

Sept. 24—A limping Ruth bats once in his final game at Yankee Stadium—a 5-0 loss to Boston.

Sept. 29—Ruth hits his 659th and final Yankees homer against Washington. He will go hitless the next day, his final in pinstripes, as the Yanks close with a 94-60 record, good for second place. Gehrig wraps up his Triple Crown season with 49 homers, 165 RBIs and a .363 average.

Nov. 21—The Yankees pay $25,000 and agree to send five players to San Francisco of the Pacific Coast League for DiMaggio.

1935

Feb. 26—Ruth is released by the Yankees, clearing the way for him to return to Boston as a member of the N.L.'s Braves.

May 25—Ruth, playing for the Braves, hits three home runs in an 11-7 loss at Pittsburgh. The third blow, a shot over the right field grandstand at Forbes Field, is the 714th and final homer of his career.

Sept. 29—The Yankees split a season-closing doubleheader with Boston, finish in second place at 89-60.

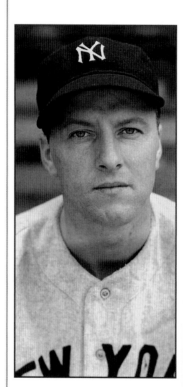

Dec. 11—The Yankees trade Johnny Allen to Cleveland for **Monte Pearson**.

1936

HALL OF FAME · *Babe* Ruth 1936

Feb. 2—Ruth is one of five Hall of Fame charter members, as selected by the Baseball Writers' Association of America.

May 3—DiMaggio, making a belated Yankees debut because of injuries, gets three hits, including a triple, in a 14-5 win over the Browns.

May 24—Lazzeri drives in an A.L. single-game-record 11 runs with three home runs, two of them grand slams. The Yanks beat the A's, 25-2.

Sept. 9—A doubleheader sweep of the Indians allows the Yankees to record the earliest pennant-clinching date in history. They will go on to finish 102-51, 19½ games ahead of the Tigers.

Oct. 2—Lazzeri hits a grand slam in the Yankees' 18-4 win over the Giants in Game 2 of the World Series.

Oct. 6—The Yankees claim their fifth World Series title with a 13-5 Game 6 win over the Giants.

Oct. 16—The baseball writers select Gehrig (49 homers, 152 RBIs, .354 average) as A.L. MVP.

1937

April 11—The Yankees sign free-agent outfielder **Tommy Henrich**.

April 20—Yankee Stadium opens its 15th season with triple-decked right field stands and a reduced center field—from 490 feet to 461.

May 25—In a somber game at Yankee Stadium, Detroit catcher/manager Mickey Cochrane is beaned by Yankee starter Bump Hadley. Cochrane suffers a skull fracture and will never return as a player.

July 7—The A.L.'s 8-3 victory over the N.L. in the annual All-Star Game comes courtesy of the Yankees. Gehrig, Red Rolfe and Dickey combine for seven RBIs and Gomez is the winning pitcher.

Sept. 23—The Yankees lose to the Browns, but clinch the pennant when Boston beats second-place Detroit. The 102-52 Yanks will finish 13 games ahead of the Tigers.

Oct. 10—A five-game World Series ends at the Polo Grounds as Gomez lifts his fall classic record to 5-0 with a 4-2 win over the Giants.

1938

May 30—A franchise-record crowd of 81,841 watches the Yankees overpower the Red Sox in a doubleheader sweep.

Aug. 27—A double victory at Yankee Stadium: DiMaggio triples three times in an opening win over Cleveland and Pearson fires a no-hitter in the nightcap, winning 13-0.

Sept. 9—Gehrig celebrates his 2,100th straight game by collecting four hits at Washington.

Sept. 18—A doubleheader loss to the Browns can't keep the Yankees from clinching their 10th pennant. They will go on to a 99-53 final record.

Oct. 9—Ruffing pitches the Yanks to an 8-3 win over the Cubs and another World Series sweep. The Bronx Bombers become the first team to win three straight championships and Gehrig collects his final World Series hit—a single.

1939

Jan. 13—Yankees owner Ruppert dies. Barrow will fill his role as team president.

Jan. 24—**Keeler** is one of three former players added to the Hall of Fame.

May 2—Gehrig voluntarily benches himself, ending his record consecutive-games streak at 2,130. Babe Dahlgren, his first base replacement, hits a double and home run in the Yankees' 22-2 win at Detroit.

June 21—The Yankees make it official, announcing Gehrig's retirement at age 36 because of a terminal illness.

July 4—Lou Gehrig Appreciation Day at Yankee Stadium. A tearful Iron Horse watches as his No. 4 is retired and then tells the sellout crowd, "I consider myself the luckiest man on the face of the earth."

Sept. 16—The Yankees clinch their fourth straight pennant with a win over Detroit. They will finish 106-45 and outdistance Boston by 17 games.

Oct. 8—The Yankees complete their second straight World Series sweep and record fourth straight championship in bizarre fashion. A 7-4 Game 4 win over Cincinnati is decided when the Yanks score three runs in the 10th inning, a rally capped by "Lombardi's Snooze."

Oct. 24—DiMaggio (.381, 30 homers, 126 RBIs) is named A.L. MVP.

Dec. 8—Bypassing the mandatory retirement rule, the baseball writers elect **Gehrig** to the Hall of Fame.

1940

July 26—Spud Chandler beats the White Sox with his arm and his bat. In a game at Chicago, Chandler knocks in six runs with two homers, one a grand slam, and a single while posting a 10-2 victory.

July 28—**Charlie Keller** hits three home runs and the Yankees post a 10-9 win over Chicago in the opener of a doubleheader.

Sept. 11—The Yankees, in search of a fifth straight championship, win the first game of a doubleheader against Cleveland and move into first place. They lose in the nightcap and fall out of first for good. They will finish in third place at 88-66, two games behind first-place Detroit.

1941

May 15—DiMaggio singles off Chicago pitcher Edgar Smith and begins his record 56-game hitting streak.

June 2—Gehrig dies in New York at age 37 of amyotrophic lateral sclerosis.

July 17—DiMaggio goes hitless in a Yankees win at Cleveland, ending the longest hitting streak in baseball history. He is robbed twice by Indians third baseman Ken Keltner.

Sept. 4—The high-flying Yankees post the earliest clinching date in history with a 6-3 win over the Red Sox. Their final 101-win total will be 17 better than second-place Boston.

Oct. 5—With a Game 4 World Series victory within grasp, the Dodgers fall 7-4 when the Yankees score four ninth-inning runs. The Yankees get new life when catcher Mickey Owen misses connections on a third strike that would have given the Dodgers a 4-3 Series-squaring victory.

Oct. 6—A 3-1 fifth-game win gives the Yankees their ninth World Series championship.

Nov. 11—DiMaggio edges Boston rival Ted Williams and captures his second A.L. MVP award.

1942

Aug. 23—In a between-games exhibition at Yankee Stadium, 47-year-old Babe Ruth belts a home run off 54-year-old Walter Johnson, sending the crowd of 69,136 into a frenzy. The exhibition, which raises more than $80,000 for war relief, is sandwiched by a doubleheader split between the Yankees and Senators.

Sept. 14—The Yankees, on their way to 103 wins, clinch their 13th A.L. pennant with an 8-3 victory over Cleveland. **Tiny Bonham** wins his 20th game.

Oct. 5—Another five-game World Series, but this time the Yankees are on the losing end. The Cardinals' 4-2 victory hands the Yanks only their fourth fall classic loss in 13 tries.

Nov. 3—Boston's Williams wins an A.L. Triple Crown, but Yankees second baseman Joe Gordon (.322, 18 homers, 103 RBIs) wins the league's MVP honors.

1943

Feb. 17—DiMaggio joins a growing list of teammates and other baseball stars who will perform military duty during World War II.

Sept. 25—The Yankees clinch their third straight pennant and seventh in eight years with a 14-inning, 2-1 win over the Tigers. They will finish with 98 wins.

Oct. 11—Sweet revenge: A two-run, sixth-inning homer by Dickey is enough for Chandler, who fires a Game 5 shutout at the Cardinals and gives the Yankees their 10th World Series championship. It is McCarthy's seventh, and final, fall classic win.

Nov. 9—**Chandler**, 20-4 with a league-leading 1.64 ERA, claims the A.L. MVP.

1944

DiMaggio (left) with his new temmates.

May 9—McCarthy, sidelined by illness for most of spring training and the early season, returns to the dugout in hopes of leading the Yankees to their fourth straight pennant.

Aug. 9—The Browns beat the Yankees 3-2 for their ninth straight win, increasing their A.L. advantage to 6½ games.

Oct. 1—The Yankees discover life on the other end as the St. Louis Browns complete a four-game sweep with a final-day 5-2 win and clinch their first pennant. The Yankees, with 83 wins, finish six games behind St. Louis and five behind Detroit.

1945

Jan. 25—Dan Topping, Del Webb and Larry MacPhail purchase the Yankees for $2.8 million from the Ruppert estate and MacPhail replaces Barrow as president and general manager.

May 20—The Yankees fall 10-1 and 5-2 to the Browns as one-armed St. Louis outfielder Pete Gray collects three first-game hits and two RBIs before making several sensational catches in the nightcap.

Sept. 30—**George "Snuffy" Stirnweiss** gets three hits on the final day and claims the A.L. batting title with a .309 average. The Yankees close out an 81-71 war-interrupted season in fourth place.

Stirnweiss (center) with **Johnny Lindell** (left) and **Henrich**.

1946

HALL OF FAME *Jack* Chesbro 1946

April 23—Iron man **Chesbro** and former manager Griffith are new Hall of Famers, courtesy of the Veterans Committee.

May 24—McCarthy, the guiding force behind eight Yankee pennants and seven championships, steps down as manager and is replaced by Dickey.

May 28—With 49,917 fans looking on, the Bronx Bombers drop a 2-1 decision to Washington in the first night game at Yankee Stadium.

Sept. 29—A third straight pennant-less season ends with the 87-67 Yankees in third, 17 games behind first-place Boston.

1947

April 27—Babe Ruth Day is celebrated at all parks throughout major league baseball. A crowd of 58,339 turns out at Yankee Stadium to honor the cancer-stricken slugger.

July 17—The Yankees, flourishing under new manager Bucky Harris, sweep a doubleheader from Cleveland and stretch their A.L.-record-tying winning streak to 19 games. The Tigers will end their run the next day.

Sept. 15—The idle Yankees clinch their first pennant since 1943 when the White Sox beat the Red Sox, 6-3. They will finish 97-57.

Oct. 2—Yogi Berra becomes the first player to hit a pinch-hit home run in a World Series game, but the Yankees lose to Brooklyn in Game 3.

Oct. 3—Yankee Bill Bevens comes within one out of baseball immortality, but his no-hit bid is ruined by a two-out, two-run, ninth-inning double by Cookie Lavagetto and the Dodgers win a dramatic Game 4, 3-2.

Oct. 5—Left fielder Al Gionfriddo's miracle catch robs DiMaggio of a potential three-run homer and the Dodgers escape with a heart-throbbing 8-6 Game 6 win that evens the Series at three games apiece.

Oct. 6—The Yankees post a 5-2 victory in Game 7 and wrap up their 11th World Series championship.

Oct. 7—MacPhail resigns as general manager and co-owners Topping and Webb announce they will purchase his one-third interest in the team. Weiss becomes the new G.M.

Nov. 27—DiMaggio (20 homers, 97 RBIs) edges Boston Triple Crown winner Williams by a single vote and wins his third MVP.

1948

Feb. 27—**Pennock** is one of two players elected to the Hall of Fame.

HALL OF FAME *Herb* Pennock 1948

June 13—The Yankees retire Ruth's No. 3 in ceremonies celebrating the 25th anniversary of Yankee Stadium. It will be the Babe's final Stadium appearance.

July 13—Yankee pitcher Vic Raschi drives in the winning runs with a bases-loaded single and gets credit for the A.L.'s 5-2 All-Star victory over the N.L. at St. Louis.

Aug. 16—Ruth dies in New York of throat cancer at age 53.

Oct. 3—The Yankees lose to the Red Sox on the final day to finish 94-60, good for third place in the tight A.L. race. Boston and Cleveland finish 96-58, forcing a one-game playoff to determine a pennant winner.

Oct. 12—The beginning of an era: Casey Stengel starts his successful managerial reign in New York.

1949

April 19—A monument honoring Babe Ruth is unveiled in center field during ceremonies preceding the season opener at Yankee Stadium, joining previous monuments honoring Huggins and Gehrig.

June 28—After missing the season's first 65 games with a heel injury, DiMaggio returns to the lineup. He will blitz the Red Sox with four home runs in a three-game Yankees sweep.

Aug. 22—The Yankees purchase the contract of slugger Johnny Mize from the Giants for $40,000.

Oct. 1—Joe DiMaggio Day at Yankee Stadium kicks off a pennant-deciding weekend for the Yankees and Red Sox. Trailing Boston by one game with two left to play, the Yankees fall behind 4-0 before rallying for a 5-4 victory on Johnny Lindell's eighth-inning homer, forcing a first-place tie.

Oct. 2—Raschi outduels Boston's Ellis Kinder in a dramatic winner-take-all final-day showdown at packed Yankee Stadium and the Yanks post a 5-3 victory that secures their 97th victory and 16th A.L. pennant.

Oct. 5—Henrich's ninth-inning home run off Brooklyn's Don Newcombe gives the Yanks a 1-0 win in the first game of the World Series.

Oct. 9—A 10-6 fifth-game win at Ebbets Field gives the Yankees their 12th championship.

1950

April 18—Rookie second baseman **Billy Martin** becomes the first player in history to get two hits in one inning in his first major league game. Martin doubles and singles in the eighth inning of New York's 15-10 win over Boston.

Sept. 29—The idle Yankees clinch their second straight pennant when Cleveland beats Detroit 12-2. They will finish the season 98-56, three games ahead of Detroit.

Oct. 7—Rookie lefthander Whitey Ford records his first World Series victory, a 5-2 decision that completes the Yankees' four-game sweep of the overmatched Phillies.

Oct. 26—Yankees shortstop **Phil Rizzuto** walks off with A.L. MVP honors.

1951

May 1—The Yankees' 8-3 victory over Chicago features the first major league home run by rookie outfielder Mickey Mantle.

July 12—Allie Reynolds holds the Indians hitless and wins 1-0 on Gene Woodling's home run off Bob Feller.

July 15—The Yankees option the slumping Mantle to Kansas City of the American Association. They will recall him for the stretch run.

Sept. 28—In the first game of a doubleheader against the Red Sox, Reynolds pitches his second no-hitter of the season, an 8-0 win at Yankee Stadium that clinches at least a tie for the A.L. pennant. In the nightcap, the Yanks, en route to a 98-56 final record, clinch as Raschi notches his 21st win.

Oct. 5—Playing right field in Game 2 of the World Series, Mantle trips over a Yankee Stadium drain cover and hurts his knee—an injury that will end his season and plague him throughout his career.

Oct. 10—Hank Bauer's bases-loaded triple and spectacular game-ending catch lift the Yankees to a 4-3 Game 6 win and their third straight championship under Stengel.

Nov. 8—Berra wins the first of three A.L. MVP awards. He also will claim the award in 1954 and '55.

Dec. 11—DiMaggio announces his retirement.

1952

Aug. 25—The Yankees are victims in the second no-hitter of the season by Detroit's Virgil Trucks. The righthander wins 1-0 and gets official scoring help when Rizzuto's third-inning infield hit is changed to an error.

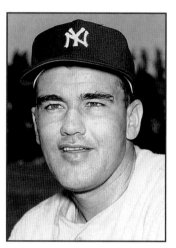

Sept. 3—Yankee pitchers **Tom Gorman** and Ewell Blackwell shut out the Red Sox, 5-0 and 4-0, in a doubleheader.

Sept. 26—The Yankees clinch their fourth straight pennant and 19th overall with an 11-inning 5-2 win at Philadelphia. They will finish two days later with a 95-59 record.

Oct. 4—Mize homers and Reynolds limits Brooklyn to four hits in a 2-0 victory that squares the World Series at two games apiece.

Oct. 7—The Yankees claim their fourth straight World Series title and 15th overall with a 4-2 seventh-game victory over the Dodgers. The day is saved by Martin, who races in to make a seventh-inning shoetop grab of a bases-loaded Jackie Robinson popup that appeared destined to fall untouched.

1953

April 17—Mantle connects against Washington's Chuck Stobbs at Griffith Stadium. The blow is measured at 565 feet.

June 14—The Yankees sweep the Indians and extend their winning streak to 18 games. It will end in their next game against St. Louis.

Aug. 4—Raschi sets a major league record for a pitcher with seven RBIs in a 15-0 win over Detroit.

Sept. 14—An 8-5 victory over Cleveland clinches the Yankees' fifth straight pennant. They will finish with a 99-52 record.

HALL OF FAME *Ed Barrow* 1953

Sept. 28—A special committee on veterans adds **Barrow**, five others to the Hall of Fame.

Oct. 4—Mantle's grand slam powers the Yankees to an 11-7 win over the Dodgers in Game 5 of the World Series.

Oct. 5—Martin's ninth-inning single, his record-tying 12th hit of the Series, gives the Yankees a 4-3 victory and their fifth straight title, breaking their own record of four straight from 1936-39.

1954

HALL OF FAME *Bill Dickey* 1954

Jan. 20—**Dickey** is one of three former players elected to the Hall of Fame.

Sept. 21—Yankees rookie Bob Grim beats Washington 3-1 for his 20th victory.

Sept. 26—The Yankees suffer a final-day 8-6 loss in the Athletics' final game representing Philadelphia. Despite a 103-51 record, the Bronx Bombers finish eight games behind the record-setting Indians and Stengel fails to win a pennant for the first time in six New York seasons.

Nov. 18—The Yankees and Orioles complete phase 1 of a shocking 17-player trade. Among the Yankee newcomers are pitchers Bob Turley and Don Larsen.

1955

Jan. 26—**DiMaggio** and Home Run Baker are among four former greats elected by the baseball writers to the Hall of Fame.

April 14—**Elston Howard**, the first black player in Yankees history, singles in his first big-league at-bat in an 8-4 loss to the Red Sox.

May 13—Mantle homers three times in a 5-2 win over Detroit. For the first time in his career, the switch hitter connects from both sides of the plate in the same game.

Sept. 23—After a second-place finish in 1954, the Yankees clinch the first of four straight pennants with a 3-2 win over Boston. They will finish 96-58.

Oct. 4—The Dodgers, losers to the Yankees in five straight World Series dating back to 1941, win their first championship in eight tries with a 2-0 decision in Game 7. Johnny Podres silences the Yankee bats and left fielder Sandy Amoros saves the game with a sensational catch on a sixth-inning drive by Berra.

1956

HALL OF FAME *Joe DiMaggio* 1955

May 30—In the opener of a doubleheader against Washington's Pedro Ramos, Mantle hits a drive off the right field facade high above Yankee Stadium's third deck. The ball misses leaving the stadium by 18 inches.

Aug. 25—The Yankees release Rizzuto, who will soon move into the team's broadcasting booth.

Sept. 18—Mantle's 50th home run, an 11th-inning shot off Chicago's Billy Pierce, triggers another Yankee pennant-clinching party. The Yanks will finish 97-57, nine games ahead of Cleveland.

Sept. 28—Mantle hits his 52nd home run in a game against the Red Sox. He will finish his Triple Crown season with a .353 average, 130 RBIs and the A.L. MVP award.

Oct. 8—Game 5 of the World Series against Brooklyn goes to the Yankees 2-0 as Larsen makes history with a 97-pitch perfect game.

Oct. 10—Berra homers twice, Bill Skowron hits a grand slam and Johnny Kucks shuts out the Dodgers 9-0 in Game 7 to give the Yankees their 17th championship.

1957

HALL OF FAME · *Joe McCarthy* 1957

Feb. 3—**McCarthy** is one of two additions to baseball's Hall of Fame.

May 7—Yankees infielder Gil McDougald hits a line drive that hits Cleveland lefthander **Herb Score** in the right eye. Score, who is removed from the field on a stretcher and hospitalized, never returns to his pre-injury form.

May 16—A birthday celebration at Manhattan's Copacabana Club turns nasty when a fight breaks out involving Yankee players and other patrons. Partiers Bauer, Martin, Berra, Ford, Mantle and Kucks will be fined and Martin, considered a bad influence on Mantle, will be traded a month later to Kansas City.

Sept. 23—The Yankees, en route to 98 wins, get pennant-clinching help when Kansas City defeats the White Sox 6-5.

Oct. 10—Extended to seven games by Milwaukee, the Yankees lose a World Series for only the sixth time. Lew Burdette spins a seven-hit shutout in a 5-0 Braves win.

Nov. 22—Mantle, a .365 hitter with 34 homers, edges Boston's Williams and wins his second straight MVP.

1958

Sept. 16—Yankee killer **Frank Lary** pitches the Tigers to a 4-2 victory—his seventh of the season over the New Yorkers. His success is unexplainable as the Yankees roll to a 92-62 record and their fourth straight pennant—their ninth in 10 seasons under Stengel.

Sept. 20—The Yankees and Larsen are no-hit victims of Orioles knuckleballer Hoyt Wilhelm, who wins 1-0.

Oct. 9—The Yankees become only the second team to recover from a three-games-to-one World Series deficit, beating Milwaukee in the seventh game 6-2 behind the relief pitching of Turley and a three-run homer by Skowron. The title is Stengel's seventh.

Nov. 12—The major league Cy Young Award goes to Turley, a 21-game regular-season winner.

1959

July 4—Turley, bidding for a no-hitter, watches helplessly as a ninth-inning bloop hit by Washington pinch-hitter Julio Becquer falls safely in the nightcap of a holiday doubleheader. Turley's 7-0 win gives the Yankees a split.

Sept. 10—Mantle goes 5-for-6 and homers in a 12-1 romp past the A's, but the Yankees will finish two weeks later with an atypical 79-75 record and third-place finish.

Dec. 11—The Yankees acquire young slugger Roger Maris from the A's in a seven-player deal that sends Larsen, Bauer, Norm Siebern and Marv Throneberry to Kansas City.

1960

Sept. 25—**Ralph Terry** (left) and **Luis Arroyo** pitch a 4-3 win over Boston that clinches the Yankees' 25th pennant and 10th in 12 years under Stengel. The Yankees will return to the World Series with a 97-57 regular-season record.

Oct. 8—Second baseman Bobby Richardson clubs the Pirates with a grand slam and two-run single in Game 3 of the fall classic, a 10-0 Yankees win. Richardson will finish with a Series-record 12 RBIs.

Oct. 13—In a dramatic conclusion to the World Series, Pittsburgh's Bill Mazeroski hits a ninth-inning Game 7 home run off Terry to secure a 10-9 victory and the Pirates' first championship since 1925. The Yanks lose only their seventh fall classic despite outscoring the Bucs 55-27.

Oct. 18—Despite his phenomenal success as Yankees manager, the 70-year-old Stengel is forced to retire by Topping and Webb. He will be replaced by 41-year-old Ralph Houk two days later.

Nov. 2—Maris (.283, 39 homers, 112 RBIs) edges teammate Mantle (.275, 40, 94) by three votes in the battle for A.L. MVP honors. Joy is subdued by the retirement of Weiss as general manager.

1961

July 17—With both **Maris** (left) and Mantle mounting a threat to the single-season home run record, commissioner Ford Frick rules Ruth's mark of 60 can be broken only if homer No. 61 is hit within 154 games. The so-called "asterisk ruling" was triggered by baseball's expanded 162-game schedule.

Aug. 16—Maris hits two home runs, giving him seven in a six-game span. After the Yankees' 5-4 win over Chicago, Maris has 48 homers to Mantle's 45. Maris will become the first player to reach the 50-homer plateau in the month of August six days later.

Sept. 20—Maris hits his 59th home run off Baltimore's Milt Pappas in New York's 155th game (including a tie). The Yankees' 4-2 win clinches their 26th pennant for rookie manager Houk.

Sept. 26—With Mantle (54 homers) sidelined by injury, Maris tags Baltimore's Jack Fisher for his 60th homer in a game at Yankee Stadium.

Oct. 1—On the final day of the season, Maris connects for record-breaking homer No. 61 off Boston's Tracy Stallard in a 1-0 win at the Stadium. The victory is the Yanks' 109th.

Oct. 8—Ford works five shutout innings in a 7-0 Game 4 win over Cincinnati, stretching his World Series-record scoreless innings streak to 32.

Oct. 9—Hector Lopez drives in five runs as the Yankees close out their 19th World Series championship with a 13-5 win over Cincinnati.

Nov. 8—Ford, coming off a 25-4 season, wins the Cy Young Award. One week later, Maris wins his second straight A.L. MVP.

1962

June 24—Jack Reed's two-run homer in the 22nd inning, the only home run of his three-year big-league career, gives the Yankees a 9-7 win over Detroit in the longest game in team history.

Aug. 19—Howard, Mantle and Skowron combine for four homers and 19 RBIs in a 21-7 win over Kansas City.

Sept. 25—Ford beats Washington 8-3 and the Yankees clinch their third straight pennant and 12th in 14 years. They will finish 96-66 and outdistance Minnesota by five games.

Oct. 10—Tom Tresh's three-run eighth-inning home run gives the Yankees and Terry a 5-3 win and a three-games-to-two edge over San Francisco in the World Series.

Oct. 16—Second baseman Richardson snares Willie McCovey's vicious ninth-inning line drive to preserve Terry's 1-0 seventh-game victory and give the Yankees their 20th championship. It is their second in a row and ninth in 14 seasons.

Nov. 20—Despite missing a month of the season to injury, Mantle wins his third A.L. MVP citation.

1963

Sept. 13—The Yankees clinch their third straight pennant under Houk behind the pitching of Jim Bouton, who stops Minnesota 2-0 for his 20th victory. The Yanks will go on to win 104 games.

Oct. 6—The Dodgers complete a shocking World Series sweep with a 2-1 victory behind the pitching of Sandy Koufax. The Yankees bat .171 and total only four runs in the four games.

Oct. 22—**Roy Hamey** steps down as G.M. of the Yankees and Houk steps up. Houk will be replaced as manager two days later by Berra.

Nov. 7—Howard becomes the first black to win MVP honors in the American League.

1964

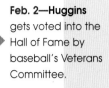

Feb. 2—**Huggins** gets voted into the Hall of Fame by baseball's Veterans Committee.

Aug. 20—With the Yankees locked in a tight pennant race with the White Sox and Orioles, tempers explode on the team bus after a loss to Chicago. Shortstop Phil Linz refuses to stop playing his harmonica and an irate Berra slaps it away before order is restored. The story makes national headlines.

HALL OF FAME
Miller Huggins 1964

Oct. 3—An 8-3 win over Cleveland clinches the Yankees' 29th pennant, fifth straight and 14th in 16 years. They will finish with 99 wins, only one better than second-place Chicago.

Oct. 10—Mantle homers on Cardinals reliever Barney Schultz's first pitch in the ninth inning to give the Yankees a 2-1 win in Game 3 of the World Series.

Oct. 15—The Cardinals post a 7-5 victory in Game 7 and claim their seventh Series championship. The Yankees' incredible four-decade postseason run comes to a disappointing end.

Oct. 16—The Yankees shock the baseball world by firing Berra, the same day Cardinals manager Johnny Keane resigns. Keane will become Yankees manager three days later.

Nov. 2—CBS purchases 80 percent of the Yankees for $11.2 million. They will buy the remaining 20 percent later.

April 9—Mantle christens Houston's wondrous new Astrodome with a home run during a preseason exhibition game.

June 18—The Yankees hit four homers and belt the first-place Twins 10-2, but they're still 10 games behind Minnesota, buried in seventh place.

HALL OF FAME *Casey* Stengel 1966

March 8—**Stengel** enters the Hall of Fame, courtesy of baseball's Veterans Committee.

May 7—With the team struggling on the field, **G.M. Houk** fires Keane and steps back into his old managerial role.

July 20—Righthander Mel Stottlemyre, en route to an impressive 20-9 record for a losing team, hits an inside-the-park grand slam to secure a 6-3 win over the Red Sox.

Oct. 3—It's official. The Yankees' A.L. reign is over. The Bombers beat Boston 11-5 to finish a 77-85, sixth-place season, their first losing campaign since 1925.

Sept. 11—John Miller becomes the first Yankee to homer in his first big-league at-bat, but the Red Sox still win 4-2. It is one of only six games Miller will play for the Yanks.

Oct. 2—The Yankees finish a down season on a high note with a 2-0 win over Chicago. Their final 70-89 record drops them to last place, 26½ games behind first-place Baltimore.

Oct. 13—Lee MacPhail is named new Yankees general manager.

Dec. 8—The Yankees trade Maris to the Cardinals for infielder Charlie Smith.

Jan. 6—Keane dies of a heart attack at age 55.

HALL OF FAME *Red* Ruffing 1967

Feb. 16—**Ruffing** is elected to the Hall of Fame.

April 14—Red Sox lefty Billy Rohr, making his major league debut at Yankee Stadium, watches his no-hit bid go down the drain in the ninth inning when Howard lines a two-out single to right-center. Rohr, who settles for a one-hit 3-0 victory, will win only two more games in the majors.

May 14—Mantle becomes the sixth member of baseball's 500-homer club when he connects off Baltimore's Stu Miller in a 6-5 win at Yankee Stadium.

Oct. 1—The Yankees close a 72-90 season (ninth place) with a 4-3 win over Kansas City behind Stottlemyre.

Sept. 17—Turnabout is fair play for the Tigers, who clinch their first pennant since 1945 with a 2-1 win over the Yankees at Detroit.

Sept. 19—Mantle connects for his 535th home run off Detroit's Denny McLain, who is en route to his 31st victory. The homer, the second-to-last of Mantle's career, gives him sole possession of third place on the all-time list.

Sept. 29—Rookie **Stan Bahnsen's** 4-3 win over Boston caps a fifth-place season as the Yankees creep back over .500 with an 83-79 record.

HALL OF FAME *Waite* Hoyt 1969

HALL OF FAME *Earle* Combs 1970

HALL OF FAME *Yogi* Berra 1972

Jan. 19—**Berra** wins election to the Hall of Fame in his second year of eligibility. The Veterans Committee adds **Gomez** two weeks later.

March 22—The Yankees get lefty reliever Sparky Lyle from Boston for Danny Cater.

Aug. 8—The Yankees sign a 30-year lease to play in remodeled Yankee Stadium beginning in 1976.

Feb. 1—**Combs** is one of two former players added to the Hall of Fame by the Veterans Committee.

Feb. 2—**Hoyt** is one of two players added by the Veterans Committee to the Hall of Fame.

March 1—Mantle announces his retirement.

June 8—Mickey Mantle Day at Yankee Stadium. As 60,096 fans look on, Mantle's No. 7 is retired and plaques honoring him and DiMaggio are hung behind the center field monuments.

Oct. 1—A 4-3 win over Cleveland gives the Yankees a final 80-81 record and fifth-place finish in the East Division of the restructured A.L.

HALL OF FAME *George* Weiss 1971

June 1—Commissioner Bowie Kuhn calls former Yankees pitcher Bouton to his office to condemn his new book, titled "Ball Four." Bouton's tell-all depiction of life as a baseball insider creates a major stir, especially his comments dealing with Mantle, sex and other formerly private issues.

Sept. 30—Fritz Peterson records his 20th victory with a 4-3 season-closing win over Boston. The Yankees rise to second in the East with a 93-69 record.

Jan. 31—**Weiss** is among the seven men tabbed by the Veterans Committee for induction into the Hall of Fame.

Sept. 30—Down 7-5 with two out in the ninth inning in the Senators' final game at Washington, the Yankees win 9-0 by forfeit when fans swarm onto the field and begin tearing up RFK Stadium. The win allows the Yanks to finish over .500 (82-80).

HALL OF FAME *Lefty* Gomez 1972

Oct. 4—The Yankees fall 1-0 to Milwaukee righthander Jim Lonborg, extending their season-closing losing streak to five games. Their final 79-76 record is good for fourth place in the A.L. East.

Nov. 27—The Yanks acquire third baseman Graig Nettles from Cleveland in a six-player trade.

1973

Jan. 3—The George Steinbrenner era begins when the shipbuilding tycoon heads a limited partnership that purchases the Yankees from CBS for $10 million.

March 5—Yankee pitchers Peterson and Mike Kekich tell the media they have swapped wives, a story that creates a national stir.

April 6—Yankee **Ron Blomberg** makes history in a game against Boston when he becomes the A.L.'s first official designated hitter. Facing Luis Tiant, Blomberg draws a bases-loaded walk.

Sept. 30—After an 8-5 loss to Detroit completes an 80-82 season, Houk resigns as manager. He will resurface as Tigers manager 11 days later.

Dec. 18—The Yankees sign former Oakland manager Dick Williams to replace Houk, but A.L. president Joe Cronin rules the signing void pending Williams' legal battle against A's owner Charlie Finley.

Ron Blomberg

1974

Jan. 3—Unable to sign Williams, the Yankees tab Bill Virdon as manager.

Jan. 16—Two new Yankee Hall of Famers: Longtime pals **Mantle** and **Ford**.

Mickey Mantle 1974

April 6—Stottlemyre beats Cleveland 6-1 as the Yanks begin a two-year stint as tenants at Shea Stadium. It is the first home game outside Yankee Stadium, which is being remodeled, since 1922.

April 14—Nettles, en route to a major league-record 11 home runs in the month of April, belts four in a doubleheader split with the Indians.

Whitey Ford 1974

April 27—The Yankees acquire first baseman Chris Chambliss from the Indians in a seven-player deal.

Oct. 1—The Yankees' 3-2 loss to Milwaukee, coupled with Baltimore's win over Detroit, clinches the A.L. East title for the Orioles. The Yanks will finish the next day with an 89-73 record.

Nov. 27—Commissioner Kuhn suspends Steinbrenner from the operation of the Yankees for two years after his conviction for illegal political contributions.

Dec. 31—The Yankees win a bidding war and land former Oakland ace Catfish Hunter, an arbitration-declared free agent, for $3.75 million over five years.

1975

Bucky Harris 1975

Feb. 3—Former manager **Harris** is Hall of Fame material, thanks to baseball's Veterans Committee.

Aug. 2—Virdon, the 1974 A.L. Manager of the Year, is replaced by Billy Martin, who begins the first of five stints as Yankees field boss.

Sept. 28—A 3-2 win over Baltimore ends a disappointing 83-77, third-place season.

Dec. 11—In separate deals with the Pirates and Angels, the Yankees acquire second baseman Willie Randolph, center fielder **Mickey Rivers** and pitcher Ed Figueroa.

1976

April 10—The second game of the season at Milwaukee ends in controversy. Milwaukee's Don Money connects for an apparent game-ending grand slam, but the home run is nullified because Chambliss had called timeout before the pitch. The Yanks hold on for a 9-7 victory.

April 15—Remodeled Yankee Stadium opens with an 11-4 New York win over Minnesota. The Twins' Dan Ford hits the facility's first and second home runs.

June 18—Commissioner Kuhn voids the sale of three A's stars: Joe Rudi and Rollie Fingers to the Red Sox and Vida Blue to the Yankees.

Sept. 25—Thurman Munson and Chambliss homer in a 10-6 win at Detroit that clinches the Yankees' first A.L. East Division title and their first postseason appearance since 1964. They will finish with a 97-62 record.

Oct. 14—Chambliss sends Yankee Stadium into pandemonium when he leads off the ninth inning of the fifth ALCS game with a home run, securing the Yanks' 30th pennant and ending an 11-year drought. Kansas City righthander Mark Littell is the victim in a 7-6 loss.

Oct. 21—Johnny Bench hits two home runs and Cincinnati's Big Red Machine rolls over the Yankees in a 7-2 Game 4 romp, completing the Reds' World Series sweep.

Nov. 16—Munson, a .302 hitter with 105 RBIs, wins A.L. MVP honors.

Nov. 29—Free-agent outfielder Reggie Jackson, the straw that will stir the Yankees' drink, signs a five-year, $2.9 million contract with the Yankees. The Bronx Zoo is open for business.

1977

Jan. 31—**Joe Sewell** gets a Hall of Fame nod from the Veterans Committee.

Joe Sewell 1977
HALL OF FAME

June 18—With a national television audience watching, Jackson and Martin nearly exchange blows in the Yankees dugout during a loss to Boston. The rift develops over Jackson's lackadaisical defensive play in right field.

Oct. 1—The Yankees, despite a 10-7 loss to Detroit, clinch their second straight A.L. East title when the Red Sox lose to Baltimore. The Yanks will close the next day with a 100-62 record.

Oct. 9—Down 3-2 entering the ninth inning of Game 5 in the A.L. Championship Series against the Royals, the Yankees rally for three runs, a 5-3 victory and their second straight A.L. pennant.

Oct. 18—The Mr. October legend is born. Jackson connects three times for first-pitch home runs as the Yankees wrap up their 21st championship with a dramatic 8-4 victory over the Dodgers in Game 6 of the World Series at Yankee Stadium.

Oct. 25—Lyle, 13-5 with 26 saves and a 2.17 ERA, becomes the first A.L. relief pitcher to win a Cy Young Award.

1978

Jan. 30—**Larry MacPhail** is selected for Hall of Fame inclusion by the Veterans Committee.

June 17—Lefty Ron Guidry sets a Yankee franchise record by striking out 18 Angels in a 4-0 victory at Yankee Stadium.

July 17—Martin suspends Jackson for five days when the slugger ignores instructions and attempts to bunt in the 10th inning of an eventual loss to Kansas City.

July 24—Martin resigns with the Yankees buried well behind Boston in the A.L. East race. Bob Lemon is named to replace Martin the next day and five days later, during Old Timers Day festivities, the Yankees announce Martin will return as manager in 1980 with Lemon moving up to general manager.

Sept. 7—The Yankees, four games behind the Red Sox, begin a weekend series that will become known as the "Boston Massacre." The Yanks, who trailed the Red Sox by 14 games at one point, will out-hit them 67-21 and outscore them 42-9 in a four-game sweep.

Oct. 2—The Yankees and Red Sox, tied at the end of regular-season play with 99-63 records, lock heads in a one-game playoff at Fenway Park. A three-run homer by short-stop Bucky Dent helps the Yanks post a dramatic 5-4, division-clinching victory and Guidry raise his record to 25-3.

Oct. 6—Munson's two-run eighth-inning homer secures a 6-5 third-game ALCS win over the Royals. The Yankees will secure their 32nd pennant the next day, 2-1, on Roy White's solo shot.

Oct. 17—A 7-2 World Series Game 6 victory over the Dodgers gives the Yankees a second straight championship and completes their rally from a two-games-to-none deficit.

Nov. 2—Guidry, who complemented his 25 wins with a 1.74 ERA and nine shutouts, earns unanimous selection as the A.L. Cy Young winner.

1979

HALL OF FAME
Larry MacPhail 1978

April 19—After a loss to the Orioles, Goose Gossage and Cliff Johnson get into a clubhouse fight. Gossage suffers a thumb injury that will sideline him until July 12.

June 18—Lemon is replaced by Martin, a half season earlier than planned. The Yankees are struggling at 34-31.

Aug. 2—Munson, 32, dies when the plane he is flying crashes en route to Canton, Ohio. His No. 15 will be retired immediately.

Sept. 30—The Yankees complete the season on a high note. A 9-2 victory over Toronto, their eighth straight win, lifts their final record to 89-71, good for fourth place in the tough A.L. East.

Oct. 23—Martin is involved in a barroom fight with marshmallow salesman Joseph Cooper. Five days later, Steinbrenner will fire Martin and replace him with Dick Howser.

Nov. 8—The Yankees sign free-agent first baseman **Bob Watson** and pitcher Rudy May.

1980

Oct. 4—The Yankees clinch their fourth A.L. East title in five years with a 5-2 victory over Detroit in the first game of a doubleheader. The Yanks will finish the next day with 103 wins and Jackson will claim a share of the A.L. home run title with 41.

Oct. 10—George Brett, a .390 hitter during the season for Kansas City, hits a three-run, seventh-inning home run off Gossage to give the Royals a 4-2 victory and a three-game ALCS sweep of the Yankees. It is the Royals' first pennant.

Nov. 21—After leading the Yankees to 103 wins and a division title, Howser resigns under fire and is replaced by G.M. Gene Michael.

Dec. 15—The Yankees sign free-agent outfielder Dave Winfield to a 10-year, $15-million-plus contract.

1981

March 11—Mize gains Hall of Fame entrance from the Veterans Committee.

May 4—Yankees reliever Ron Davis strikes out the final eight batters in a 4-2 win over the Angels. He ties Nolan Ryan's consecutive-strikeout record.

Aug. 6—The Yankees, A.L. East leaders when baseball's 50-day strike began, are declared first-half division leaders and guaranteed participation in a special best-of-five postseason division playoff series that will set up LCS matchups.

Sept. 6—Lemon returns to manage the Yankees, replacing Michael.

Oct. 4—The Yankees lose 5-2 at Baltimore to complete a 59-48 strike-shortened regular season.

Oct. 11—Jackson homers and the Yankees record a 7-3 fifth-game victory over Milwaukee in a special playoff to decide division champions.

Oct. 15—Dave Righetti, Davis and Gossage combine on a five-hitter and Randolph homers in a 4-0 ALCS-clinching Game 3 victory over Oakland.

Oct. 25—After watching his Yankees lose 2-1 to the Dodgers in Game 5 of the World Series, Steinbrenner gets into a scuffle with two fans in a hotel elevator and suffers a swollen lip and injured hand.

Oct. 28—The Yanks, who enjoyed a two-games-to-none lead at one point, lose their fourth straight game and the Series to Los Angeles. Reliever George Frazier suffers the 9-2 loss, his record-tying third defeat of the Series.

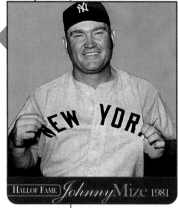

HALL OF FAME *Johnny* Mize 1981

1982

Jan. 22—Jackson ends his sometimes-rocky Yankee stint by signing a free-agent contract with the Angels.

April 25—Just 14 games into the season, Steinbrenner fires Lemon and replaces him with Michael, the man Lemon replaced in 1981.

Aug. 3—Steinbrenner watches the White Sox sweep a double-header at Yankee Stadium and fires Michael, replacing him with pitching coach Clyde King.

Oct. 3—Boston completes a season-ending sweep of the hated Yankees with a 5-3 victory, dropping the Bombers into fifth place with a 79-83 record.

Gene
Michael

1983

Jan. 11—Martin returns for a third time, replacing King, who will move to the front office.

Feb. 8—Mantle is banned from baseball by Kuhn after taking a promotions job with a New Jersey casino.

May 31—A.L. president Lee MacPhail suspends Steinbrenner for a week because of his repeated criticism of umpires. The Yankees owner will not be allowed at the ballpark during the suspension.

July 4—Righetti pitches the first Yankees no-hitter since Larsen's perfect game in the 1956 World Series. A holiday crowd of 41,077 watches him stop the Red Sox 4-0.

July 24—Kansas City's Brett hits his infamous "Pine Tar Homer" off Gossage in the ninth inning of a game at Yankee Stadium. Umpires nullify the apparent game-winner, but a Royals protest will be upheld and the umpires' decision overturned. The Royals will complete their 5-4 win on August 18.

Aug. 4—Winfield's errant warmup throw between innings of a game at Toronto kills a seagull, an endangered bird in Canada. Winfield is arrested after the game and charged with cruelty to animals. The charge eventually will be dropped.

Oct. 2—A final-day 2-0 loss to Baltimore completes a 91-71 season and third-place finish.

Dec. 16—Steinbrenner fires Martin again, replacing him with Berra. Martin moves into the front office.

1984

Jan. 5—Veteran knuckleballer Phil Niekro, a future Hall of Famer, signs a two-year free-agent contract with the Yankees. He will become a starter with Righetti moving into the bullpen to replace Gossage.

March 30—Third baseman Nettles is traded to the Padres for rookie pitcher Dennis Rasmussen and a player to be named.

Sept. 30—In a season-ending 9-2 win over Detroit, Don Mattingly goes 4-for-5 and edges teammate Winfield for the A.L. batting title, .343 to .340. The Yankees finish in third place at 87-75.

Dec. 5—The Yankees acquire left fielder **Rickey Henderson** from the A's in a seven-player deal.

March 7—**Enos Slaughter** is one of two former players added to the Hall of Fame by the Veterans Committee.

Enos Slaughter 1985
HALL OF FAME

April 28—The Yankees lose to the White Sox and Berra gives way to Martin, who begins his fourth term as Yankees manager.

Aug. 4—Tom Seaver, pitching for the White Sox, earns his 300th career win with a 4-1, six-hit effort against the Yankees on Phil Rizzuto Day at Yankee Stadium.

Sept. 14—While watching his Yankees lose a key game at Toronto, Steinbrenner goes on a press-box tirade in which he sarcastically refers to Winfield as "Mr. May."

Sept. 22—One night after another barroom scuffle at Baltimore, Martin suffers a broken arm during a fight with pitcher Ed Whitson. The righthander will become a target for fan abuse in New York—abuse that gets so passionate the team will be forced to keep him out of games at Yankee Stadium.

Oct. 6—Niekro, at age 46, wins his 300th game on the final day of the season—an 8-0 blanking of Toronto. The win is New York's 97th, but the Yanks still finish in second place, two games behind the Blue Jays.

Oct. 27—Martin is fired for a fourth time and replaced by former Yankees star **Lou Piniella.**

Nov. 20—Mattingly, a .324 hitter with 145 RBIs, wins the A.L. MVP award.

Dec. 14—Maris, at age 51, dies in Houston.

March 28—In an exchange of designated hitters, the Yankees get Don Baylor and give up Mike Easler.

May 14—Jackson, now playing for the Angels, connects off Boston's Roger Clemens and moves past Mantle (537-536) on the all-time home run list.

July 9—Whitson, unable to perform before abusive fans at Yankee Stadium, is traded to the Padres for pitcher Tim Stoddard.

Oct. 2—Mattingly gets his 232nd hit, a Yankees record, in a 6-1 win over the Red Sox. He will finish the season with 238 and a .352 average.

Oct. 4—Righetti records saves in both ends of a doubleheader sweep of the Red Sox, giving him a major league-record 46 for the season. The Yanks will close the season the next day in second place at 90-72.

Jan. 14—The baseball writers select **Hunter** for Hall of Fame inclusion.

June 17—Former Yankees and Royals manager Howser dies of a brain tumor in Kansas City at age 51.

Catfish Hunter 1987
HALL OF FAME

July 18—The Yankees' 7-2 loss to Texas is tempered by another home run by Mattingly. The first baseman now has homered in a major league record-tying eight consecutive games— a streak that will end the next day in a loss to the Rangers.

Sept. 29—**Mattingly** hits his record sixth grand slam of the season in a 6-0 Yankees victory over Boston and lefty Bruce Hurst. The Yanks will finish an 89-73 season five days later in fourth place.

Oct. 19—Martin returns as Yankees manager for a fifth time, pushing Piniella into the front office.

June 23—Despite his team's 40-28 record, Steinbrenner fires Martin for the fifth time, returning Piniella to the hotseat. Martin's managerial career is over.

Oct. 2—A 4-3 season-ending loss at Detroit gives the Yankees an 85-76 final record and fifth place, but they finish only 3½ games behind division winner Boston in the tight A.L. East.

Oct. 7—Piniella is out and Dallas Green is in as Yankees manager.

1989

Feb. 3—Longtime Yankees broadcaster Bill White is elected president of the National League.

June 21—The Yankees, going nowhere fast, trade leadoff man Rickey Henderson back to the A's for Eric Plunk, Greg Cadaret and Luis Polonia. Henderson will lead the A's to a World Series championship.

Aug. 4—A two-out, ninth-inning double by the Yankees' Roberto Kelly ruins a perfect-game bid by hard-luck Toronto righthander Dave Stieb, who settles for a two-hitter and a 2-1 victory. It is the third time Stieb has lost a no-hitter with two out in the ninth.

Aug. 18—The merry-go-round continues. **Green** is fired and replaced by former shortstop Dent.

Oct. 1—A 5-3 final-day loss to Detroit drops the Yankees to 74-87, their worst mark in 22 years. They finish fifth in the A.L. East.

Oct. 13—Bob Quinn resigns as Yankees general manager.

Dec. 25—Martin, 61, dies in a Christmas Day car accident near his home in Binghamton, N.Y.

1990

May 11—Steinbrenner ends his stormy relationship with Winfield by trading the left fielder to California for pitcher Mike Witt. Winfield at first refuses to report but eventually accepts the deal.

June 6—Stump Merrill, manager of the Yankees' Columbus affiliate, replaces Dent as New York field boss.

July 1—An error and walk-filled eighth inning costs Yankee pitcher **Andy Hawkins** in a 4-0 loss—even though Hawkins pitches a no-hitter against the White Sox. He becomes the second pitcher to lose while pitching a no-hitter.

July 30—Commissioner Fay Vincent orders Steinbrenner to resign as general partner and bans him from operation of the team for life. The ruling is the result of Steinbrenner's $40,000 payment to a confessed gambler for damaging information about former Yankee star Winfield.

Sept. 9—Oakland's 7-3 win completes a 12-game season sweep of the Yankees. It's that kind of season for the New Yorkers, who will go on to finish last in the A.L. East with a 67-95 record.

1991

HALL OF FAME *Tony* Lazzeri 1991

Feb. 26—The Veterans Committee adds **Lazzeri** to the Hall of Fame.

August—Vincent asks the eight-man committee for statistical accuracy to remove the parentheses noting that Maris' 61 homers in 1961 were compiled during a 162-game season. The committee eventually will agree to stop listing Ruth as holder of the single-season home run record.

Aug. 15—Mattingly refuses G.M. Michael's order to get a haircut and is temporarily benched. Tension remains high for the remainder of a difficult season.

Oct. 7—Merrill is fired as manager and replaced by **Buck Showalter**. Merrill, who led the team to a 71-91 record and fifth-place finish, is the first Yankees manager to last an entire season since Piniella in 1987.

1992

June 8—Lefthander Steve Howe is suspended from baseball for a seventh time because of substance abuse. The bullpen will struggle without its closer.

July 24—Vincent announces Steinbrenner's reinstatement as managing general partner of the Yankees, effective March 1, 1993.

Oct. 4—A season-ending 8-2 loss at Boston completes a 76-86 season and leaves the Yankees tied for fourth.

Nov. 3—The Yankees acquire outfielder Paul O'Neill from the Reds in a three-player deal.

Reggie Jackson 1993

HALL OF FAME

Jan. 5—Jackson is the only player elected by the baseball writers to the Hall of Fame.

Aug. 14—Reggie Jackson Day at Yankee Stadium. Jackson's No. 44 is retired and the Yankees go on to beat Baltimore, 4-2.

Sept. 4—One-armed lefthander Jim Abbott fires a 4-0 no-hitter at the Indians. It is the team's first no-hitter at Yankee Stadium since Righetti's gem in 1983.

Sept. 19—Only three games behind first-place Toronto entering a game against Boston, the Yankees lose 8-3. It is the first of five straight losses that will drop them out of contention.

Oct. 3—The Yankees post a 2-1 final-day win over the Tigers at Yankee Stadium, ending a stretch of four straight losing seasons. Their 88-74 mark is good for second place behind A.L. East champion Toronto.

HALL OF FAME *Phil* Rizzuto 1994

Feb. 25—The Veterans Committee adds **Rizzuto**, Leo Durocher to the Hall of Fame.

June 17—O'Neill's average drops below .400 during an 8-1 loss to Milwaukee. He will go on to win the A.L. batting title with a .359 mark.

July 23—Mattingly collects career hit No. 2,000 off California's Russ Springer during a 7-2 Yankees victory.

Aug. 11—Despite a 13-inning, 8-7 loss to Toronto, the Yankees complete their strike-shortened season with an A.L.-best 70-43 record—their best mark after 113 games since 1963. They also capture the mythical championship of the reconfigured A.L. East Division, finishing 6½ games ahead of Baltimore.

July 28—The Yankees acquire David Cone from Toronto for three pitchers.

Aug. 13—Mantle dies of cancer in Dallas at age 63.

Oct. 1—Mattingly and Randy Velarde homer in a 6-1 regular season-ending win at Toronto and the 79-65, second-place Yankees clinch the A.L.'s new wild-card berth. It will be Mattingly's first postseason appearance after 1,785 regular-season games.

Oct. 8—Game 5 of an intense Division Series ends when Seattle scores twice in the bottom of the 11th inning for a 6-5 win. Ken Griffey Jr. contributes his fifth home run, tying Jackson's 1977 postseason single-series record.

Oct. 18—Michael resigns as Yankees general manager. He will be replaced five days later by Watson.

Oct. 26—Showalter, after leading the Yankees to their first postseason appearance since 1981, steps down as manager. He will be replaced by Joe Torre.

Dec. 7—The Yankees acquire first baseman Tino Martinez and pitcher Jeff Nelson from the Mariners in a five-player deal.

May 14—Dwight Gooden pitches the eighth regular-season no-hitter in Yankees history, stopping the Mariners 2-0 at Yankee Stadium.

June 16—Mel Allen, the legendary voice of the Yankees, dies at age 83.

Aug. 25—The Yankees unveil a new monument honoring Mantle in Yankee Stadium's Monument Park.

Sept. 25—A 19-2 and 6-2 doubleheader sweep of the Brewers clinches the A.L. East title for the Yankees. They will finish four days later with a 92-70 record.

Oct. 9—The Yankees, Division Series winners over Texas, win the ALCS opener against Baltimore, 5-4, on Bernie Williams' 11th-inning homer. The Yanks force extra innings on a controversial eighth-inning homer by shortstop Derek Jeter, who gets an assist from young fan Jeffrey Maier.

Oct. 13—The Yankees, behind 21-game winner Andy Pettitte, post a 6-4 Game 5 ALCS win over the Orioles and advance to their first World Series since 1981.

Oct. 26—A 3-2 sixth-game victory over Atlanta secures the Yankees' 23rd Series championship and first since 1978. After losing the first two games, they win four straight, including a Game 4 thriller that features Jim Leyritz's game-tying, Series-turning, three-run homer.

1997

Jan. 22—Mattingly, after taking the 1996 season off to ponder his future, officially announces his retirement.

April 2—**Martinez** hits three homers and drives in seven runs in a 16-2 win at Seattle. He will go on to hit 44 home runs, the most of any Yankee since 1961.

June 16—The first Subway Series gets off to a sour note for the Yankees, who drop a 6-0 decision to the Mets at Yankee Stadium. The Bronx Bombers will rebound to win the next two games and the first interleague series between the New York teams.

Sept. 20—The Yankees clinch their third straight postseason berth with an 11-inning, 4-3 win over Toronto. They will win eight of their final nine games, finish second in the A.L. East with a 96-66 record and enter the playoffs as a wild-card team.

Oct. 6—The Indians hold on for a 4-3 victory in Game 5 of the A.L. Division Series, ending the Yankees' hopes for a second straight championship.

Tino
Martinez

1998

LeeMacPhail 1998
HALL OF FAME

March 3—Lee MacPhail is a Veterans Committee choice for the Hall of Fame.

May 17—Lefty **David Wells** pitches the only regular-season perfect game in Yankees history and the first at Yankee Stadium since Larsen's 1956 World Series perfecto. The Twins lose, 4-0.

Sept. 9—The Yankees clinch the A.L. East title with a 7-5 victory at Boston, their 102nd win.

Sept. 25—A 6-1 victory over Tampa Bay at Yankee Stadium is the Yankees' 112th, an A.L. record. They will finish the season two days later with 114.

Oct. 2—Cone, Graeme Lloyd, Nelson and Mariano Rivera combine on a three-hit, 4-0 shutout of Texas to complete a three-game Division Series sweep. The series is played under emotional strain when Darryl Strawberry is diagnosed with colon cancer.

Oct. 21—The Yankees complete the most prolific season in baseball history with a 3-0 World Series Game 4 win over San Diego. The sweep secures the Yanks' 24th championship and lifts their incredible season record (regular and postseason combined) to 125-50.

1999

March 8—DiMaggio dies at age 84 in Hollywood, Fla.

April 25—A new momument honoring DiMaggio is added to Yankee Stadium's Monument Park.

June 1—**Clemens** becomes the fourth pitcher in history to record 20 consecutive wins with an 11-5 victory over Cleveland. He will lose his next start against the Mets.

July 18—On Yogi Berra Day at Yankee Stadium, Cone retires all 27 Expos he faces in a 6-0 interleague victory. Ironically, Cone's perfect game follows the ceremonial first pitch of Larsen, who pitched a perfecto in the 1956 World Series.

Sept. 9—Hunter dies at age 53 in Hertford, N.C.

Sept. 30—The Yankees' 96th win, a 12-5 rout of Baltimore in the second game of a doubleheader, clinches their third A.L. East title in four years. They will go on to win 98 games.

Oct. 18—The Yankees get two-run homers from Jeter and Jorge Posada and outstanding pitching from Orlando Hernandez to defeat the Red Sox 6-1 in Game 5 of the ALCS and claim their 36th pennant.

Oct. 27—The last major league game of the century goes to the Yankees and gives them their record 25th championship. A 4-1 fourth-game win over the Braves also gives them a 12-game Series winning streak, matching the team's success in the 1927, '28 and '32 fall classics.

2000

May 9—A 4-3, 10-inning win over Tampa Bay gives the Yankees a 22-9 record and four-game lead in the East. The fast start is critical because the Bombers are only 15 games over .500 and 3½ games ahead of Boston on September 29 when they clinch their third straight title with a 13-2 win at Baltimore.

July 8—The Yankees complete an unusual home-and-home doubleheader sweep of the Mets with a 4-2 win at Yankee Stadium. Tempers flare when Clemens hits Mets slugger Mike Piazza in the head with an errant pitch.

Oct. 8—A bases-loaded double by Martinez keys a six-run first inning that carries the Yankees to a 7-5 victory at Oakland in decisive Game 5 of the A.L. Division Series.

Oct. 14—Clemens, allowing only a seventh-inning double to Seattle's Al Martin, posts a 5-0 victory in Game 4 of the ALCS and gives the Yankees a commanding three-games-to-one lead.

Oct. 17—David Justice's dramatic three-run homer keys a six-run seventh inning, lifting the Yankees to a 9-7 victory over the Mariners in Game 6 of the ALCS at Yankee Stadium. The Yankees become the first team since the 1988-90 Oakland A's to win three straight pennants.

Oct. 26—Luis Sojo's ninth-inning single drives in the winning run in a 4-2 Game 5 victory over the Mets, allowing the Yankees' to become the first team to win three straight World Series since the 1972-74 Oakland A's.

Sept. 2—**Mike Mussina's** no-hit bid ends on a ninth-inning single by Boston's Carl Everett, but he completes his one-hitter and a three-game Yankees sweep at Fenway Park. The 1-0 victory gives the Yanks a nine-game edge over the Red Sox in the A.L. East.

Sept. 19—Clemens, with relief help from Rivera, defeats Chicago 6-3 for his 16th straight win, lifting his record to 20-1. At 39, Clemens becomes the oldest 20-game winner since Early Wynn in 1959 en route to winning his record sixth Cy Young Award.

Sept. 25—On an emotional night at the Stadium, the Yankees, playing their first home game since September 11, lose 4-0 to Tampa Bay. Despite the loss, the Yanks clinch the East Division when Boston loses to Baltimore.

Oct. 7—**Rivera** records his franchise-record 50th save in a 1-0 final-day victory at Tampa Bay.

Oct. 13—Down two-games-to-none and facing elimination in the A.L. Division Series, the Yankees post the first of three straight season-saving victories at Oakland, a 1-0 win behind Mussina and Rivera. Jeter saves the game in the seventh inning when he hustles after a Shane Spencer overthrow and guns down Jeremy Giambi at the plate.

Oct. 21—The Yankees grab a three-games-to-one lead over Seattle in Game 4 of the ALCS when second baseman Alfonso Soriano hits a two-run, ninth-inning homer for a 3-1 victory. The Yanks wrap up their fourth straight pennant the next night with a 12-3 win at Yankee Stadium.

Oct. 31—Martinez hits a stunning two-out, two-run ninth-inning homer off Arizona closer Byung-Hyun Kim to tie Game 4 of the World Series at 3-3 and Jeter homers in the 10th to give the Yankees a home-field miracle. The 4-3 win squares the Series at two games apiece.

Nov. 1—Miracle No. 2. Scott Brosius hits a two-out, two-run ninth-inning homer off Kim to tie Game 5 at 2-2 and Soriano wins it in the 12th with an RBI single. The 3-2 win puts the Yanks on the verge of a fourth straight championship.

Nov. 4—The Diamondbacks score two ninth-inning runs in Game 7 and win their first World Series. The 3-2 Arizona victory, decided on a single by Luis Gonzalez, comes at the expense of Rivera, who had converted 23 straight postseason save opportunities.

April 1—The Yankees' quest for a fifth straight A.L. pennant starts slowly when Clemens allows eight runs, issues five walks and serves up a grand slam to Tony Batista in an opening day 10-3 loss to the Orioles.

June 8—The Giants, playing the Yankees for the first time since the 1962 fall classic, win Game 2 of their interleague series, 4-3, when Barry Bonds hits a three-run homer—his first in Yankee Stadium.

June 10—Rookie Marcus Thames, making his major league debut, hits the first pitch he sees from Arizona lefty Randy Johnson for a third-inning home run and the Yankees go on to beat the Diamondbacks, 7-5.

June 15—The day after **Robin Ventura** beats his former team with a 10th-inning home run, Mike Piazza homers and the Mets pound Clemens and the Yankees, 8-0, at Shea Stadium.

Aug. 18—The Mariners end center fielder **Bernie Williams'** consecutive-hit streak at 11, one short of the big-league record, but the Yankees record an 8-3 victory.

Sept. 11—A crowd of 35,183 watch the Yankees dedicate a monument to "victims and heroes" of September 11 in Monument Park during emotional pregame ceremonies. The Yanks need 11 innings to beat the Orioles, 5-4, on Nick Johnson's single.

Sept. 14—A crowd of 44,795 lifts the season attendance to a Yankee Stadium-record 3,331,787, but Clemens is battered in an 8-1 loss to Chicago.

Jason Giambi

Sept. 21—Andy Pettitte raises his record to 12-5 and injured closer Mariano Rivera makes his first appearance since August 15 as the Yankees record a 3-2 win over Detroit and clinch their fifth straight A.L. East title. They will finish the season a week later with 103 wins.

Sept. 24—First-year Yankee **Jason Giambi** hits home runs 39 and 40 in a 6-0 win over Tampa Bay at Yankee Stadium.

Oct. 5—The Anaheim Angels complete a stunning four-game rout of the Yankees in the A.L. Division Series, ending New York's bid for a fifth straight pennant with a 9-5 victory. The Angels batter Yankee pitching for 56 hits and 31 runs.

*Yankee*Voices

It was hard to beat the broadcasting team of (far left, left to right) Mel Allen, Red Barber and Phil Rizzuto. Other key Yankee voices included Frank Messer (center) and Bill White (near left).

Younger generation fans associated the resonant, soothing and distinctive voice of Mel Allen with his long-running "This Week in Baseball" television show, but that's only a partial sampling of one of the game's broadcasting pioneers. In his first baseball life, the colorful and descriptive Allen was the "Voice of the Yankees" for 25 seasons and a huge part of the team's early championship mystique.

From 1939-64, fans literally hung on the words of the man who brought the game right into their living rooms from his front-row seat in the "Big Stadium's" radio booth. Allen's pitch-by-pitch narrative was engrossing; his commentary was colored by such trademark phrases as "How about that!" and "Going, going, gone"—his then-unique home run call.

Allen was at the microphone for many of the memorable moments in Yankees history—from the daily drama of Joe DiMaggio's 56-game hitting streak in 1941 to the instant excitement of Don Larsen's World Series perfect game in 1956. Everything was flavored with his Alabama charm and the downhome style that made him seem like a personal friend to millions of New Yorkers.

From 1954 through 1964, Yankees fans were blessed with the pairing of Allen and Red Barber—a fellow Southerner who had spent 15 years infatuating Dodger fans with his special broadcasting style. With Allen and Barber sharing the booth, Yankee followers experienced a wonderful contrast of emotions—from Allen's roaring enthusiasm and penchant for communicating a game's excitement to Barber's low-key reporting genius and ability to make listen-

ers understand baseball subtleties.

No broadcast booth in baseball could match that ultimate pairing. And Yankee fans of the era were treated to a third voice, one that could not match the others in diction and communicative skills but eventually would challenge them in local popularity and exceed them in longevity.

Hall of Fame shortstop Phil Rizzuto was added to the broadcast team in 1957, replacing Jim Woods, and spent most of the next decade learning from Allen and Barber. He was raw, grammatically incorrect at times, but he also was peppy and upbeat, much like his style as a player. By the time Allen was fired in 1964, Rizzuto was gaining polish and his "Holy Cow!" enthusiasm was generating fan support. When Barber left in 1966, Rizzuto became the dean of Yankee broadcasters—a distinction he would hold for the final three decades of his 40-year broadcasting career.

Seventeen of those years were spent with Frank Messer and 18 with Bill White, who later became president of the National League. Over the years, Rizzuto also worked with such partners as Jerry Coleman, Joe Garagiola, Fran Healy, Bobby Murcer, Tom Seaver and Tony Kubek. John Sterling and Michael Kay have been members of the Yankees booth for 14 years.

No discussion of voices would be complete without Bob Sheppard, who has brought a special dignity to Yankee Stadium for more than 50 years. The eloquent linguist, who speaks with perfect diction in his clear, distinctive style, is the public address announcer—as much a part of every Yankees game as the thousands of players he has introduced.